Public Journalism and Political Knowledge

Public Journalism and Political Knowledge

Edited by Anthony J. Eksterowicz
and Robert N. Roberts

ROWMAN & LITTLEFIELD PUBLISHERS, INC.
Lanham • Boulder • New York • Oxford

ROWMAN & LITTLEFIELD PUBLISHERS, INC.

Published in the United States of America
by Rowman & Littlefield Publishers, Inc.
4720 Boston Way, Lanham, Maryland 20706
http://www.rowmanlittlefield.com

12 Hid's Copse Road, Cumnor Hill, Oxford OX2 9JJ, England

An earlier version of portions of chapter 1 appeared in Anthony Eksterowicz, Robert Roberts, and Adrian Clark, "Public Journalism and Public Knowledge," *The Harvard International Journal of Press/Politics* 3, no. 2 (spring 1998):74–95.

British Library Cataloguing in Publication Information Available

Library of Congress Cataloging-in-Publication Data

Public journalism and political knowledge / edited by Anthony J. Eksterowicz and Robert N. Roberts.
    p. cm.
    Includes bibliographical references and index.
    ISBN 0-8476-9539-5 (cloth : alk.)—ISBN 0-8476-9540-9 (paper : alk.)
      1. Journalism—Social aspects—United States. 2. Journalism—Political aspects—United States. I. Eksterowicz, Anthony J. II. Roberts, Robert North.

PN4749 .P83 2000
302.23—dc21   00-02851

Printed in the United States of America

♾™ The paper used in this publication meets the minimum requirements of American National Standard for Information Sciences—Permanence of Paper for Printed Library Materials, ANSI/NISO Z39.48-1992.

Contents

Part III: The Impact and Future of Public Journalism

The Disease to Please

The Disease to Please

Curing the People-Pleasing Syndrome

Harriet B. Braiker, Ph.D.

McGraw-Hill

New York   San Francisco   Washington, D.C.   Auckland   Bogotá
Caracas   Lisbon   London   Madrid   Mexico City   Milan
Montreal   New Delhi   San Juan   Singapore
Sydney   Tokyo   Toronto

McGraw-Hill

A Division of The McGraw-Hill Companies

1 2 3 4 5 6 7 8 9 0 AGM/AGM 0 9 8 7 6 5 4 3 2 1 0

ISBN 0-07-136410-2

This book was set in Minion by North Market Street Graphics.

Printed and bound by Quebecor / Martinsburg.

This publication is designed to provide accurate and authoritative information in regard to the subject matter covered. It is sold with the understanding that the publisher is not engaged in rendering legal, accounting, or other professional service. If legal advice or other expert assistance is required, the services of a competent professional person should be sought.
> —*From a declaration of principles jointly adopted by a committee of the American Bar Association and a committee of publishers.*

This book is printed on acid-free paper

McGraw-Hill books are available at special quantity discounts to use as premiums and sales promotions, or for use in corporate training programs. For more information, please write to the Director of Special Sales, Professional Publishing, McGraw-Hill, Two Penn Plaza, New York, NY 10121. Or contact your local bookstore.

To the memory of my beloved mother and father
To Amanda, my most cherished blessing
and
To Steven, for giving me his shoe

I hope I have pleased you.

Contents

Preface

In July 1999 I appeared as a guest expert on *Oprah* to discuss "The Disease to Please." Oprah told her audience that this "disease"—the people-pleasing syndrome—is an issue that is very important and personal to her. It is a problem that she has struggled long and hard to overcome. And she believes, as I do, that there are epidemic numbers of women—and men, too— plagued by the self-imposed pressure to please others at the expense of their own health and happiness.

My interest in this topic began many years ago. I have been a practicing clinical psychologist for more than 25 years. Over this time, I have treated hundreds of women *and* men people-pleasers whose lives become impaired by this compulsion to put others' needs first, to never say "No," to strive endlessly for everyone's approval, and to try to make everyone *else* happy.

My first book, *The Type E Woman: How to Overcome the Stress of Being Everything to Everybody,* highlighted people-pleasing as a core cause of women's stress problems. Since then, I have written other books and articles on related topics.

But, my decision to write this book was prompted directly by Oprah Winfrey. Twice, during the taping of the show, Oprah turned to me and said, "Harriet, *this* should be the topic of your next book." I am grateful for Oprah's suggestion and encouragement.

The Disease to Please is not about nice people who occasionally go too far in trying to make others happy. The Disease to Please, in fact, is a debilitating psychological problem with far-reaching, serious consequences.

In conjunction with the publication of this book, I am starting a Web site—**www.diseasetoplease.com**—which will provide more information, help get support groups started in local communities, allow messages to be placed, questions to be asked and answered, and much, much more. Visit the Web site and join other recovered people-pleasers as well as those striving for recovery.

I hope you will contact me through the Web site to ask any questions you might have and to share your own experiences with the Disease to

Please. Let me know how the program is working in your personal recovery process.

I wrote this book to help. I fervently hope that it does.

Harriet B. Braiker, Ph.D.
Los Angeles, California

Acknowledgments

Over the past 25 years that I have been in clinical practice, my patients have been a constant source of knowledge and inspiration to me. The many people-pleasers—women *and* men—I have treated have greatly enhanced my understanding of the toll this problem takes on its sufferers' health, relationships, and quality of life. My patients have consistently affirmed my belief that, with focused effort and the *desire* to change, the human spirit can overcome this and many other obstacles to happiness.

The case studies in this book are based on the clinical histories of the people I have had the privilege of treating. Naturally, the names and particulars have been changed to protect confidentiality. I believe the book has been enriched by the color and depth that only real life stories can provide.

I also want to thank my patients for accommodating to my schedule during the time that I was writing. I am deeply grateful for my personal assistant and other "right hand," Sonja Simmons. Her loyalty, commitment, good humor, and constant moral support are deeply appreciated.

I am particularly appreciative of Oprah's input and encouragement when I appeared on her show about the Disease to Please, which first aired in July 1999 and provided much of the impetus for this book.

I want to thank my first editor at McGraw-Hill, Betsy Brown, who saw Oprah's show on people-pleasing and recognized the need of so many for help with this problem. I am grateful that she and McGraw-Hill have given me the opportunity to offer that help by writing this book.

It has been my very good fortune and privilege to work with Claudia Riemer Boutote. Her enthusiasm, keen intelligence, and extraordinary efforts in the very capable editing of the manuscript have been of tremendous value to me.

Of course, I thank my agent, Alice Martell, for her encouragement, availability, and wise counsel.

Last, but never least, I thank my family for loving me so much and so well.

My husband, Steven, is my in-house editor-in-chief and the love of my life. He provides the guidance, wisdom, humor, and strength that keep me going. My little girl and best friend, Amanda, has massaged both my aching back and, on occasion, my flagging spirits through the laborious process that writing a book entails.

Finally, thanks to Brandy, our quintessential people-pleaser, for keeping my feet warm while I wrote.

Introduction: A User's Guide for Getting the Most Benefit from This Book

This book is based on small steps, and step-by-step you *will* recover from your Disease to Please. Here's how to begin:

First, you do not have to read this book from cover to cover to benefit from it. If you are like most people-pleasers I know, you probably are too busy right now, anyway. The book was written with you and your crushing time demands in mind.

Read the first chapter and take the revealing quiz, "Do You Have the Disease to Please?" This quiz will help you pinpoint the most important underlying causes of your own Disease to Please syndrome and, therefore, into which type or grouping you best fit. Specifically, the quiz will reveal whether your people-pleasing issues are primarily based in compulsive behavior, distorted thinking, or the avoidance of negative feelings. (You are very likely affected by all three—most people-pleasers are—but one type is probably more dominant than the others.)

Once you know your own type, if you do not have time right now to read the book all the way through, simply go immediately to the section that most pertains to you: People-Pleasing Mindsets, People-Pleasing Habits, or People-Pleasing Feelings. Then, when you are ready, you may proceed directly to the 21-Day Action Plan for curing the Disease to Please. The most effective approach to the Action Plan is to start on Day 1 and proceed *one day at a time* for the next three weeks of the action plan. Remember: Take small steps—don't rush.

This book is best read with a highlighter or a pen in hand. You should highlight and mark up those sections, passages, stories, lines, and epiphanies that hit close to home and have personal meaning to you. Feel free to write in your copy of the book. Add your own thoughts and "Amens" to the margins. Keep your copy of the book close for comfort, guidance, and security when you most need it.

Throughout the book, look for little arrows (▶) that indicate something to which you should pay particular attention. Make your own arrows or stars when you come across something that is particularly important to you.

When you have begun your recovery and you have the time, go back and read those portions of the book you skipped the first time, as well as re-read those sections that are most helpful to you.

Be assured that you are not alone. There are millions of people-pleasers out there just like you. Talk openly to your friends and family and you'll find you are not alone. Consider starting support groups in your community so you and others like you can help each other.

Visit the Web site at **www.diseasetoplease.com** to connect with other recovering people-pleasers. Talking about the problem will strengthen your commitment to recover.

CHAPTER 1

The Disease to Please Triangle: The Price of Nice

Do You Have the Disease to Please?

I f you are like most people-pleasers, you probably already know the answer to this question. And if the Disease to Please plagues you, you will more likely be interested in the cure than in the diagnosis.

But don't be too quick to skip this chapter. You'll find the brief quiz that follows useful. It not only will help you to evaluate the relative depth or seriousness of your people-pleasing problems, but also will allow you to determine the most important underlying causes of your own Disease to Please problem.

As you will soon learn, these causes fall into three major groupings: People-Pleasing Mindsets, People-Pleasing Habits, and People-Pleasing Feelings. Knowing your dominant cause will help you focus your efforts so that you can achieve the biggest impact on curing your people-pleasing syndrome as quickly as possible.

The quiz contains 24 items that measure your people-pleasing tendencies as well as the underlying reasons that you find yourself on the slippery slopes of the Disease to Please triangle. Read each item and decide whether the statement applies to you. If the statement is true or mostly true, circle "T." If it is false or mostly false, circle "F." Do not overthink or try to analyze each question. Your answers need only reflect your quick, global judgment of how much each statement applies to you.

Do You Have the Disease to Please? Quiz

1. It's extremely important to me to be liked by nearly everyone in my life.   T or F

2. I believe that nothing good can come from conflict.   T or F

3. My needs should always take a backseat to the needs of the people I love.   T or F

4. I expect myself to rise above conflict and confrontation.   T or F

5. I often do too much for other people or even let myself be used so that I won't be rejected for other reasons.   T or F

6. I have always needed the approval of other people.   T or F

7. It's much easier for me to acknowledge negative feelings about myself than to express negative feelings toward others.   T or F

8. I believe that if I make other people need me because of all the things I do for them, I won't be left alone.   T or F

9. I'm hooked on doing things for others and pleasing them.   T or F

10. I go to great lengths to avoid conflict or confrontation with my family, friends, or coworkers.   T or F

11. I'm likely to do all the things I can to make others happy before I do anything just for myself.   T or F

12. I almost never stand up to others in order to protect myself because I am too afraid of getting an angry response or provoking a confrontation.   T or F

13. If I stopped putting others' needs ahead of my own, I would become a selfish person and people would no longer like me.   T or F

14. Having to face a confrontation or conflict with anybody makes me feel so anxious that I almost get physically sick.   T or F

15. It is very difficult for me to express criticism even if it is constructive because I don't want to make anyone angry with me.   T or F

16. I must always please others even at the expense of my own feelings.   T or F

17. I have to give of myself all the time in order to be worthy of love.   T or F

18. I believe that nice people get the approval, affection, and friendship of others.   T or F

19. I must never let other people down by failing to do everything they expect of me even when I know that the demands are excessive or unreasonable.   T or F

20. Sometimes I feel like I'm trying to "buy" the love and friendship of others by doing so many nice things to please them.   T or F

21. It makes me very anxious and uncomfortable to say or do anything that might make another person angry with me.   T or F

22. I rarely delegate tasks to others.   T or F

23. I feel guilty when I say "no" to requests or needs of others.   T or F

24. I would think that I am a bad person if I didn't give of myself all the time to those around me.   T or F

How to Score and Interpret Your Answers

Do You Have the Disease to Please? The answer to this question depends on your overall score. Simply total the number of your "True" responses; that total is your overall score. To interpret the meaning of your overall score, refer to the range of your score below:

♦ *Overall score between 16 and 24:* If your score is in this range, your people-pleasing syndrome is deeply ingrained and serious. You probably already know that the Disease to Please is taking a heavy toll on your emotional and physical health, as well as on the quality of your relationships with others. However, your current level of distress can serve as a powerful motivation in your recovery program, but you must act now to cure the problem and reclaim control over your life.

♦ *Overall score between 10 and 15:* If your total score is in this range, your Disease to Please symptoms are already moderately severe. The destructive pattern requires your immediate attention and effort to change before it grows any worse.

♦ *Overall score between 5 and 9:* If your total score is in this range, you have a moderate Disease to Please problem. You already have developed some strengths and resistance to your own self-defeating tendencies. However, your people-pleasing habits can still pose a disruptive threat to your health and well-being. Build on your strengths and aim for full recovery.

♦ *Overall score 4 or less:* If your total score falls here, you may have only mild people-pleasing tendencies—or even none at all—at present.

However, be forewarned that the Disease to Please is a self-perpetuating cycle that can develop quickly and overtake your sense of control in your own life. As a preventative measure, you may wish to develop your awareness of the problem and to learn the techniques of recovery.

Which Type Are You?

In order to determine the dominant cause of your own Disease to Please syndrome, you will need to add up your scores on those items that measure each of the three underlying causes.

1. To see if you are more controlled by your *thoughts*—or, People-Pleasing Mindsets—add together the number of True responses to questions 1, 3, 5, 8, 13, 17, 18, and 24.

2. Now add the number of True responses to questions 6, 9, 11, 16, 19, 20, 22, and 23 to see if People-Pleasing Habits—or *behaviors*—are dominant for you.

3. Finally, add the number of True responses to questions 2, 4, 7, 10, 12, 14, 15, and 21 to discover if People-Pleasing Feelings—or *emotions*—are the leading cause for you.

The highest score reveals which is the dominant cause of your Disease to Please problems:

♦ You are a Cognitive people-pleaser if your highest score is on the mindsets or thought scale;

♦ You are a Behavioral people-pleaser if your highest score is on the habits or behavioral scale; and

♦ You are an Emotionally Avoidant people-pleaser if your highest score is on the feelings or emotional scale.

Finally, if two or all three of your scores are tied for #1, it simply means that you do not have just one dominant cause for your syndrome. For you, two or even all three causes are equally important as reasons for your people-pleasing problems.

The Disease to Please Triangle

Now that you have determined the dominant underlying cause of your own syndrome, let's examine how these three psychological components or pieces to the Disease to Please puzzle fit together. These three components are: (1) People-Pleasing Mindsets, or distorted ways of *thinking;* (2) People-Pleasing Habits, or compulsive *behaviors;* and (3) People-Pleasing Feelings, or fearful *emotions.*

Together, the parts join in a *triangle* in which each side—behavior, thoughts, or feelings—operates as both a *cause* and a *consequence* of the others (see Figure 1). For example, compulsive behavior is driven by the avoidance of feared emotions and supported by distorted, flawed thinking. Similarly, anxious feelings create avoidance behaviors that, in turn, are linked to flawed or incorrect ways of thinking.

> ▶ *The Disease to Please triangle shows how you can achieve big gains in curing your people-pleasing problems by making small changes in the way you think, act, or feel. Because of their interconnections, small changes in any side of the triangle will generate change in the whole syndrome.*

Now that you know the main underlying cause of your own triangle, you will be able to direct and prioritize your personal change process.

People-Pleasing Mindsets

People-pleasers whose distorted thinking is the predominant cause of their syndrome are ensnared in burdensome and self-defeating mindsets that perpetuate their Disease to Please problems. If you are in this group, your

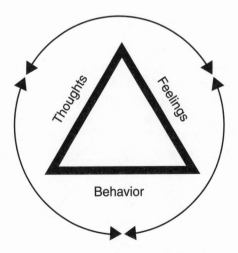

Figure 1. The Disease to Please Triangle

people-pleasing is driven by a fixed thought that you need and must strive for *everyone* to like you. You measure your self-esteem and define your identity by how much you do for others whose needs, you insist, *must* come before your own.

When you have People-Pleasing Mindsets, you believe that being *nice* will protect you from rejection and other hurtful treatment from others. And, while you impose demanding rules, harsh criticism, and perfectionist expectations on yourself, you simultaneously yearn for universal acceptance. In short, you have *thought* your way into the problem and, to a significant extent, you will need to *think* your way to recovery. So, your change efforts should first be directed toward understanding and correcting your People-Pleasing Mindsets.

People-Pleasing Habits

People-pleasers whose Disease to Please is predominantly caused by habitual behavior are driven to take care of others' needs at the expense of their own. If you are this type, you do too much, too often for others, almost never say "no," rarely delegate, and inevitably become overcommitted and spread too thin. And, while these self-defeating, stress-producing patterns take their toll on your health and on your closest relationships, they maintain a firm grip on your behavior because they are driven by your excessive, even addictive, need for everyone's approval. If you fit this description, your initial focus will be best spent on understanding and breaking your self-defeating people-pleasing habits.

People-Pleasing Feelings

People-pleasers whose syndrome is primarily caused by the avoidance of frightening and uncomfortable feelings comprise the third type. If you are in this group, you will recognize the high anxiety that merely the anticipation or possibility of an angry confrontation with others evokes.

Your Disease to Please syndrome operates primarily as an avoidance tactic intended to protect you from your fears of anger, conflict, and confrontation. But, as you may already know, the tactic is faulty. Your fears not only fail to diminish, they even intensify, as the avoidance patterns persist.

Because you avoid difficult emotions, you never allow yourself to learn how to effectively manage conflict or how to deal appropriately with anger. As a consequence, you relinquish control too easily to those who would dominate you through intimidation and manipulation.

So, if the main cause of your Disease to Please is based in emotional avoidance, your personal change process will be best directed first on your people-pleasing feelings. Your efforts to overcome your fears and to better understand and manage anger and conflict will yield big returns.

Finally, you may be among those people who do not have *one* cause or one side of the triangle that is most dominant in their Disease to Please syndrome. If so, People-Pleasing Mindsets, Habits, and Feelings all play about equal roles as underlying causes of your problem. As a result, you may begin your change process in any of the three areas with equal impact.

While most people-pleasers can identify a dominant causal feature in their problem, it is important to remember that the Disease to Please syndrome is composed of *all three* sides of the triangle. You want and need to find effective solutions to this troubling problem as soon as possible. Locating your dominant side is the fastest method to help prioritize and begin your personal change process.

Eventually, however, in order to make a full and lasting recovery, you will need to address your issues in all three areas: thinking, behavior, and feelings. To this end, the 21-Day Action Plan for curing the Disease to Please takes a wide and inclusive aim at correcting the faulty mindsets, breaking the habits, and overcoming the fearful feelings that collectively comprise this difficult and frustrating syndrome.

The Hidden Cost of People-Pleasing

People-pleasing is an odd problem. At first glance, it may not even seem like a problem at all. In fact, the phrase "people-pleaser" might feel more like a compliment or a flattering self-description that you proudly wear as a badge of honor.

After all, what's wrong with trying to make others happy? Shouldn't we all strive to please the people we love and even those we just like a lot? Surely the world would be a happier place if there were more people-pleasers . . . wouldn't it?

> ► *The truth is that "people-pleasing" is a sweet-sounding name for what, to many people, actually is a serious psychological problem.*

The Disease to Please is a compulsive—even addictive—behavior pattern. As a people-pleaser, you feel controlled by your need to please others and addicted to their approval. At the same time, you feel out of control over the pressures and demands on your life that these needs have created.

If you have the Disease, your need to please is not limited to just saying "yes" to the actual requests, invitations, or demands initiated by others. As a people-pleaser, your emotional tuning dials are jammed on the frequency of what you believe other people want or expect of you. Just the perception that another might need your help is enough to send your people-pleasing response system into overdrive.

The dilemma you face is that in staying so finely tuned to the real and perceived needs of others, you often turn a deaf ear to your own inner voice that may be trying to protect you from overextending yourself and from operating against your own self-interests.

When you have the Disease to Please, your self-esteem is all tied up with how much you do for others and how successful you are at pleasing them. Fulfilling the needs of others becomes the magic formula for gaining love and self-worth and for protection from abandonment and rejection. But, in reality, it's a formula that simply doesn't work.

Driven by an excessive need to gain the approval of other people—of everyone—people-pleasers will strive to do so at almost any cost to themselves. But this approval addiction can paralyze action. For example, when you feel pulled in more than one direction trying to meet the needs of several people, your fear of disapproval (the flipside of the need for approval) can freeze you up, leaving you in a quandary: Whom should you please? How should you choose? What if you end up pleasing no one?

When Being Nice Is Too High a Price

People-pleasers become deeply attached to seeing themselves—and to being certain that others see them—as *nice* people. Their very identity derives from this image of niceness. And, while they may believe that being nice protects them from unpleasant situations with friends and family, in actuality, the price they pay is still far too high.

First, because you are so nice, other people may manipulate and exploit your willingness to please them. Your niceness may even blind you to the fact that others are exploiting you. Further, keeping a front of niceness all the time prevents you from showing anger and displeasure, however justified they may be.

Second, you avoid criticizing others so that you won't be criticized. To avoid confrontation, it is all too easy to take the path of least resistance that psychologists call *conflict avoidance*. Like criticism, confrontation and anger are also dangerous emotional experiences that you wish to avoid at nearly any cost.

Driven by Your Fears

▶ *At the core of your niceness is a deep fear of negative emotions.*

In fact, people-pleasing is largely driven by emotional fears: fear of rejection, fear of abandonment, fear of conflict or confrontation, fear of criticism, fear of being alone, and fear of anger. As a people-pleaser, you hold the belief that by being nice and always doing things for others you will avoid these emotions in yourself and others. This defensive belief has a two-way effect. First, you use your niceness to deter and dodge negative emotions aimed at you from others—as long as you're so nice and always try to do things to please others, why would anyone want to get angry, or reject or criticize you? Second, by being so invested in your own niceness, you don't allow yourself to feel or express negative emotions toward others.

▶ *The more you identify with being nice, instead of being real, the more you will find yourself plagued by nagging doubts, insecurities, and lingering fears.*

Being accepted and getting approval from others always will seem just out of reach. And, even if you succeed at pleasing others, you find that your fears of rejection, abandonment, or angry confrontation will not diminish or be alleviated. In fact, they grow stronger over time.

The Disease to Please creates a psychological blockade against both sending and receiving these negative emotions. For this reason, it cripples the very relationships you slave to satisfy and try so hard to protect. If you cannot express negative feelings, your relationships will simply lose their authenticity. You will come across as a one-dimensional cardboard figure rather than a rich multidimensional human personality full of interesting facets and sides.

In any relationship, if your niceness prevents you from telling others what is making you unhappy, angry, upset, or disappointed—or from hearing their complaints—there is little chance of fixing what has gone wrong. Conflict avoidance is not an ingredient of successful relationships. Rather, it is a serious symptom of dysfunctional ones. It's better to recognize that negative emotions between people are inevitable, and you must learn to deal with them effectively.

Negative emotions are built into the hardwiring of human beings. We are programmed biologically to feel fear and anger, and to respond defensively when others seek to harm us or hurt those we love. When conflict is handled constructively and anger is expressed appropriately, they can be powerful communication tools for dealing with people in the real world. Handled responsibly, these emotions enable you to maintain your relationships in good working condition with problems minimized and pleasures optimized.

In fact, you ignore these negative feelings at your own peril. How many of us have found ourselves in situations where outwardly we deny our anger and resentment toward another, while on the inside, we find ourselves feeling anxious, panicked, and depressed?

Repressed negative feelings may emerge in the form of migraine or tension headaches, back pain, stomach pain, high blood pressure, or any of a host of other stress-related symptoms. And, under the surface, resentment and frustration bubble and churn, threatening to erupt in open hostility and uncontrolled anger. Eventually, these physical and emotional problems take their toll on your health and your closest relationships.

You are not alone. Millions of *nice* women and men just like you suffer from the Disease to Please and can testify to the effect it has on their emotional, physical, and relationship health. Compulsively striving to meet the needs of others at the expense of your own only serves to make you prone to debilitating stress and exhaustion. People-pleasers may be tempted to turn to self-medication with alcohol, drugs, and/or food to continue to be able to push their limits in order to do even more for others. It is easy to see how the Disease to Please plays a major role in chronic fatigue syndrome, alcohol and substance abuse, eating disorders, and weight problems.

As a veteran people-pleaser, despite your persistent efforts to make everyone else happy, you will rarely if ever feel satisfied with the job you are doing. You continually expand the circle of others whose needs you try to meet. The pressure this produces and the inevitable drain on your energy create profound feelings of guilt and inadequacy that you will attempt to repress by trying harder to please even more.

▶ *Unless you act to stop this dangerous cycle of pleasing others at the expense of yourself, you will eventually hit the proverbial wall. Your energy will be exhausted and you may feel like giving up altogether.*

You don't have to let things reach the desperation point. You don't want the disappointment, rejection, and anger that you have labored so hard to avoid to come spewing forth in a torrent of overt hostility. Nor do you want your anger to remain covert and turn inward, creating a paralyzing depression.

If you let the Disease to Please cycle play out, feelings of inadequacy, guilt, and failure can build. Over time, long-suppressed anger and resentment turn toxic and might even cause cherished relationships to weaken or fail. In the end abandonment—the ultimate fear for a people-pleaser—which you sought to avoid may become a terrifying reality.

"After everything I've done for everyone else," one patient of mine says bitterly, "nobody is there for me. I've been so *nice* to everyone, and people just take me for granted."

Clearly, viewed in this light, people-pleasing is no benign problem. If you have the Disease to Please, you cannot afford to continue thinking of yourself as just a nice person who goes overboard by trying to make too many other people happy or doing too much for the people you seek to please.

But how does something that, on its face, sounds so innocent—indeed, even benevolent—become so problematic and dangerous? How and why does people-pleasing transform into its pathological form—the Disease to Please?

As you now know, the Disease to Please is a set of self-defeating *thoughts* and flawed beliefs about yourself and other people that fuel *compulsive behavior* that, in turn, is driven by the need to avoid forbidden negative *feelings.* This triple combination of distorted thinking, compulsive behavior, and the need to avoid fearful feelings creates the syndrome of people-pleasing and forms the Disease to Please triangle.

But, there is good news: You *can* stop the progression of the Disease to Please and you *can* change *now.* To do so, you need only begin with a small change in any one area—your behavior, thoughts, or feelings. As one change at a time inevitably builds on the next, you will soon see rapid results as your people-pleasing habits, like stacked dominoes, fall over in defeat.

Will more changes in the way you feel, think, or act yield better results? Certainly. But you should begin with small steps and at your own pace.

Part One

People-Pleasing Mindsets

We now turn to an exploration of the first side of the Disease to Please triangle: People-Pleasing Mindsets. These mindsets comprise that portion of your personal "thinking equipment" that is used when you think about people-pleasing. A quick check of the equipment reveals many types of mental tools: patterns of thinking, beliefs, self-imposed rules and expectations about yourself and others, evaluations of your self-concept and self-esteem, and, critically, ways of processing all the data of thought.

> ▶ *People-Pleasing Mindsets are logically flawed and incorrect. In addition to being incorrect, they are damaging and dangerous because they contribute to feelings of depression, anxiety, self-blame, and guilt and perpetuate a self-defeating stress cycle.*

The way you think and process information has an immensely strong impact on how you feel. And, as a rational person, you exercise control of your behavior by relying on your thinking to shape and influence your actions. People-Pleasing Mindsets are psychologically insidious because they permit you to rationalize, justify, support, and perpetuate your people-pleasing habits. They also allow you to continue your avoidance of negative, fearful feelings with the consequence that you never learn to overcome or manage them.

As you will see, some of the People-Pleasing Mindsets may have been appropriate and even beneficial in your childhood. But, today, most are operating against you as an adult. You need to repair and correct your thinking errors because your current ways of thinking are just not working for you anymore. On the contrary, they're keeping you stuck in the Disease to Please trap.

In a figurative sense, your mind has been poisoned, or at least contaminated, by flawed and erroneous ways of processing your own thoughts. In the current techno-speak, your mind has a people-pleasing *virus* that is messing up big portions of your hard drive including how you feel and how you continue to behave with other people.

For example, People-Pleasing Mindsets are anchored firmly in a mandatory self-concept of being *nice*. You not only expect others to accord you universal acknowledgment of your incomparable niceness, but you expect somehow always to *feel* nice on the inside too.

Niceness is the psychological armor of the people-pleaser. In a deep part of your personality, you believe that by being nice, you will gain love and affection, and that you will be protected from meanness, rejection, anger, conflict, criticism, and disapproval. But, when (not *if*) you are exposed to a negative experience with another person—which happens inevitably (and repeatedly) as part of everyone's life—your thinking patterns will leave *you* holding the blame bag. This is because in the People-Pleasing Mindsets, if you are rejected or hurt, you believe it is because you weren't *nice enough*. It's just a short hop from this kind of thinking to self-sabotaging depression.

You will learn about the magical thinking left over from your childhood, in which *niceness* is imbued with the power to protect you. As a child, your magical thinking was normal, charming, and likely harmless. But now, this same magical thinking is immature and inappropriate. As such, it doesn't work for you anymore either.

Also critical to the People-Pleasing Mindset is that no one—including yourself—thinks of you as a selfish person. But, your definition and scope of the term *selfish* are overly broad and essentially wrong in important ways. There is a big, important difference between exercising enlightened self-interest and being selfish. You may choose to be a martyr and sacrifice your own needs on the altar of those of your family and friends. But, in doing so, you are neither demonstrating nor proving that you are unselfish, but merely self-destructive.

Simply by redefining and correcting your interpretation of terms such as *selfish* or *nice*, for example, you will be taking the first step to springing yourself loose from the Disease to Please trap.

You may have lived with these people-pleasing thoughts and beliefs for so long that they just seem correct to you now. But, before you turn to the next chapter, you need to focus on the fact that People-Pleasing Mindsets are wrong.

As you proceed into this section, make it your goal to understand *why* and *how* your thinking is flawed. Assert firmly to yourself that your thinking can and should be corrected. Every Mindset chapter ends with an Attitude Adjustment section that provides solid, concrete directions for correcting and changing self-defeating thought patterns.

As you read about many of the people-pleasers I have treated in my practice, you may find yourself identifying with their cases. Sometimes, we can see in others what we can't see clearly in ourselves. As you reflect on these case studies and my discussions of them, think about how the information can be applied directly to you and your thought patterns. The material will help you develop some important insights into the price you pay for using a faulty mental program to manage something as important as your relationships with other people.

When you change your thinking, you *will* change how you feel and how you act. Remember, just making one correction in your thinking—taking just one small step—will start a chain reaction of change that will culminate in your recovery from the Disease to Please.

Toxic Thoughts

W hile people-pleasers may think they excel at making others happy, their real talent lies in making themselves feel miserable and inadequate.

By now, maybe you realize just how good you are at making yourself feel bad. As a people-pleaser, you push yourself around with commanding orders, burden yourself with a strict, rigid code of personal rules, and measure yourself against unrealistic, judgmental standards. And, you do all this in order to be a *nice* person!

But, why can't you be nice to yourself?

Sabotaging Shoulds

▶ *The reason is that your thinking is contaminated and distorted with demanding and erroneous* should *statements.*

This virus that corrupts your mental computer—the infiltration of *shoulds, musts, oughts,* and *have to's* into your thought process—is sabotaging your emotional capacity to feel happy, satisfied, adequate, or successful.

Instead, you have become a victim of dictatorial control under your own mind's constant pressure and harsh judgment. When you fall short of perfect compliance with your internal commands, you set yourself up to

feel guilt, self-blame, discouragement, and depression. When others don't comply with the expectations implicit in your rules, you feel anger, frustration, disappointment, and reproach.

The Ten Commandments of People-Pleasing

Perhaps you don't fully realize how tough you are on yourself. But take a look at The Ten Commandments of People-Pleasing listed below. Who wouldn't feel constant stress from trying to live up to these requirements?

The Ten Commandments of People-Pleasing

1. I should always do what others want, expect, or need from me.
2. I should take care of everyone around me whether they ask for help or not.
3. I should always listen to everyone's problems and try my best to solve them.
4. I should always be nice and never hurt anyone's feelings.
5. I should always put other people first, before me.
6. I should never say "no" to anyone who needs or requests something of me.
7. I should never disappoint anyone or let others down in any way.
8. I should always be happy and upbeat and never show any negative feelings to others.
9. I should always try to please other people and make them happy.
10. I should try never to burden others with my own needs or problems.

There is really a hidden eleventh commandment as well: I should fulfill all of these *should and shouldn't* expectations of myself completely and perfectly.

The Seven Deadly Shoulds

The people-pleasing syndrome involves a number of expectations about the way other people *should* treat you, given how nice you are and how hard you try to make them happy.

Many of these expectations about others fall into the category of "hidden shoulds"; that is, they are implicit in, or follow from, the more explicit commandments above. However, The Seven Deadly Shoulds about others are compelling demands nonetheless that set you up to have negative feelings when others fail to fully meet them.

But, of course, the expression of negative feelings toward others—such as anger, resentment, or disappointment—is prohibited by the Eighth Commandment of People-Pleasing: You *should* always be happy, and never show any negative feelings toward others. The net result of this self-imposed trap is that you: (1) feel guilty about having negative feelings toward others, and (2) blame yourself for not pleasing others enough to elicit consistently positive treatment from them in return.

Here are the people-pleasing rules about how others *should* behave:

The Seven Deadly Shoulds

1. Other people should appreciate and love me because of all the things I do for them.

2. Other people should always like and approve of me because of how hard I work to please them.

3. Other people should never reject or criticize me because I always try to live up to their desires and expectations.

4. Other people should be kind and caring to me in return because of how well I treat them.

5. Other people should never hurt me or treat me unfairly because I am so *nice* to them.

6. Other people should never leave or abandon me because of how much I make them need me.

7. Other people should never be angry with me because I would go to any length to avoid conflict, anger, or confrontation with them.

These rules about how others should and should not behave reveal the defensive character of people-pleasing. There is little doubt that pleasing, helping, or fulfilling the needs of other people gives you pleasure and affords you gratification. However, the defensive people-pleasing formula that seems to deter negative responses from others in exchange for your niceness serves as an even stronger motivation.

The formula, however, is flawed.

Stop "Should-ing" and "Must-urbating"

All of The Seven Deadly Shoulds can easily be restated as preferences. For example, "I would prefer that others wouldn't reject me," is a more realistic statement than the injunction that prohibits others from doing so. It also allows for the possibility that another might reject you for reasons that have to do with that individual's biases or prejudices rather than with your shortcomings.

Stating your preference, "I would prefer that others, especially those I love, stay with me and not abandon or reject me," is a more rational statement than one that essentially forbids others to leave because you say they cannot. The latter command implies that you are fully in control of what other people can and cannot do—which you emphatically are not. The preference statement, on the other hand, contains a tacit and accurate acknowledgment that others have free will to make choices even though they might disappoint or hurt you.

Dr. David Burns and other practitioners of Cognitive Therapy[1]—a widely used treatment aimed at changing the flawed thinking that produces negative moods and emotions—identify the presence of demanding *should* statements as a characteristic error in patients' thinking that causes depression, anxiety, and other mood problems. (The term *should statements* is used as an umbrella to include all command phrases that begin with *should, ought, must* or *have to,* as well as the negative forms, *shouldn't, must not,* etc.) Patients are taught to replace their rigid commands with more flexible and accurate statements of preference, acceptance, and tolerance.

The notion that the excessive use of should statements sabotages emotional health and happiness did not originate with the advent of Cognitive Therapy in the 1970s. Thirty years or so earlier, one of the great pioneers of psychoanalysis, Dr. Karen Horney,[2] coined the term *the tyranny of the should* to refer to the enslaving force of personal rules.

Dr. Albert Ellis, founder of Rational-Emotive Behavior Therapy[3] (a forerunner of modern Cognitive Behavior Therapy), invented the word-play verb forms, *should-ing* and *must-urbating,* to convey the prodding, destructive impact of personal demands.

According to Ellis,[4] "nice neurotics"—an all-inclusive term used by him to embrace nearly everyone who suffers from anxiety, depression, and other negative mood states—are "self-upsetting creatures" who make themselves miserable by believing three main musts or shoulds:

1. "I *must* do well, please others, or be liked by significant others or else I will be worthless." (This imperative creates depression and anxiety.)

2. "You *must* treat me kindly, sweetly, or approvingly or else you are wrong and mean." (This imperative creates anger, blame, and disappointment. People-pleasers may blame themselves for not being nice or pleasing enough to earn others' approval or kindness.)

3. "Conditions in life *must* or *should* be the way I want or it's horrible, catastrophic, or disastrous." (This imperative leads to frustration, fear, confusion, blame, anger, anxiety, and depression.)

Because these musts and shoulds are based on strong needs and desires, Ellis maintains that it is innate in human nature to believe them. The problem, then, does not lie in a desire or need itself, but rather in framing it as a mandatory requirement or demanding insistence on the way things *must* or *should* be.

Ellis, along with other cognitive therapists, suggests replacing *should* commands with corrective statements that reflect your desires or wishes—as demonstrated a moment ago when I showed how easily The Seven Deadly Shoulds could be restated as preferences, rather than shoulds. When this is done, the negative emotional responses that occur when reality hits up against inaccurate expectations also will be modified and often eliminated altogether.

For example, there is no rational reason why other people *must* love and appreciate you, even if you stand on your head to please them. But, it would be nice if you received love. It would even be more desirable if others loved you for the person that you are—including the kindness you display in your treatment of others—rather than for all the things you feel so compelled to do for them.

Similarly, you may wish to be a reliable friend on whom others can depend. However, to command that you *should never* say "no" or let other people down is an excessively rigid requirement that, given life's unexpected events and needs, you simply cannot guarantee. However, by stating your intention and preference to be reliable and supportive to your friends, you allow for the realistic possibility that, sometimes, you may need to say "no," due to factors outside your control or due to mere self-preservation.

▶ *Try as you may, you cannot impose your will on the world.*

When you persist with rigid expectations of how you, others, the world, or life in general should be, it only serves to produce confusion, frustration, discouragement, and worse.

When you demand that other people and the world or life treat you in a certain way, you set yourself up to feel angry, disappointed, and depressed when, inevitably, they do not or cannot submit to your will. And, when you demand certain behavior or feelings from yourself—especially when your demands are unrealistic or unattainable—you set yourself up to feel guilty and inadequate.

The bottom line is that the only thing you really *should* do is eliminate as many shoulds from your thinking as possible. When you replace the demanding shoulds with alternative statements about your requests, desires, or preferences, you will reap the benefits emotionally.

Are You Giving Advice or Imposing Your "Shoulds" on Others?

While you may be somewhat aware of the harsh rules you impose on yourself, you probably don't view yourself as critical and judgmental of others. But, when you share your own strict rules in the form of advice to others about what they should and shouldn't do, your well-intended helpfulness can easily be misread as smug disapproval, superiority, harsh criticism, or even censure.

Joan, 48, has two married sons and a daughter in college. She decided to seek therapy for the first time in her life because of a gnawing depression that set in during the past holiday season. Joan says her mood problems started on Christmas as a direct result of the family's conversation during their annual holiday dinner.

"My whole family had come home for the holidays," Joan explained. "We were eating the beautiful dinner I'd prepared. My two daughters-in-law, my sons, my daughter, my husband, and our little granddaughter were all there."

"During dinner, I made some comment to the effect that I see myself as a kind, accepting, and tolerant person. The whole family started laughing. I was the only one who didn't get the joke."

"I insisted that they tell me what was so funny. My sons and daughter voiced the opinion that I was the most judgmental, opinionated, and controlling person they know! They told me I was filled with 'free advice' all the time that nobody wanted to hear. My daughter called me a 'walking talking should machine.' She actually mimicked me, 'You should do this and you shouldn't do that,' apparently to everyone's great amusement but my own. That really stung!"

"My daughters-in-law were a bit more gentle, but even they agreed. They said they knew that I meant well and that it was my way of trying to be supportive and to help people solve their problems. But they both said that I make them feel like they don't measure up to my high standards and that my way is the only right way of doing things. And they resent being told how to make my sons—their husbands— happy."

"I was devastated," Joan concluded. "I never realized the negative effect my 'help' was having on people. I love my family and friends. My husband always tells me I do too much for everyone. Now and then, I realize that one of my kids or friends seems to get angry or annoyed with me but I never understood why. I used to think it was because I wasn't doing enough to be helpful and supportive, or that maybe I was just being too honest with my opinion. Now, it seems like all my efforts have backfired. I feel so terrible about myself I can hardly get out of bed."

Joan turned the corner in her therapy when she understood that her intentions were good, but her methods were flawed. She also recognized that her "should" rules came from her own mother who, she admitted, created similar feelings of inadequacy and resentment among Joan and her sisters with her continual string of maternal "helpful advice and constructive criticism."

When Joan concluded therapy, she remarked, "Even though it was very painful, I think my family may have given me the best Christmas present of all that night. They let me know how I was ramming my rules down everyone's throats and that's the last thing I want to do to the people I love."

You may share Joan's intention to be supportive to friends and loved ones when they have problems. But, the unintended effect of imposing your *shoulds* on others may be to frustrate and irritate them by making them feel like they are doing things poorly because it's not *your* way.

You may also be pushing solutions or jumping prematurely to the "fix," when others simply need you to be a sympathetic listener. Often, the most effective support is to be a good sounding board, reflecting back what you hear and creating a safe context for your friends and family members to think and work through problems at their own pace and direction.

The Power of Accurate Thinking

In addition to the strict and inappropriate commands they contain, The Ten Commandments of People-Pleasing and The Seven Deadly Shoulds include other elements of erroneous thinking that contribute to negative feelings. *Should* statements contain exaggerated language such as *always, never,* or *everyone* that make fulfilling the unrealistic commands even more difficult and unlikely.

Absolute words and exaggerated language are indicative of distorted thinking. And, distorted thinking plays an important causal role in the creation of depression, anxiety, and other negative mood states. While feelings are neither right nor wrong, your thoughts *can* be accurate or inaccurate. By keeping your thinking as rational, reasoned, and accurate as possible, you can minimize or reduce emotional discomfort and negative feelings.

When your beliefs about yourself and about others are accurate, they create a useful road map of your inner life as well as the social world. With a good map, you know where you are and where you're going, especially with other people. In contrast, when your thoughts are not accurate, your ability to understand yourself and others is impaired, just as your sense of direction and geographical bearing is thrown off by an inaccurate road map.

Of course, it is the excessiveness of people-pleasing that makes it problematic. When you are capable of being selective and moderate in your attempts to make others happy, you will be on your way to curing the Disease to Please.

By replacing *always* and *never* with more moderate language, such as *most of the time, sometimes,* or *rarely,* in your people-pleasing thoughts, you will alleviate much of the stress and pressure you now feel from trying to meet such exaggerated time requirements.

Finally, The Seven Deadly Shoulds contain conditional clauses that link your expectations about how others *should* treat you to obligations you believe have been created by your people-pleasing efforts on their behalf. These conditional rules reveal a sense of entitlement and even an underlying scent of manipulation on your part.

Imagine, for example, how another person would respond if you were to instruct them directly, "You *have to* like me because of all the nice things I do for you." The coercive quality of your rules becomes evident when you speak them out loud.

Unless other people have explicitly agreed to like you or treat you in a positive manner in exchange for your pleasing them, your conditions are one-sided and probably destined to fail. It might be pleasant to have other people like and appreciate you, but they have no built-in requirement to do so no matter how nice you have been to them.

> ▶ *Holding on to conditional beliefs about how people should behave toward you because of all you do for them will only set you up to feel disappointment, anger, and resentment to people in particular as well as disillusionment about others in general.*

Further, conditional thinking is a trap that will ensnare you in self-blame and recrimination. If you stick with the false logic that others will be good to you only if you do enough to please them, then you are left with thinking you have only yourself to blame when others let you down.

Voices from the Past

When you hear the commanding *should* in your thoughts or self-talk, you are hearing the voice of your judging conscience. That voice is the amalgamation of your parents, teachers, older siblings, coaches, or other authority figures that, at various points in your life, laid down rules that have stayed with you throughout your life.

As a people-pleasing adult, your conscience still orients you to the expectations of others. By your demonstrated willingness to put others' needs before your own, you continue to accord other people a position of authority over you. Even though you may be taking care of others in what often feels like a parental capacity, and meeting your adult obligations and responsibilities, your conscience still treats you like an obedient or disobedient child.

When you conform to your demanding *should* rules, your conscience gives you a figurative pat on the back. But, when you fall short of following them, your conscience is self-reproaching and generates guilt.

As a people-pleaser, your conscience is doubly punishing. Since you measure your performance according to a standard of whether others are pleased with you—and not just whether you are pleased with yourself—your guilt is further compounded by feelings of shame. While guilt results when you disappoint yourself, shame occurs when you believe that others feel disappointed with and by you.

Although as a people-pleaser, you abhor both giving and receiving criticism from others, you can be brutal when the attack is self-directed. Typically, in addition to more *shoulds* and *shouldn'ts*, ("I should have done more," "I shouldn't be angry or resentful," etc.), your self-critical monologues are likely laden with other depression-producing language and distorted thoughts.

You may use labels such as "selfish," "self-centered," and "unlovable" or, more primitively, "jerk," "stupid," or "dumb" to berate and insult yourself. And, like a telescopic mental trick, you will tend to magnify or exaggerate the scale of your own judged inadequacies and shortcomings while you minimize the magnitude of misdeeds or faults in others.

People-Pleasing Perfectionism

People with the Disease to Please are rarely—if ever—truly pleased and satisfied with themselves. As a people-pleaser, you want and need everyone's approval yet withhold approval from yourself.

Each new day you strive yet again to prove your value through all the things you do to please others. Apparently there are no reservoirs of good deeds in your psychological economy. Whatever worth you may have earned in days or years past by the myriad of your nice and giving actions, you respond today as though your value is perpetually in question, tested anew with each fresh request or expression of need that you must rise to meet. It's as if you start each day with nothing in the bank.

What spurs the constant striving to please others is a pervasive sense of inadequacy composed of nagging doubt and the chronic suspicions that you have not done quite enough, tried hard enough, given enough, or said "yes" enough to have truly satisfied others.

But this disquieting sense of inadequacy does not come from a shortfall of effort or ability to please on your part. Its true source lies in the hidden perfectionism lurking between the lines of your *should* rules.

Remember the eleventh postscript commandment: "I *should* fulfill these *should and shouldn't* expectations of myself completely and perfectly." The perfectionist standards to which you hold yourself are measured at two levels.

First, you require yourself to please everyone, all the time. Second, you demand that you maintain a positive emotional temperament at all times. Thus, you are to exude a happy and upbeat demeanor even while you exhaust and deplete yourself pleasing others and denying your own needs. If your mood should inadvertently slip, you are never to show your negative feelings to others.

▶ *Holding yourself to perfectionist standards like these is nothing short of self-imposed emotional cruelty.*

If that sounds too dramatic or extreme, imagine a mother instructing her child to meet such requirements: "You must always please me," says the woman sternly to the young child. "You are to fulfill each and every request or order I issue, no matter what you are doing or how you feel. And, you must smile and be happy all the time. If I ever hear you complain or show any signs of an emotion other than happiness, you will be punished. If you fail to do these things perfectly, I will not love you anymore. Any questions?"

This sounds like the deranged dialogue of the mean stepmother character in a fairy tale. Alternatively, in darker, real-life terms, the speaker might be a narcissistic "Mommy Dearest," subjecting her child to emotional and psychological abuse. While admittedly your self-talk may not be quite as stark as this imaginary "mother," the perfectionist expectations and evaluative standards that you apply to yourself are directly comparable.

> ► *There is nothing inherently wrong or unhealthy about setting high standards in various arenas of life. However, striving for perfection is a demoralizing and guaranteed formula for failure. Striving for excellence, on the other hand, is motivating because reaching it is attainable.*

Attitude Adjustment:
The Sabotaging Shoulds of People-Pleasing

Concentrate on the corrections below for countering your sabotaging *shoulds*. As you do so, keep in mind Albert Ellis's advice to stop *should-ing* on yourself and others, and avoid *must-urbating* as much as possible.

♦ Whenever your thinking is contaminated by shoulds, musts, oughts, and have to's, it is rigid, inflexible, and extreme. Rational thinking that will serve you better is flexible, moderate, and balanced.

♦ Imposing your shoulds on others is coercive and controlling. Instead, try using phrases such as, "I would prefer if . . . ," or "It might be better if . . . ," or, "I would like it if you . . ." instead of the manipulative and coercive "you should" and "you shouldn't" statements.

♦ The Ten Commandments of People-Pleasing and The Seven Deadly Shoulds are rigid rules that are nearly impossible to fulfill and will not make you happy. You will be far better off with more attainable, realistic guidelines and principles about how you would like to treat others and how you would prefer others to treat you.

♦ You don't have to do anything *perfectly,* including pleasing others or having perfectly positive emotions. Striving for perfection is demoralizing. Striving for excellence is motivating.

CHAPTER 3

It's *Okay* Not *to Be Nice*

If the personality of a people-pleaser had to be summed up in one word, that word would be *nice*. But, if you have the Disease to Please, *nice* isn't just a personality description. Being nice is shorthand for a full-blown belief system that dictates how to act with other people so that bad things won't happen to you.

Unfortunately, though, the formula doesn't always work. Bad things happen to nice people all the time, as you probably already know. While they may not deserve it, nice people are sometimes rejected, abandoned, disdained, disliked, or hurt by others. And, nice people also are frequently beset by seemingly self-imposed emotional burdens such as worry, anxiety, depression, and even panic attacks.

Carolyn was nine when her mother was diagnosed with breast cancer. She recalls clearly the conversation she had with her father and with her mother's doctor about the importance of keeping her mother happy and unstressed in order for her to recover. Terrified that her mother would die, she believed that her mother's survival depended on Carolyn's being a good and nice little girl.

A few weeks prior to the discovery of the lump in her mother's breast, Carolyn had been seriously reprimanded by her teacher for teasing and making fun of a disabled child on the school playground. The teacher wrote a stern letter to Carolyn's parents recounting the

incident and requesting that her parents come to school for a confer-
ence about their daughter's behavior.

When Carolyn's parents received the letter, they were extremely
upset with their daughter.

"We have tried to teach you to be a good person and to be nice to
everyone," her mother said tearfully. "Now, I find out that you were
downright cruel and mean to that sweet little girl in the wheelchair.
Your father and I are ashamed of you," she concluded.

As a punishment, Carolyn was required to give up playing outside
for a week and to stay in her room instead in order to think about how
much she had hurt the little girl's feelings by not being nice. Carolyn's
parents also instructed her to write three letters of apology: One to the
disabled child, one to the child's parents, and a third to her own parents for disappointing them so deeply.

In her letters, Carolyn stated that she was sorry and ashamed about
"not being nice" and for hurting the other girl's feelings. She vowed to
her own parents that she would never be mean or unkind to anyone
again. Carolyn recalls feeling extremely guilty and remorseful.

In her young mind, Carolyn believed that she was directly to blame
for her mother's illness because of how upsetting the playground incident had been to both her parents. After all, hadn't the doctor said that
her mother needed to stay calm and happy in order to fully recover?
Carolyn reasoned that if no stress could help cure her mother, then
causing her to become so stressed and upset must have made her
mother get sick initially.

During the months of her mother's illness, Carolyn vowed in her
daily prayers that she would always be a nice girl, if only her mother
would survive. She promised herself that she would never again be
mean or tease anyone, including her younger brother, if only her Mom
wouldn't die.

Happily, Carolyn's mother did survive. But, Carolyn became a
world-class people-pleaser. Even as an adult, Carolyn continued to
believe that by being nice, she could prevent bad things from happening. Conversely, she feared that dire consequences would ensue on those
rare occasions when she would slip and say an unkind word or be
otherwise short-tempered with her family, friends, or employees.

Though Carolyn's reactions are somewhat extreme, virtually every
people-pleaser holds tenaciously to the self-concept of being a nice person.
Despite what other people may say or do to people-pleasers their essential

niceness prohibits them from saying negative things in response. Often, the nice people-pleaser cannot even acknowledge having negative thoughts or feelings toward others.

But, there is a substantial price to being nice which you should no longer be willing to pay. When you can endorse this seemingly simple statement, "It's okay *not* to be nice," you will have made giant inroads on curing your own Disease to Please problems.

First, though, the quiz below will help you assess the degree to which your current thinking contains a commitment to being nice.

What Is Your "Nice-Q?" Quiz

Read each statement and decide whether or not it applies to you. Circle "T" if the statement is true, or mostly true. Or, circle "F" if it is false, or mostly false.

1. I pride myself on being a nice person.   T or F

2. It is very difficult for me to reject another person no matter how much she or he may deserve it.   T or F

3. I probably go overboard in doing nice things for other people. T or F

4. It's much easier for me to acknowledge negative feelings about myself than to express negative feelings toward others.   T or F

5. If something goes wrong, I often feel that I'm to blame.   T or F

6. I believe that I should always be nice.   T or F

7. I might do too much for others, be overly nice, or even let myself be used so that I won't be rejected for other reasons.   T or F

8. I really believe that nice people get the approval, affection, and friendship of others.   T or F

9. I don't think it's nice to express anger toward others.   T or F

10. I shouldn't get angry or upset with the people I love.   T or F

11. I am afraid that if I'm not nice to others, I will be ignored, rejected, or even punished.   T or F

12. I believe that I should always be nice even if it means allowing others to take advantage of my good nature.   T or F

13. Being nice and doing things to please others is my way of protecting myself from rejection, disapproval, and abandonment.   T or F

14. I wouldn't think of myself as a nice person if I criticized other people, even if they deserved it.   T or F

15. I try to make other people like me by being a nice person.   T or F

16. Sometimes I feel like I need to "buy" the love and friendship of others by doing nice things to please them.   T or F

17. Often, being nice prevents me from expressing negative feelings toward others.   T or F

18. I believe that others would describe me as being polite, pleasing, and agreeable.   T or F

19. I think my friends should like me because of all the nice things I do for them.   T or F

20. I want everyone to think of me as a nice person.   T or F

How to Score and Interpret Your Answers

Add up the number of times you circled "T" to obtain your total score.

♦ *If your score is between 14 and 20:* You are nice to a fault. It is likely that your interpersonal relationships as well as your emotional health actually are negatively affected by your good intentions. You are paying far too high a price for being nice. When you replace nice at the core of your self-concept with less self-defeating traits, the rate of your recovery will speed up.

♦ *If your score is between 8 and 13:* Your people-pleasing problems are strongly associated with your excessive need to be nice to others, too often at the expense of being good to yourself. Letting go of your *nice* self-concept will speed the rate of your recovery.

♦ *If your score is between 5 and 7:* You still have a concern with being viewed as nice by others, though somewhat less so than most people-pleasers. Build on your strengths—but remember that being nice isn't one of them. You are still close to dangerous psychological territory and should monitor your tendencies to be nice at your own expense.

♦ *If your score is between 0 and 4:* You have an unusually low concern with being nice for someone with the Disease to Please. Check to be sure you are not falling into the trap of denial. But, if you've really overcome your need to be nice at your own expense, then you've already traveled some notable distance on the path to recovery. Build on your strengths.

Pleasing = Nice

As a practicing psychologist for the past 25 years, I can assure you that personalities generally are far too interesting and complicated to be reduced to any single word or description, such as *nice*. Nonetheless, I do know that if a certain personality trait is assigned to you at an early age and, therefore, becomes a core part of your self-concept, that label will have a strong impact on your thoughts, feelings, and behavior throughout life.

Nice is a label that parents, teachers, and other adults affix to a well-behaved child. "What a nice little girl you are!" or "There's a nice boy" are frequently heard forms of praise. Perhaps you use these phrases yourself.

Nice is also used prescriptively by parents and other significant adults—as in, you *should* be nice—because it connotes being well-bred, polite, well-mannered, and, ultimately, socially acceptable. It is also used proscriptively, especially with adolescent girls, to differentiate morally sound actions from those that are immoral or amoral, as in "*Nice* girls don't go to bars" or "*Nice* girls don't 'go all the way.' "

However, it is interesting to note how often the attribute of "niceness" when applied to adults is actually discounted and sometimes even disparaged. Consider, for example, how often a qualifier follows the subjective phrase as in, "She's nice, but . . ." or "He's a nice guy, but . . ." The discounting *but* generally heralds some reference to a negative character quality.

Dictionaries define *nice* as pleasing or agreeable. In general, nice people tend to be viewed as flat and two-dimensional instead of three-dimensional with depth and definition. They are rather innocuous, lacking sharp edges or clear definition to their personalities. In groups or organizations, nice individuals simply don't make waves. And, while they do not offend others, nice people rarely impress others either. (When my daughter was young, she once explained that she liked the Disney villains more than the "nice" heroes because the villains were "much more interesting.")

In fact, some *nice* people are even disparaged for the very qualities of compliance, ingratiation, and agreeability that are largely synonymous with their defining trait. Jane Austen captures this subtle but negative response to *niceness* in her description of a female character in one of her stories:

> *She was nothing more than a mere good-tempered and obliging young woman; as such we could scarcely dislike her—she was only an object of contempt.*

Since, by literal definition, *nice* means *pleasing*, it understandably lies at the core of your self-concept as a people-pleaser. On the other hand, since *nice* seems, at best, to be of equivocal value as a character trait and source of self-esteem, why does it feel so compelling as a guideline for your actions? And, why do actions that are incongruous with *nice* create so much anxiety and discomfort?

Niceness as Emotional Armor

The answers lie in understanding the protective value of being nice in your belief system as a people-pleaser. Viewed in the context of the interpersonal cover it provides, *nice* takes on a considerably higher worth than it holds as a trait of character.

> ▶ *Specifically, people-pleasers believe that by being nice, they will avoid painful experiences, including rejection, isolation, abandonment, disapproval, and anger. After all, if you don't make waves or rock the boat, the other passengers shouldn't want to throw you overboard.*

But, people-pleasers typically go the extra distance to ensure that they will be viewed as not just ordinarily nice, but as extraordinarily so. To this end, people-pleasers often go to excessive lengths, overdoing their efforts in extravagant gestures of care and consideration. In extreme niceness lies the perceived protection: Who, after all, would want to hurt you if you are *so* nice and giving to them?

Consider your responses to the quiz earlier in this chapter, and specifically your responses to statements 7, 8, 11, 13, 15, 16, and 19. If you recognize yourself in at least some of these statements, you are using *niceness* as a form of interpersonal protection, at least to some degree. If you endorsed all seven items, you clearly expect that by being nice to others, you will earn their gratitude, affection, and acceptance. In turn, you believe (and hope) that you will be protected by your niceness and the goodwill it creates from being rejected, abandoned, disapproved of, or otherwise hurt emotionally.

On its face, this belief system appears logical and reasonable. In fact, the eminent scientist-philosopher Dr. Hans Selye, the father of modern concepts of stress and stress-induced illness, endorsed a qualified version of this belief. Selye argued that the best way for human beings to protect themselves from interpersonal stress was to be kind and giving to others. Selye believed that this was critically important as a way to live because the stress caused by other people is deadly.[5] (Several years ago I wrote a book, *Lethal Lovers and Poisonous People: How to Protect Your Health from Relationships That Make You Sick,*[6] which dealt with these kinds of toxic relationships.)

Selye called his philosophy of stress management "altruistic egoism." This mouthful of a phrase is intended to mean that by earning the good-will of others through the generosity of your character and action, you are actually acting in your own self-interest. If you are kind and giving to others, Selye argued, other people will tend to be kind in return and, therefore, won't be as likely to cause you stress.

So, what are the distinctions between the people-pleasers' version of niceness-as-protection and Dr. Selye's wise counsel on altruistic egoism? Dr. Selye understood that niceness would not protect you from everyone, all of the time. He was adamant that certain people could and would cause harm to you emotionally—regardless of whether you treated them kindly or not. This might occur because the other person is intrinsically hateful, prejudiced, or bigoted; or because he or she holds an old grudge and is out to settle a score by punishing you; or simply because the other person is not emotionally healthy or mature enough to be loved and to love in return.

People-pleasers, in contrast, believe in niceness as an article of faith. They invest being nice with a kind of magical power to avert meanness or hurtfulness from others. In people-pleasing logic, if niceness fails to protect you from an interpersonal slight or hurt, *you* must not have been *nice enough, and you must do even more!*

Do You Remember Your "Magical" Thoughts?

This compelling, but ultimately flawed belief that being nice will protect you from being hurt by others is rooted in the magical thinking of child-hood. The term *magical thinking* refers to a mindset in which thoughts and actions are indistinguishable. As such, thoughts are every bit as potent as actions.

If this were true, of course, it would bestow magical powers to virtually anyone who could think. In the thrilling calculus of childish thought, just a simple wish is enough to make it so.

Young children often use their innate magical thinking to ward off fears. In the child's mind, conditional agreements are formulated in order to maintain the illusion of control. For example, the child might make a deal with the imaginary monsters in the closet: "If I go to sleep and leave all the lights on, you can't come out or hurt me."

Similarly, a child may try to fend off the all-too-real possibility of a parental divorce by bargaining, "If I'm good and do all the things my parents want, they won't split up." It is easy to understand how "being nice" could be incorporated into a child's set of magical conditions that promise to provide protection from harm.

In normal development, by about age seven to eight, the child learns that, indeed, there is a difference between thinking and doing, between wishing and making something happen in reality. By puberty, most magical thinking has transformed into reality-based plans and action or into culturally acceptable forms, including faith and prayer.

However, there are some childlike ways of thinking—some magical thoughts—that can stay with you even as an adult. In particular, when such thoughts provide relief from fear and anxiety, they can endure for decades. When you strictly examine them, under the harsh light of logic and adult reality, you may know that they don't hold sway. Nevertheless, you still hold on to their protective promise.

The belief in the protective power of niceness, then, is a holdover from a childhood era of magical thinking. Fears of rejection, abandonment, isolation, or disapproval—and of the depression and emotional pain such experiences can produce—are now the "monsters" that require containment. But, the dread of rejection, alienation, and loneliness are reality-based fears, not fantasy-based fears, like the imaginary inhabitants of a child's closet.

Do You Still Have "Magical" Thoughts?

For children, the connection between being nice or good and avoiding bad outcomes is not just magical, it has a strong reality basis as well. Most children learn through direct experience that if they comply with parental rules and preferences—that is, if they are *nice* girls and boys—they will receive praise and/or avoid punishment. On the other hand, children are repeatedly shown that if they are *not nice* because they break rules or challenge the parental or school order, they will be disciplined and punished. In a very real sense, then, being nice prevents at least *some* bad things from happening.

Young children often compound the protective power of niceness by adding magical thinking and childish omnipotence to the reality base. This means that being *nice* may be invested with the imagined power to fend off bad consequences that are not within the child's actual control. Such a child, for example, might try to prevent the parents from divorcing by promising in his or her mind to *be nice.*

As we saw earlier in the case of Carolyn, when a particularly disruptive, painful, or traumatic early life experience is associated with a belief in the protective power of niceness, it can have long-lasting impact. This is especially true if being nice is linked in a child's mind with the actual prevention or amelioration of a bad experience; or, conversely, if doing or thinking something that was not nice is connected to the occurrence of a trauma.

Many people-pleasers that I have treated over the years can trace their need to be nice to their childlike analysis of why a particular trauma occurred. In some cases, such as Carolyn's, a serious illness afflicts a family member or even the child directly. In others, there may have been a fatal or disabling accident or a premature death of a parent or sibling.

It is a normal psychological response to severe stress to try to regain a semblance of control, particularly when the stakes are high. Under such circumstances, a child might bargain with a higher power promising to "be nice" and "good" in order to influence the outcome of an illness or accident.

In therapy, Carolyn uncovered the connection between being nice and saving her mother's life. And she came to understand that when she wasn't nice to someone, her old "magical thinking" sparked the immediate fear that something bad would happen as a consequence.

Carolyn's case is a dramatic illustration of the psychological protection value of being nice. In Carolyn's young mind, her promise to always be nice was rewarded by her mother's survival. As a result, Carolyn held tightly to her belief that niceness was imperative in ways that eventually became self-defeating.

As a perennially nice person, Carolyn had little ability to express negative feelings in constructive ways. Carolyn knew that people took advantage of her nice nature but she was unable to stand up for herself. When her doctor referred Carolyn to see me, she was exhausted and depleted from her people-pleasing efforts, but too fearful to say "no" or set any boundaries because doing so "wouldn't be nice."

Carolyn's attachment to being nice is linked to a good outcome: her mother's survival. But, in other cases, bad outcomes of traumatic experiences prevail. A parent may die prematurely or a sibling may become permanently disabled from an accident. Parents may get divorced, despite their children's sense of excessive responsibility and misplaced efforts to keep them together.

Nevertheless, many adult people-pleasers maintain a compulsion to be nice even though their own childhood traumas had unhappy endings. Some can trace their niceness to the thought that being nice will prevent more bad things from happening. Or, sadly, some adult people-pleasers carry forward the childhood guilt that the bad events might never have happened if only they had been *nicer* and better kids.

Chronic, long-term people-pleasers often go about their people-pleasing behavior without a clue that their Disease to Please virus began to grow and spread during their childhood.

By definition, superstitious or magical thinking is not accurate. Believing that your niceness should or could protect you from rejection, isolation, or other negative life experiences including trauma, places an onerous responsibility on your mood and behavior. It simply isn't human to live up to the burden of being nice all the time to everyone; nor is it always appropriate.

▶ *It's okay not to be nice all the time.*

When Bad Things Happen to Nice People

While your belief in the protective power of niceness may seem harmless on its face, it is actually a cognitive minefield.

▶ **The biggest problem with believing in the absolute protective power of niceness is that it simply does not work. You may be the nicest person alive, and somebody out there won't like you— maybe precisely because you're so darned nice.**

The fact remains that no matter how nice you are, there are no guarantees against being rejected, insulted, excluded, disapproved of, and even abandoned by others. A person who is prejudiced against you because of your race, ethnicity, gender, or sexual preference will likely reject you for his or her own irrational, hateful reasons. Your relative niceness won't make any difference. Or, if another is jealous of you, she may take a stand against you in spite of all the nice things you may have done for her. It's not fair, but neither is life.

Take another look at your assumptions about whether you believe life is or ought to be fair. The belief that being nice should protect you from being hurt by others is firmly grounded in a root expectation that life is fair.

So, the dilemma nice people like you face is that, when the world doesn't work the way it is supposed to and other people hurt you even though you are nice to them, you are likely to feel confused and frustrated. Your reactions also include anger because, in part, your expectations of how others *should* treat you if you are nice to them are also being violated. Of course, you are too nice to direct that anger toward others who may have wronged you. Instead, more than likely you will turn it inward and blame yourself for not being nice enough or for deserving the mistreatment for some other reason. That way, life remains fair in your mind. However, the price you will pay for turning the anger against yourself will be depression.

Think about it for a minute. In a fair world, only good things would happen to nice people because they deserve to be happy. If life were fair, bad things would only happen to bad people, because they deserve problems and unhappiness.

Now, here's the reality wrinkle: Bad things do happen to nice people, even nice people just like you.

If you believe that life is fair and that niceness should protect you from bad things, you are setting yourself up for a wallop of self-blame and depression when a bad thing happens to you, as it inevitably will.

There are some dangerous but seductive syllogisms or false logic lurking behind the belief that niceness should protect you from being hurt by others. The faulty reasoning leads to depressing and guilt-inducing conclusions:

If life is fair, people get what they deserve.
A bad thing (e.g., rejection, abandonment) happened to me.
Therefore, I deserve it.

or

If I'm nice, nobody will reject or hurt me.
I just got rejected and hurt.
Therefore, I'm not as nice as I think; or, I'm not nice enough.

This downward spiral of mood and thought can sink you into a tailspin of negativity. Moreover, this faulty logic leads you into making even greater efforts to please and be nice to others, thereby feeding the vicious cycle of the Disease to Please.

Modifying the initial assumption that life is fair will go a long way toward correcting this depression-producing thinking. But if you hold on stubbornly to a belief that niceness should protect you, you will likely devolve into self-blame, guilt, and depression when—not if—life deals you a painful blow. Remember, correcting just one thought in the Disease to Please triangle will interrupt the cycle and eventually lead you to the path of recovery.

Don't Reward Abusive Treatment

You may also use being nice as a trump card that could overcome the unkind treatment of another. In this case, however, niceness is really the weakest suit.

Being nice is not an appropriate response to someone who is hurting you emotionally. On the contrary, being nice to someone who is using you as a verbal punching bag only rewards his or her abusive behavior. In effect, niceness gives the other person permission—and even encouragement—to mistreat you.

The tendency to always be nice, to avoid conflict or confrontation at any cost, and to submit to the will of critical and controlling partners or bosses, places you at significant risk to emotionally abusive relationships.

In a conflict situation—even if the attack is one-sided—people-pleasing is equivalent to unilateral psychological disarmament. Being nice when you are under attack leaves you defenseless and unacceptably vulnerable.

Paradoxically, if you are the target of verbal and emotional abuse, your niceness not only will fail to protect you, it will strengthen the person who is hurting you or treating you unkindly.

This is not to say that people-pleasing *causes* others to be abusive toward you in the first place. Those causes lie within the personality and life history of the abuser. Research shows, for example, that children who were abused grow up to be abusive adults.

But, while you are not the cause of the mistreatment you may be getting, your niceness and people-pleasing certainly maintain the cycle of abuse. You may think that by trying even harder to please someone who is being unkind, you are challenging the cycle. But, in fact, you are playing right into it.

You may ardently hope that your niceness, kindness, and love will eventually carry the day and change the other person's behavior toward you. Sadly, despite your good intentions, this approach almost never works. Instead, your continued participation and inadvertent reward of the abusive behavior will only embolden the abuser and erode your self-esteem. Eventually, you may even come to believe that unkind, hostile, or abusive treatment is all you really deserve anyway.

Of course, you must learn the skills to speak up appropriately when your right to kind and respectful treatment is violated. However, first, you must change your mistaken belief that niceness will protect you or that it will overcome abusive or unkind treatment.

Niceness and the 3-Letter "F" Word

Susan is a people-pleasing pro. At 38, she is the mother of three and the daughter to two elderly parents whose care falls to her as the only girl in the family. She teaches the fifth grade at the local school where her children attend and she is a leading force in the PTA.

In addition, Susan does the bookkeeping for her husband's small consulting business. She entertains her husband's clients at lovely home dinner parties for which she does all her own cooking. Susan is an active volunteer in a charitable organization where she heads the fundraising committee and does the bulk of the work.

Susan admits that she cannot remember the last time she said "no" to anyone. She realizes that she is under a lot of stress, and that she should probably stop doing so many things. She knows that many of her relationships are very unbalanced, and that she is putting out far more effort than she is getting in return.

Susan has struggled with a significant weight problem since childhood. She jokes, with a tear in her voice, that she has gained and lost the same 50 pounds about 100 times in her life. She understands the link between her people-pleasing patterns and her weight issues.

"I've always felt that I need to be super-nice to people and do whatever I can to make them happy, or else they won't like me because I'm heavy. It seems like I'm trying to convince people not to reject me from the minute I first meet them. I'm really afraid that if I do get rejected, someone will call me the 'F' word—the 3-letter one: F-A-T."

"My feelings were constantly hurt when I was a child. The other kids teased me and called me fat names like 'Tubby' or 'Fatso.' My only defense was to try to make them like me for other reasons."

"As a child and later as a teenager, I was willing to do anything for other kids just so they wouldn't reject me because I was fat. I really let people use me. I did their homework, forged notes that were supposed to come from parents, let them copy from my tests—anything anybody asked, I would do."

"When I was a teenager, I was sexually promiscuous. I was willing to have sex with nearly any boy, just to avoid being rejected."

"Needless to say, I was rejected a lot anyway. But, as an adult, I'm still doing the same things, going overboard to be nice to everyone. Only now, I don't even wait for someone to ask for something. I figure out what they need, and I give it to them."

There are many people like Susan who suffer from the Disease to Please because they *expect* to be rejected. Some aspect of their appearance or character makes them feel unworthy and mars their self-esteem.

The perceived "flaw" can be physical in nature such as overweight, an apparent disability or deformity, an unattractive face or facial feature, bad hair, or short stature. Or, the "flaw" can be psychological such as feeling unintelligent, undereducated, unsuccessful, or ashamed about not having a lot of money.

Like Susan, you may feel compelled to be nice because you anticipate and expect rejection from others due to a real or imagined "flaw" you find in yourself. In psychological terms, you are *projecting* your own negative feelings about yourself onto others. You also may be using your niceness defensively to compensate for what you perceive to be a serious inadequacy in your appearance or character. By being nice, pleasing, and inoffensive, your hidden motivation may be to manipulate others into liking you or at least into not rejecting you.

The real flaw lies in this strategy rather than in your appearance or character. It backfires because it continually erodes your self-esteem, thereby thrusting you further into the cycle of the Disease to Please. If people do accept you, your self-esteem will still remain impaired because you will attribute their acceptance to the nice things you do for them rather than to your value as a human being. ("She only likes me because I'm nice and do so much for her.") At the same time, your belief that niceness works as both protection and compensation for your perceived "flaw" is reinforced along with the rest of your people-pleasing habits.

On the other hand, if people reject you, your erroneous belief that you are fundamentally unworthy will be confirmed in your mind. When this happens, the rupture in your self-esteem deepens. Moreover, you will feel the need to be even nicer in the future in order to protect against further painful rejection.

▶ *The solution lies in recognizing that the person whose acceptance you most need is your own. When you address the real issues that make you feel unworthy and separate your essential value as a person from some attribute of your appearance or fact of your background, the wound in your self-esteem will begin to heal and your people-pleasing problems will loosen their grip.*

Attitude Adjustment: It's Okay Not to Be Nice

Here are some corrective thoughts to replace the toxic idea that you *need to be nice,* at any price. Replacing just one toxic thought with a corrective statement can start the process of curing your people-pleasing syndrome.

♦ Being nice won't always protect you from unkind treatment from others. Thinking that it will is likely to make you feel guilty and responsible if others treat you badly.

- Don't reward people who treat you badly or unkindly by acting nice and pretending that it's okay.

- If you have to compromise your own values, needs, or identity as a special and unique individual, then the price of nice is just too high.

- It is far better for you to say what's on your mind, even if you must communicate some negative feelings, than to stuff your thoughts inside and become depressed, anxious, or emotionally ill in other ways just to stay nice.

- *It's okay not to be nice.*

CHAPTER 4

Putting Others First

At the core of the people-pleasing syndrome is the central belief that others must come first. As a people-pleaser, you almost certainly know that you put others' needs ahead of your own. And you most likely believe that to do otherwise would be selfish.

What you probably do not realize, however, is the disturbingly negative picture of other people's motives and dispositions that underlies these beliefs. Viewed psychologically, the world of the people-pleaser is a dangerous place filled with powerful others who are controlling, demanding, rejecting, exploitative, and punishing. Furthermore, the needs of these demanding others hold a position of primacy that must be served and satisfied, even at the expense of your own.

Before we uncover and examine these buried beliefs, take the quiz below to measure the extent to which you agree that others *must* come first.

Do You Put Others First? Quiz

Read each statement below and decide whether or not it applies to you. Circle "T" if the statement is true, or mostly true, for you; circle "F" if it is false, or mostly false, for you.

1. I focus a great deal on meeting the needs of others, even at the expense of my own needs or desires.   T or F

2. My needs should always take a backseat to the needs of people I love.   T or F

3. I have to give of myself to others all the time in order to really be worthy of love.   T or F

4. My first concern in life is to make other people happy.   T or F

5. In any given situation, I am far more likely to take the perspective of other people than to consider my own.   T or F

6. When other people in my life are upset, I think it is up to me to do something about it.   T or F

7. I should always do what others want or expect of me.   T or F

8. My greatest need is to take care of the people in my life.   T or F

9. I usually adopt the beliefs and attitudes of those closest to me. T or F

10. I try to live my life according to the belief that it is much better to give than to receive.   T or F

11. I am likely to do all the things I can to make others happy before I do anything just for myself.   T or F

12. It is extremely difficult for me to ask others for help or to express my needs in any way.   T or F

13. I feel that I need to earn other people's love by doing things to make them happy.   T or F

14. I am comfortable doing things for others without asking or expecting anything in return.   T or F

15. If I stopped putting others' needs ahead of my own, I would become a selfish person and people wouldn't like me.   T or F

16. I expect to give far more in relationships than I expect to get back. T or F

17. I must always please others even if it is at the expense of my own feelings or needs.   T or F

18. I often feel that others expect too much from me, but I always try not to disappoint them or let them down.   T or F

19. When my own needs conflict with those of others, I always put my needs last.   T or F

20. I would feel very guilty if I didn't make the needs of others more important than my own.   T or F

21. I sometimes feel resentful that so many people make demands on me or need me, but I never let my resentment show.   T or F

22. At times I feel taken for granted and disappointed that others aren't there for me when I need help.   T or F

23. My friends and family often come to me for advice and help with solving their problems.   T or F

24. I often feel drained, stressed, and exhausted by meeting the needs of so many other people.   T or F

25. I sometimes feel worried that if I expressed my needs to others, I'd be rejected, ignored, or punished.   T or F

How to Score and Interpret Your Answers

Add up the number of times you circled "T" to obtain your total score.

♦ *If your score is between 17 and 25:* Your people-pleasing problems are strongly based in your belief in the primacy of others over yourself. At this point, you probably can't even identify your own needs independent of your needs to take care of others. It is likely that you feel highly stressed by putting others before yourself, and far more resentful and angry than you can even acknowledge. You will make a significant breakthrough in your recovery when you change your thinking about *always* putting others' needs ahead of your own.

♦ *If your score is between 10 and 16:* Your thinking has the characteristic people-pleasing bent toward putting others' needs ahead of your own. While you seem to exercise some degree of moderation over the belief that others *must* come first, you are wise to keep a watchful eye on this core assumption behind the Disease to Please. Changing this self-defeating belief in the primacy of others is a key to curing the Disease to Please.

♦ *If your score is 9 or lower:* You have only mild tendencies to believe that others' needs should always come before your own. However, if you have the Disease to Please, your behavior suggests otherwise. Although you may not consciously believe that others are more important than you, your people-pleasing habits reflect that belief. Work on becoming more aware of how your thoughts fit with your tendency to cater to others. Strengthening the view that your needs are as important as others' will help speed your recovery.

Training Others Not to Take Care of You

Sarah, 40, was the ultimate people-pleasing wife and mother of four. She was a homemaker and stay-at-home mom. Because her husband worked hard to make a good living for the family, Sarah believed that it was her responsibility to take care of his every need from the time he walked through the door in the evening to the time he went to bed. And she catered to her children as well.

Because she had grown up in relatively poor circumstances in which both her parents worked alternate day and night shifts, Sarah wanted to give her own children the benefits of having a mom at home and a dad who made a nice living for them. So Sarah believed that her children should have very few household responsibilities in order for them to do well in school and to have fun as kids.

But, despite her benevolent intentions, Sarah's people-pleasing backfired.

For years, Sarah kept up the pace of taking care of everyone's needs in the family without ever asking for help or support. Then, she was diagnosed with acute rheumatoid arthritis that required a brief hospitalization followed by six weeks of mandatory bed rest. Sarah's doctor, a good personal friend, ordered her to "stop waiting on your family hand and foot like a maid."

When she returned from the hospital, Sarah was shocked and profoundly hurt by her family's reaction. Instead of being kind and happy to reciprocate the years of Sarah's nurturance, they displayed irritation and resentment for the inconvenience caused by Sarah's illness.

At first, Sarah felt guilty for being sick and a burden to her family. But soon she was overcome with feelings of anger and resentment.

Sarah's short-term solution was to ask her own mother to come stay with the family in order to take care of them and her until she was well. When she recovered, however, Sarah sat down with her family and, mustering all her courage, told them what she had been thinking about while she was recuperating in bed.

"I feel 100 percent responsible for creating selfish, self-centered brats as children, and a spoiled, ungrateful husband," she told her shocked family. "But now things are going to be very different."

Sarah announced further that she was officially "on strike." She stated that she would do nothing more for them until each of them assumed a measure of responsibility for his or her own needs, as well as for one another.

"It was sad that I had to get so sick to see the mistakes I was making," Sarah said. "I thought I was being a good wife and mom by being such a people-pleaser. I never let anyone in my family think I needed anything from them until I got sick. I trained them to ignore me and to think only of themselves."

As Sarah worked in therapy to overcome her people-pleasing syndrome, she reflected on the role model she had been presenting to her two daughters and two sons.

"My intentions were to take care of the household work so that my kids could focus all their energy on school and on their activities. I want my kids to achieve their full potential—all my kids, the girls and the boys. I've always told them to shoot for the stars, to be anything they want to be."

"But I'm truly horrified when I think what I have been showing them by my example. I've been teaching my daughters that women are doormats! Even worse, I've been showing my sons how to wipe their feet on them. That's the last message in the world I want my kids to learn."

"I realize now that if I don't treat myself with respect, my kids won't learn to respect me or themselves either."

"When my mother came to take care of me, she gave me a serious attitude adjustment. She reminded me that when growing up in my own family, even though we were pretty hard up financially, we loved and took care of one another."

"I realized that I was raising a bunch of lousy human beings. So I decided there and then that things were going to change. And they have, but very slowly. Periodically, I have to go on strike again to remind everyone to live up to his or her responsibilities."

"The best part is that I really believe my family respects me and loves me more for making them into better people," she concluded.

In one sense, Sarah's illness was fortuitous. By getting sick, Sarah was able to take the first step on the road to curing her Disease to Please.

Sarah's story is also a good illustration of how people-pleasers can easily lose track of their own needs by always making others more important than themselves. People-pleasers train themselves to deny their own needs while, at the same time, they inadvertently teach others not to take care of them either.

Sarah, like many other people-pleasers in a maternal or parental role, received a great deal of cultural and social reinforcement for putting her children first and for being a "Super-Mom." Other people praised her competence and she enjoyed fulfilling the role she had defined for herself until she realized the price she was paying.

You can easily become a victim of your own competence. The more you demonstrate that you can do, the more others expect or allow you to do. Eventually, though, the vicious cycle of people-pleasing and putting others first will render you stressed, exhausted, depleted, and depressed. At this point, in sheer desperation, your needs will be screaming to be heard. But, like Sarah's, your needs might be screaming in the dark with no one to answer them.

Is It Selfish to Take Care of Yourself?

Most people-pleasers think in highly polarized, distorted terms about taking care of others' needs versus taking care of themselves. Even the word *versus* in the preceding phrase suggests an either/or, all or nothing choice in the matter.

The two alternatives appear to be either that (1) you can be utterly *unselfish*—to the point of being truly *selfless*—always putting other people's needs before your own; or, (2) you can be completely *selfish*, always putting your needs first and foremost, even stepping over or squashing others who get in the way of what you want.

Obviously, as a people-pleaser, you opt for the first alternative. After all, always putting others' needs first, even at your own expense, captures the essence of the people-pleasing syndrome. Yet, if you knew that by being so selfless, you were actually putting the needs of others at serious risk of *not* being fulfilled by you at all, would you still persist?

Consider this analogy: Imagine that you are given exclusive responsibility for feeding seven hungry toddlers for one month. Your mission is to make sure that the children don't go hungry.

To accomplish your purpose, you give the children as much food as they wish to eat at each meal. Instead of feeding yourself, you decide to save your portion along with any leftovers in case the children should become hungry again before the next meal.

You become so compelled by the primacy of the children's hunger over your own, that you teach yourself to ignore your own hunger signals. In fact, since you identify feeding the children as *your* primary need, you decide to forgo eating altogether.

Eventually, however, you become so weakened by starvation that you can no longer prepare the children's food nor feed them. Thus, notwithstanding your benevolent and altruistic intentions to put the children's needs ahead of your own, your mission fails. Clearly, there is a flaw in your strategy.

In a parallel way, your principal need as a people-pleaser is to take care of the needs of others. But, by not tending to your own welfare, you too are endangering those you love, albeit unintentionally and unconsciously, by endangering yourself, the caretaker.

> ▶ **When you constantly stress and exhaust yourself by caring for others at your own expense, you are courting illness, depression, stress, and other serious trouble. As a result of your good intentions, those who depend on you will suffer as well.**

There is a third alternative that will best serve everyone, and that is for you to operate in a state of *enlightened self-interest*. What this means is that you will take good care of yourself, even putting your needs first at times, while simultaneously considering the needs and welfare of others. In this way, you will still be attending to the needs of others who benefit by your taking care of yourself. Enlightened self-interest, unlike selfishness, precludes making others suffer at your expense.

Paradoxically, in order to truly meet your obligations to others who are closest and most important to you, you must be able to take care of yourself. But, the problem you now face is that years of people-pleasing have made you nearly deaf to the inner voice of your own needs.

Nobody Loves an "Over-Giver"

One of the hardest lessons people-pleasers have to learn is that making yourself a martyr is no way to make friends. In fact, it is very difficult for most mortals to like the self-appointed, holier-than-thou "saint" who walks among them.

As a people-pleaser, you may feel more secure in relationships where you give far more than you receive in return. You may also subscribe to the mistaken belief that it is *always* far better to give than to receive, even among your friends and family.

While charity and altruism are positive and admirable, the mistake lies in applying the terms of self-sacrifice and unrequited giving to your personal relationships. When you constantly give of yourself to friends and family and do not permit others to give back to you in return, you actually are being manipulative and rejecting, whether you intend to be or not. By maintaining a stubborn posture as a giver who refuses to receive anything in return, you deny others the pleasure and good feelings to which they are also entitled by giving back to you in return.

> ▶ **When you give too extravagantly and remain unwilling to receive anything in return, your motives become suspect.**

While your intention may be to share your good fortune, you may inadvertently diminish the receiver by making him or her feel inadequate to reciprocate in kind. Or, your intention may be read as an outright attempt to "buy" the friendship of another, in which case both giver and receiver are devalued.

People-pleasers who give to the point of utter selflessness or self-effacing excess can create the unintended effect of making others feel embarrassed, uncomfortable, and even disdainful. When you put others' needs so far ahead of yours that your self-denial becomes apparent, the effect on others can be doubly guilt producing. While others may characterize you as a "true giving spirit," they may also desire you to give of your spirit elsewhere.

Finally, when you do favors and kind acts for others but refuse to allow others to give back to you in return, you create the unintended but nevertheless ill effects of making others indebted or obligated to you. While you may be operating out of the best of intentions, others on the receiving end of your efforts may feel resentful and angry because you have manipulated them into a position with which they are uncomfortable.

► *By allowing others to repay your kindnesses and reciprocate your giving, you will be doing a bigger favor for others than by leaving them beholden or in your debt.*

The Hidden Cost of Catering to Others

How common is the story of Sarah and people-pleasers like her? Actually, stories like hers are not unusual. It seems that whatever the people-pleaser's motives may have been when she started down the path of catering to the needs of others, the outcome is almost inevitably *not* what was intended. In fact, as Miranda repeatedly discovered, the results are often quite sad. Most sad, though, is that the results are actually predictable.

At 35, Miranda can't understand why she still is single. She seems to have no trouble attracting men or getting men to ask her out on dates. In fact, most of the men she dates are quite enthusiastic about her . . . at least for a while. But none of Miranda's relationships have lasted. Sooner or later, every man with whom she's involved has broken off the relationship.

What really perplexes and upsets Miranda is that having a successful relationship with a man is the most important desire in her life. She just can't understand what she is doing wrong because, especially when it comes to men, Miranda is a committed people-pleaser.

The irony is that by always putting the men first, and failing to attend to her own needs, Miranda creates the very outcome she is trying hardest to avoid. Still, despite years of recurrent break-ups, Miranda lacks any insight into how self-defeating her compulsive people-pleasing and nearly mindless catering to her men have become.

"I have to put men first and do everything I can to please them," she maintains adamantly. "Otherwise, they won't love me."

So, as soon as Miranda finds herself attracted and interested in a new man, she puts herself in a subservient, submissive position. She lavishes men with attention, adoration, and praise. Miranda believes that to be worthy of a man's love, she must prove that she will always put his needs first.

To this end, Miranda will agree to do anything, go anywhere, and comply with any request or desire to make her partner happy. She will see any movie or watch any television show that her partner prefers; she will eat any kind of food, at any restaurant that her partner selects. If he prefers, she will cook for him or skip eating altogether if he isn't hungry.

When Miranda's man of the moment works out at the gym, she becomes an exercise devotee. If he is idle, she joins the couch potato ranks. Miranda dresses to please her partner and will willingly change her hairstyle, makeup, or other facets of her appearance to comply with her boyfriend's taste.

Miranda's opinions always take a secondary seat to her man's positions. In fact, she "finds" herself in agreement with nearly everything her partner believes, making sure to tell him how intelligent and fascinating he is.

At first, almost all the men that Miranda dates are flattered and pleased by her apparent adoration. She has the ability to make each man feel special as she tells him how intelligent, talented, fascinating, and attractive she finds him to be. But, as time goes on, her partners' initial enthusiasm and interest begin to wane.

The hard reality is that with Miranda, as Gertrude Stein once said about Oakland, California, "there's no there there." Men discover, after a relatively short time, that Miranda's toadying flattery and submissive conformity transform her into a crashing bore.

Without an opinion or idea of her own, Miranda offers no true intellectual compatibility, merely a mirror image of her partner's thoughts. Since her interests and activities change each time she changes partners, Miranda has never really developed an enduring passion, nurtured a talent, or even identified a need of her own other than to be some man's "other half." But instead of being a complementary and independent

half, Miranda merely becomes a replica or carbon copy of her partner,
only in female form. Consequently, she offers little to enlarge a man's
experience or to broaden his horizon of knowledge.

Miranda's people-pleasing ultimately becomes as burdensome to her
partners as dead weight. She believes that by putting a man first, she is
willing to give him anything and everything he could desire. But the
truth is that she cannot offer the one thing a healthy man wants and
needs the most: the ability to truly share herself because she knows and
values who she is.

Tuning into Others' Demands

As a people-pleaser, your perceptual antennae are attuned to the needs, preferences, desires, requests, and expectations of others. The psychological "volume" of other people's needs is turned up high, while the relative volume of your own needs is very nearly muted altogether.

Sometimes, the needs or requests of others are stated explicitly. At other times, however, no explicit demands are made of you. Yet you still feel the requirement to respond to implicit demands.

Your psychological radar is constantly scanning the interpersonal space to pick up both explicit *and* implicit demands of other people. These subtle, unspoken needs are overlaid on the continuous clamor of demands from others whom you have trained to require and expect your attention.

While the number and range of demands from others is, in theory, limitless, your resources to respond are finite. You are only one person; your available time can only expand to the number of waking hours in a day, and your energy, however robust, is not boundless. Yet, because you prioritize according to the simple but self-defeating principle that *others must come first*, and, therefore, that you come last, you do not delegate often or effectively. You rarely if ever ask for help or support, anticipating punishment or rejection if you do. And, you almost never negotiate the terms of a demand or request because doing so requires putting your own needs forward and, consequently, risking disapproval or accusations wherein you might be dubbed the dreaded "s" word: *selfish*.

Without the ability to say "No," or to effectively delegate, prioritize, negotiate, or ask for help, the stream of continuous demands from others goes unfiltered and unregulated. And, your compulsive—albeit largely vain—attempts to please all the people, all of the time merely increase the number and weight of demands from others. Under this excessive load, your ability to respond becomes compromised and severely strained.

The psychological effects of the strain are serious. First, the intense stress produced by so many demands threatens both your emotional and physical health. Second, your self-esteem plummets as you feel inadequate to meet the ever increasing demands from others that your own people-pleasing habits encouraged. Still, the controlling compulsion to put others first remains undeterred.

Earning Love in a Dangerous World

In the face of such high psychological and physical costs, why is the core belief that others must come first etched so deeply into your mind? To answer this question, we need to examine what cognitive psychologists refer to as the "silent assumptions" or the underlying thoughts that anchor the *others must come first* tenet.

Embedded in your belief that others must come first is a latent threat: If you don't put others' needs ahead of your own, you will be rejected, viewed as selfish, abandoned, disapproved of, or punished in some other manner. Taken one level deeper, the embedded threat derives from a view that the world of others is essentially a dangerous place. That place, according to your silent assumptions, is inhabited by powerful others who are controlling, demanding, rejecting, exploitative, and punishing. You must serve and satisfy their needs at all times, even and often at the expense of your own. It's no wonder, then, that even thinking about your own needs before you satisfy those of others fills you with feelings of dread, anxiety, and guilt.

One of the best ways to uncover your anchoring thoughts and silent assumptions is to ask yourself what would happen if you didn't give of yourself to please others all the time. What would happen if you didn't put others first or if you didn't do whatever you could to make others happy?

If you are like most people-pleasers, you believe that if you don't put others first, you will be viewed as selfish. Further, you believe that if you were selfish, you wouldn't be worthy of love. Ultimately, selfish, unlovable people are abandoned, left alone to be miserable. So the silent assumptions that underly this value system are:

1. The world of others is not a safe place; if you don't satisfy others' needs, you will suffer negative consequences;

2. Love and caring must be constantly earned by always giving of yourself and doing things to please others;

3. If you don't give of yourself to others and make their needs more important than your own, you will be viewed as selfish; and

4. Selfish people are abandoned, left to be alone and miserable.

These anchoring assumptions promote the supremacy and primacy of others as an article of faith. In other words, in your worldview as a people-pleaser, it is a given that other people and their needs are, by definition, more important than your own.

But, what if your worldview is wrong? It does sound a bit exaggerated to the negative, doesn't it?

Attitude Adjustment: Putting Others First

Here are some corrective statements to counter the toxic idea that others must come first. Remember, changing just one thought can start the whole process in motion to cure your Disease to Please.

- ♦ If you always put others' needs ahead of your own and fail to take care of yourself, there is a very good chance that you won't be able to take care of those who matter the most to you.
- ♦ It is entirely possible to care about others *and* to look after yourself.
- ♦ There is a big difference between being selfish and acting in your own enlightened self-interest.
- ♦ You are not compelled to be with others who are controlling, punitive, rejecting, and exploitative. You have choices about the people with whom you surround yourself.
- ♦ You become a slave to others only if you enslave yourself with self-defeating, people-pleasing beliefs and behavior.
- ♦ It is not always better to give than receive; the best balance in relationships is both to give *and* to receive.
- ♦ Your own needs, desires, and ideas are just as important as anyone else's. To you, they can be even more important.
- ♦ You're setting yourself up for trouble and disappointment if you fail to teach the people you love that you have needs, too, and that they have some responsibility to help fulfill your needs.

CHAPTER 5

There's More to You Than How Much You Do

I f you are like most people-pleasers, you have a peculiar relationship with time. There is never enough of it for you to relax, have fun, do pleasurable things, or just have some to yourself. On the other hand, your time seems to expand to make room for tasks—especially when the tasks involve things that you do for others.

You probably make Herculean sized "to do" lists, which you likely use to take note of all the things you don't get around to doing by the end of any given day. You rarely give yourself enough credit for all you do accomplish and drive yourself relentlessly with "shoulds," "musts," and perfectionist standards of self-evaluation.

In fact, as a people-pleaser, your sense of identity, your self-esteem, and even your worthiness to be loved derive from doing things for others. In fact, it often seems like you *are* what you *do*.

Doing It All Yourself

One of the consequences of overderiving self-esteem from what you do for others is a failure to delegate. The risky result of not delegating is the creation of debilitating stress both in your personal life and at work. If you do all the work by yourself without sufficient help and support, your time and resources will eventually and inevitably become depleted. Tapped out of reserve, you will find yourself laboring under severe stress, pushing yourself further and further to compensate for the deepening sense of inadequacy the stress itself is producing.

Stress has contagion effects, too. It spreads to those around you, endangering not only your physical and emotional well-being but that of your family, coworkers, friends, and virtually everyone with whom you come into contact. And, stress can exert such a distorting, negative influence on your carefully cultivated *nice* personality as to turn you into a screaming, short-tempered nightmare version of your usually people-pleasing self.

Your reasons for not delegating, particularly at work, may be complex. First, you may seek to retain tight and total control over your work or projects. By not delegating, you may be lured into the seductive promise of taking—or being given—all the credit for a successful outcome. But remember, you will also bear all the blame if a project goes badly.

You may rationalize your unwillingness to delegate by protesting that nobody will do the work as well or carefully as you will. And, while this may even be true, doing all the work by yourself has significant downsides, especially in settings where coworkers or subordinates wish to assist you.

When you maintain tight control on the work and never delegate full responsibility and accountability, you preclude others from learning, developing their skills, furthering their careers, or deriving a similar benefit to their self-esteem from accomplishment. You may be caught wholly unprepared for the resentment and disloyalty from your subordinates that your unwillingness to truly delegate can breed.

Failing to delegate effectively also keeps you mired in the micromanagement of details. While you may feel safe and even less anxious dotting all the *i*'s and crossing all the *t*'s yourself, you run the substantial risk of being viewed by those in the executive level as always a manager, never a leader.

This damaging image works to keep that proverbial glass ceiling right over your head. As hard as it may be to admit, there is the perception that micromanagers and others who dwell in the land of detail do not think in strategic, forward-planning terms, as executive leaders must do. In corporate organizations, the executives think and plan strategically and the ranks (and managers) tactically implement the executive's directives. In which group do you want to belong?

In psychological terms, ability and effort are considered compensatory traits. This means that a person who is perceived as having high ability is expected to have to work *less hard* than someone with lesser ability. Conversely, when a person of lesser ability does get ahead, they are typically viewed as having had to exert a substantial and extraordinary effort.

Now, by extrapolation, consider the possible backfire effects of being a corporate manager who is perceived as working harder and longer than everyone else. Contrary to what you may have believed, the actual impact on observers is to *discount the ability* of the person who is seen as *needing* to work so hard in order to compensate for their lower competence. Unfortunately, this tendency is especially strong when the hard worker in question is a woman. And you thought that hard work would be the guaranteed formula for success and promotion. Think again.

There is yet another illusion created by doing all the work yourself that has left many mid-level managers and vice presidents in a state of shocked disbelief when their positions are eliminated in a merger or their "functions are outsourced," to use contemporary corporate-speak. The illusion is that if you make yourself indispensable by virtue of how hard you work and how much you do, your promotions and your job security will be insured. This is a dangerous and entirely false belief.

In any business setting, allowing any one person—CEO included—to become indispensable is just plain poor management. In fact, it can be tantamount to creating a crisis and waiting for it to happen, as Kay painfully learned in the case that follows.

> Kay is special projects manager for a small but successful public relations agency. Her job entails the planning and coordination of all special events for the agency's clients.
>
> Kay is extremely dedicated to her boss who hired her 10 years ago at age 42, just a few months after her husband died. "My boss took a real chance on me at a time when I needed a break," Kay says. "When my husband died, I didn't need to work for the money; but the job gave me a sense of value and purpose."
>
> Kay refuses to delegate to others anything that she considers "important" even though there are two full-time employees hired to be her assistants. Kay considers every single detail of the project to be vitally important to the outcome. Unwilling to relinquish control over any part of her work, Kay winds up doing everything herself except for the most mundane or menial jobs, such as stuffing invitations and licking envelopes, or walking packages or mailings to the mailroom.
>
> "That way," Kay rationalizes, "I have no one to blame but myself if something important goes wrong."
>
> But Kay's assistants feel devalued and stymied in their career development. They complain to management that they do not appreciate the menial work she assigns to them. They remind the boss that they were hired to learn how to do special project production, but are treated by Kay as "glorified clerks, flunkies and go-fers."

Generally, Kay has a sweet, people-pleasing disposition—except when she's under a lot of stress. Before every special event, Kay creates a pressure cooker of stress for herself and the rest of the agency staff.

During this period, Kay works nearly around the clock, checking and rechecking every detail. The entire office staff suffers the effects of stress contagion. Behind her back, the other employees refer to Kay as "hell on wheels" or call her "Sybil" because of her seeming altered personality under stress. If something goes wrong, she screams at vendors, cries in her office, hurls insults, uses foul language, barks orders, and even blames the same assistants that she cut out of the loop of responsibility and information. On four occasions, assistants have even quit on the spot, leaving Kay more frazzled as the event day approaches.

After the opening event takes place, Kay is remorseful about her "bad behavior." She buys apology flowers or other gifts for her coworkers and assistants. She begs for their understanding and forgiveness, promising to "stay calmer" next time. But the cycle merely repeats itself.

The president of the agency never disciplines Kay. He apologizes to his staff on her behalf, and makes excuses for her inappropriate behavior while he reminds people that "nobody can pull off the job like Kay."

Kay's events are generally very successful, garnering compliments from clients and excellent coverage from the real estate and commercial press. Because of Kay's ability to please clients, her boss has been willing to tolerate her histrionics under stress. He believes that nobody could replace Kay, and feels that maintaining her is probably worth the turnover in other employees and the morale crash that her stressed-out behavior produces.

Now, however, the costs may have risen too high. Six of Kay's assistants—present and past—have served the agency with a lawsuit alleging, among other things, harassment and discrimination due to Kay's "abusive treatment" of them and the management's "preferential treatment" of Kay.

Kay feels miserable, guilty, and depressed. She has been placed on an indeterminate leave of absence to get treatment for her problems. While Kay is on leave, the agency has been subcontracting the special events planning to an outside firm. To her dismay, the boss has now discovered that perhaps Kay isn't indispensable after all.

Nobody is.

Do You Prove Your Worth by How Much You Do?

Do your identity and sense of self-worth depend on how much you do for others? Do you consider yourself indispensable? Take the following quiz and find out.

Does Your Value Depend on How Much You Do? Quiz

Read the statements below and decide whether or not each applies to you. If you agree or mostly agree, circle "T" for true; if you disagree or mostly disagree with the statement, circle "F" for false.

1. I believe my value depends on the things I do for other people. T or F

2. I have to give of myself to others by doing things for them in order to really be worthy of love.   T or F

3. I often feel like there just is not enough of me to go around.   T or F

4. I feel that I need to prove myself to others by doing things to make them happy.   T or F

5. I would feel worthless if I were unable to do things for others or make them happy.   T or F

6. My sense of self-worth and value come from how much I do for others.   T or F

7. I would think of myself as a bad or selfish human being if I didn't give of myself all the time to those around me.   T or F

8. I believe I must earn the love of others by doing things to please them.   T or F

9. I believe that other people would question my value as a person if I couldn't do things for them.   T or F

10. Even though I try my hardest to do everything I can to please others, I still often feel inadequate or like I'm failing.   T or F

11. I rarely delegate tasks to others.   T or F

12. Even though I believe that I'm basically a good person, I still feel that I must prove myself every day by the things I do for others.   T or F

13. I believe that my friends like me because of all the things I do for them.   T or F

14. I try not to let fatigue prevent me from doing the most I possibly can for others.   T or F

15. I sometimes feel resentful that so many people make demands on my time, but I would never express my negative feelings.   T or F

How to Score and Interpret Your Answers

Total the number of times you circled "T" to determine your overall score.

♦ *If your score is 8 or higher:* Your identity and self-esteem depend too much on your ability to do things for others. This mindset can result in debilitating stress and, therefore, can even put your health at risk.

♦ *If your score is between 4 and 7:* You still may be in a dangerous area where a shock to your self-esteem may drive you to do more for others as a way of regaining what you feel has been lost. Be careful.

♦ *If your score is 3 or under:* You are doing well in *not* overestimating your indispensability to others. This is a strength to build on in your recovery.

All Work, No Play

When you equate your worth with what you do for others, you run the risk of becoming an "all work, no play" kind of person. Your time always seems to expand to accommodate others' needs and requests, but shrinks or disappears altogether when it comes to taking care of yourself.

▶ *Putting a premium on accomplishment and productivity creates a bias against the value of pleasurable activities and relaxation.*

You may even endorse the self-defeating beliefs that having fun, taking a nap, and going for a leisurely walk are "wastes of valuable time." These beliefs are self-defeating because relaxation and unwinding are not only good for your overall health and well-being, they are necessary to maintain optimal levels of productivity and quality of accomplishment.

Nevertheless, you probably delay and procrastinate your relaxation and other pleasurable activities until you have finished doing all the things that you think you *have* to do. The problem with this formula, of course, is that you almost *never* finish all the things you have to do for others and, therefore, rarely take or make time for yourself.

Or, if you do find a small bit of time for yourself, you may have converted activities that are supposed to be stress reducing into mandatory obligations that now produce stress until they are accomplished. Exercise is a good example. Has exercise become one more thing on your lengthy "to do" list that must be accomplished in order for you to avoid feeling guilty? If so, then you are likely deriving far fewer benefits from exercise than you may believe. While you may be building muscles and burning fat or calories, you are also canceling out the stress reduction value—arguably one of the most important payoffs of regular exercise—by surrounding it with feelings of obligation, pressure, and guilt.

You are no doubt harder on yourself than you would ever be on any other person. Most people-pleasers, for example, rarely allow themselves to feel satisfied with how much they have accomplished in a given day. You may be reluctant to pat yourself on the back, give yourself credit for your accomplishments, or feel happy and satisfied with yourself for fear that you will grow complacent. Without the "edge" of discontent, you may fear that your performance will fall even shorter of some imagined high mark than it does now.

You may also believe that by staying "hard" on yourself and denying yourself pleasure and relaxation, you will somehow appear more worthy and giving to others. What is more likely is that you will merely appear unhappy to others, and possibly bitter as well.

One of the ways that you may be hard on yourself is by ignoring your body's internal signals that say it is time to stop and rest. While your people-pleasing skills would make you attentive and nurturing to another who complained of headache, body aches, exhaustion, or other physical symptoms, you are quite likely to misread or ignore altogether similar messages from your own body's wisdom.

If you are the one with the symptoms, you are likely to try to push past what you view as weakness, inadequacy, or limitations in order to continue to do things for others. In fact, some people-pleasers become highly depressed and anxious when illness does become disruptive enough to incapacitate their functioning, even if only for a few days.

When your self-worth is so closely tied to what you do for others, being sick and requiring care yourself can make you feel worthless, useless, burdensome, guilty, and largely irrelevant. These self-defeating negative thoughts, in turn, may only complicate your illness and delay your recovery.

The Mind-Reading Trap

You may feel resentful and disappointed that other people in your life don't seem to know how to take care of you as well as you take care of them—or, as well as you think you do. If you harbor such feelings, you are most likely also holding on to the stubborn and self-defeating rule that you should not have to tell people what you need or teach them how to best care for you. They should just know.

Marcia and Peter have been married for three years. While Marcia takes pride in her constant efforts to please her husband, she started to feel resentful when Peter did not seem to reciprocate by knowing exactly what she needed and wanted without being told. In fact, Marcia even made this a test of Peter's love.

"I cook what Peter likes for dinner. I give him great back massages before he goes to sleep. On Sunday mornings, I bring him breakfast in bed with the newspaper," Marcia brags. "And, don't get me wrong. I love taking care of him. It makes me feel as happy or happier than him!"

After just a few months of marriage, though, Marcia noticed that Peter wasn't figuring out her desires accurately and, consequently, she felt let down and disappointed. Marcia also felt guilty for even having needs that weren't being met by her husband. And, she held the self-defeating and erroneous belief that if marital partners really wanted to please each other, it wouldn't be necessary for either one to ever tell the other what they wanted and needed.

For example, Marcia felt upset because Peter always seemed to interpret any overtures of affection from her as a signal to become sexual.

"You know, sometimes I just want to cuddle and hold each other," she explained. "But Peter thinks if I get affectionate, I want to make love. Sometimes I do, but a lot of times, I just don't want to have sex. I think he should be able to tell the difference without my having to spell it all out to him."

Marcia refused to talk to Peter about the sex-affection issue.

"I don't see why I have to tell him what I want and don't want. Why doesn't he try to figure it out on his own like I do? If he were really in tune with my needs, he would know what I want and just give it to me," Marcia stated angrily.

Marcia and Peter eventually wound up in therapy because she became sullen and depressed. At first, even in therapy, Marcia was reluctant to tell Peter what she was feeling. She maintained that her fantasy of a "perfect marriage" was one in which telling each other what was needed would be unnecessary because both partners "would just know."

However, once they began discussing their relationship openly, Marcia learned that Peter actually did not like some of the things that she did for him.

"I didn't want to hurt her feelings by telling her I didn't like some-thing she cooked, or something she did for me," Peter explained. "I know she prides herself on 'knowing' me and on being such a natural at giving me what she thinks I want. And, she's pretty good. But even she isn't always right."

Marcia and Peter learned in therapy that, in the best relationships, part-ners teach one another how best to give and receive love. Communication, not mental telepathy, is the hallmark of a satisfying, successful marriage.

By taking the unreasonable and unrealistic position that if Peter loved her, he would be able to read her mind, Marcia was setting up psychologi-cal traps in which both she and her husband were becoming ensnared. Each time Marcia focused on an implicit rule that her husband should know what she needed in any given situation, she supplied herself with the justification—albeit a faulty one—to become angry and hurt when he failed to meet her expectations.

Marcia and Peter are now much better partners to one another. Because they communicate their needs, both feel more successful at making the other happy and satisfied.

Attitude Adjustment: There's More to You Than How Much You Do

Believing that you are indispensable and that your identity and self-esteem depend on how much you do *yourself* for others will keep you stuck in your people-pleasing rut. Give yourself permission to delegate and do it effec-tively. By delegating *and* by asking for what you need and want without fear of disapproval or punishment, you will open the exit door to the people-pleasing syndrome and begin to reclaim control of your life.

Here are some corrections to counter the toxic idea that you are what you do:

♦ It is more important for you to effectively delegate than to main-tain total control or to receive all the credit (or all the blame).

♦ By not delegating, not asking for help, and not saying "no," you are just asking to be buried in stress and to be overwhelmed with pres-sure.

♦ The quality of your accomplishments and everything you do for others will be improved if you take time to play, have fun, relax, and do pleasurable things.

CHAPTER 6

Nice People Can Say "No"

Here's a conundrum: people-pleasers never have enough time to do all the things they have to do, nor to take care of themselves. But, they never say "no" to a request to do one more thing for somebody who needs them.

Take this quiz to determine the extent to which you fit this description.

Can You Say No? Quiz

Read the statements below and decide whether or not each applies to your way of thinking. If you agree or mostly agree, circle "T" for true; if you disagree or mostly disagree, circle "F" for false.

1. I can't really take the time to relax until I finish all the things I have to do.   T or F

2. It is very difficult for me to turn down a request from a friend, family member, or coworker.   T or F

3. My sense of identity is based on what I do for other people.   T or F

4. I very seldom say "no" to anyone who needs my help or wants me to do a favor.   T or F

5. On a daily basis, I almost never really feel satisfied with how much I have accomplished.   T or F

6. I am often so depleted by taking care of others that I have no time or energy left to enjoy my own life.   T or F

7. I would feel guilty if I took time to relax or just to do something pleasurable for myself.   T or F

8. I believe that nobody would really care about me if I stopped doing all the things I now do for others.   T or F

9. I almost never ask anybody to do things for me.   T or F

10. I often say "yes" when I would like to say "no" to requests from others.   T or F

How to Score and Interpret Your Answers

Total the number of times you circled "T" to determine your overall score.

♦ *If your score is between 7 and 10:* You place a higher priority on pleasing others than on trying to take care of yourself. You just don't say "no."

♦ *If your score is between 4 and 6:* You should keep a careful watch to make certain you don't lose your footing on the slippery slope of *niceness*. You are not saying "no" to others often or selectively enough.

♦ *If your score is 3 or less:* You have already figured out some of the solutions to becoming a recovered people-pleaser. Build on your strengths to say "no" and keep your own needs in balance with those of others.

Is Saying "No" Like Speaking a Foreign Language?

While the word *nice* may be the singular description of people-pleasers, the word *no* generally does not appear in their vocabularies.

If you are a people-pleaser, it is a safe bet that you have difficulty saying "no" to just about any request, expressed need, desire, invitation, or demand—implicit or explicit—from nearly anyone.

Saying "no" probably makes you feel guilty or selfish because you equate it with disappointing and letting others down. After years of saying, "yes," you have taught others to expect you to comply. Now, you may feel that "yes" is simply your only option.

Just the idea or possibility of saying "no" may be enough to make you feel uncomfortably tense and anxious. And, each time you give into your fears and say "yes," the short-term anxiety reduction merely strengthens your yes-saying habit. But, the longer-term consequences of your knee-jerk compliance are costly.

> ► *Like most people-pleasers, your aversion to saying "no" is probably grounded in the negative, angry responses that you anticipate your denial might elicit. In this sense, you have empowered the word to such a degree that you are now afraid to even use it.*

If you always say "yes," especially when you want to say "no," you eventually will find yourself joylessly going through the motions of living, yielding control over your precious time and resources to the will of whoever asks for it. In effect, your continuous yes-saying will enslave you to others.

Why Does Saying "No" Make You Feel So Anxious and Guilty?

Your avoidance of "no" may also be linked to the self-esteem you think you earn by doing things for others. In this sense, by saying "no" to a request, you will also be denying yourself an opportunity to add one more count to the sum of tasks and favors you accomplish on behalf of others. Since your self-worth seems to depend on the things you do for other people, your reluctance to turn down a chance to add another point to your tally of accomplishments is understandable.

But the dilemma you face as a chronic people-pleaser is that, despite your impressive ability to meet almost everyone's needs so far, the time inevitably will come when your energy will run out. Depleted by your own good intentions and desire to please, you will confront a breaking point after which you will no longer be able to do all the things for others on which your value has come to so crucially depend.

> ► *The only way to avoid that breaking point and to preserve your ability to say "yes" to the people that matter most is to learn to say "no" convincingly and effectively to at least some of the people, some of the time. In fact, learning to say "no" is imperative to curing your people-pleasing syndrome.*

Saying "no" will require you to reframe the feeding source to your self-esteem. As a people-pleaser, you have taught yourself to feel good *because* of all the things you do for other people, in spite of the fact that you have lost control over how you spend your precious time and energy.

As a recovered people-pleaser, you will have to learn to feel good *because* you have reclaimed control over your life. This control is due, in part, to your new ability to make conscious, deliberate choices over what you will and will not do, in spite of the fact that you will necessarily have to say "no" some of the time.

But, why does saying "no" make you feel so guilty, anxious, and uncomfortable now? What you probably don't realize is that years of suppressing your urge to say "no" have been generating continuous frustration. Given the chance to vent, that frustration could erupt into raging anger.

It is no small wonder, then, that the mere prospect of lifting the ban on saying "no" floods you with anxiety. Your fear has far more to do with your own long-suppressed resentment and with the intensely angry and offensive way that you might finally say "no"—or, rather, scream "*NO!!!*"—than with the mere use of the word itself.

Saying "no" is about establishing your boundaries. Consider the analogy of someone who violates your physical boundaries by literally stepping on your toes.

You would probably be able to maintain your composure and calmly inform the individual that your toes have been stepped on, if you do so right away. However, in a misguided but well-meaning attempt to spare the other person's feelings, you elect to stay quiet. If you fail to tell the violator that he or she has stepped on your toes after repeated stomps, you will likely reach a threshold beyond which you are no longer able to be polite. The longer you try to remain amicable and compliant, allowing the other individual to step on your toes, the more strained your self-control will become.

On the final "I-can't-take-it-anymore" stomp, you will very likely raise your voice in anger. You might even reflexively push the person off your foot as you loudly inform him or her of the oafish, boorish, and repeated injury to your now substantially sore foot.

It appears, in retrospect, that you would have saved the other person's feelings, as well as your foot, by clearly establishing your boundaries as soon as they had been violated.

Because you are a people-pleaser, you wait too long to say "no" to nearly everyone. Your proverbial toes are black and blue from the constant invasion of your personal boundaries. Since you have avoided saying "no" and have not established clear and firm limits on your time and energy, you may now find yourself perilously close to the limits of your patience and self-control.

But the solution does not lie in forestalling further opportunities to say "no." As the analogy illustrates, the longer you delay saying "no," the bigger the risk that the lid will blow off your mounting resentment and frustration.

▶ *Once you merely give yourself permission to say "no"—just to some of the people, just some of the time—you will have taken the most important step toward curing your people-pleasing syndrome.*

Attitude Adjustment: Nice People Can Say "No"

By giving yourself permission to say, "no," you will be removing a heavy burden from your shoulders. Remember these corrective thoughts the next time you start to say "yes," but you want to say "no."

♦ You need to say "no," to *some* people, *some* of the time, in order to preserve your ability to give to the people that really matter most in your life.

♦ You need to treat yourself as well as you treat others.

♦ Saying "yes" when you want to say "no" in order to protect your emotional, physical health or well-being should make you feel guilty—not the other way around.

♦ Your value as a human being does *not* depend on the things you do for others. Saying "no" some of the time to some of the people will in no way diminish your value or worth in their eyes. It probably will enhance it.

Part Two

People-Pleasing Habits

A s you turn to this page, you also turn the first corner of the Disease to Please triangle moving from People-Pleasing Mindsets to People-Pleasing Habits. On this side of the triangle, we will examine the *behavior* that comprises the Disease to Please syndrome.

Actually, the word *habits* is a euphemism to describe the compulsive behavioral cycle in which you find yourself trapped. More accurately, your people-pleasing habits have reached the level of *addiction*. The "fix" or reward for your people-pleasing addiction is twofold.

First, you have become hooked on people-pleasing in order to *gain approval* from significant others as well as from everyone and anyone who will give it to you. Second, you are also hooked because you have "learned" to believe that your people-pleasing behaviors will *avoid disapproval* from others.

In fact it is the avoidance of disapproval—more than the attainment of approval—that moves people-pleasing behaviors from compulsive habits to bona fide addiction. When the driving force for a habitual behavior is to avoid the occurrence of something painful or negative (such as disapproval) more than to attain something positive or rewarding (such as approval) the compulsive habit transforms into an addiction.

In behavioral terms, the Disease to Please syndrome entails taking on too much and spreading your finite resources too thin because you rarely say "no" and fail to delegate effectively. As a result of these habits, the circle of others whom you seek to please—or to avoid displeasing—grows ever wider until it becomes burdensome and severely stressful.

Your approval fix comes in many forms—appreciation, praise, acceptance, love. The disapproval you seek to avoid also comes in varied forms—rejection, abandonment, criticism, or withholding of love and affection.

Like other addictions, People-Pleasing Habits are rewarded on a random, occasional basis rather than continuously. Just as a gambler at a slot machine becomes hooked by the *periodic* and *random* jackpot, you are addicted to the praise *and* absence of criticism or rejection that you receive for some but not all of your people-pleasing efforts. For this reason, you find yourself compelled to please more and more people, acquiescing to more and more requests and needs in order to increase the frequency of your rewards. Like the gambler who ultimately loses more money than he ever wins back, you too become depleted and drained by your expanding efforts to make everyone like and accept you.

This intense need for approval causes you to give up power and control over your time and energy as well as to give up power and control to others in close relationships. The need for approval stems from childhood when parents doled out the praise you learned to crave as well as the criticism, disapproval, and rejection you learned to avoid through the development of People-Pleasing Habits. Learning to please significant, powerful grown-ups may have been useful and beneficial behavior when you were a child. But, like the People-Pleasing Mindsets in the previous section, compulsive approval-seeking and disapproval-avoiding habits are not working for you anymore now that you are an adult.

You may still be hooked on a frustrating quest for your parents' approval. But now, your need for love and acceptance can also make you easy prey to the painful roller coaster of romantic addiction. Moreover, your Disease to Please can make you the unwitting accomplice of a hostile partner. The chapters that follow will help you realize that your People-Pleasing Habits actually reward and perpetuate your angry partner's mistreatment and abuse.

Alternatively, you may use your people-pleasing as a kind of benevolent manipulation of your partner in order to avoid your greatest fear: abandonment. In this form, your People-Pleasing Habits find you knocking yourself out to meet your partner's every need in order to prove that you are essential to his very existence. If you make him need you enough, you erroneously reason, he'll never leave you. Sadly, this formula often fails.

As in the previous section, each chapter that follows will conclude with a Behavior Adjustment directing you to concrete steps you can take *now* to break the addictive cycle of the Disease to Please. Remember, the power of the triangle is the impact of just one change—one small step—on any side to unleash a chain reaction of progress leading toward your recovery.

CHAPTER 7

Learning to Please: Approval Addiction

*M*arilyn can't recall exactly when her people-pleasing behavior began. More accurately, she can't remember a time when she wasn't a people-pleaser.

"I've been this way my whole life," Marilyn explains. "I think I learned it first from my mother. She drilled into my head that being a 'nice girl' means that you take care of other people. In fact, my mom's way of asking me to do something was, 'Honey, be a nice girl and do [a favor or chore]' or, 'Sweetie, be a good girl and do [another chore or favor].' "

Marilyn's relationship with her father, however, was more difficult. He was highly critical of her behavior and appearance, especially when she became an adolescent. Her father also had a volatile temper, and Marilyn learned not to challenge his authority in any way. Marilyn recalls that she "got around" her father's anger by "keeping a low profile, anticipating his needs, and doing favors for him." In her family, Marilyn refined her people-pleasing skills because they provided protection from her father's anger and criticism and gained his highly conditional approval.

Like many women, Marilyn learned her people-pleasing behavior in early childhood. Because she loved and identified with her mother, Marilyn felt good to emulate her mother's behavior through role modeling. And, she was taught directly that by being "nice" and pleasing *others, she would gain her mother's love and, on a good day, her father's approval as well.*

Almost all of us enjoy gaining the approval of other people who are important in our lives. But, for people-pleasers, earning others' approval and avoiding their disapproval are primary driving forces. In fact, if you have the Disease to Please, avoiding their disapproval is likely even a more paramount concern than gaining their approval.

Are You Hooked on Approval?

It is no exaggeration to say that most people-pleasers are addicted to approval and to avoiding disapproval. Are you?

Take the "Are You Hooked on Approval?" quiz and find out how much your people-pleasing problems are driven by these compulsive habits.

Are You Hooked on Approval? Quiz

Read each statement below. Circle "T" if the statement is true or mostly true. Or, circle "F" if the statement is false or mostly false.

1. If someone disapproves of me, I feel like I am not very worthwhile. T or F

2. It's extremely important to me to be liked by nearly everyone in my life. T or F

3. I have always needed the approval of other people. T or F

4. When someone criticizes me, I usually get very upset. T or F

5. I believe I need the approval of others more than most people do. T or F

6. I need others to approve of me in order to really feel worthwhile. T or F

7. My self-esteem seems to greatly depend on what other people think of me. T or F

8. It bothers me a lot to learn that someone doesn't like me. T or F

9. Other people have a great deal of control over my feelings. T or F

10. I want everyone to like me. T or F

11. I need the approval of others in order to feel happy. T or F

12. If I had to choose between gaining the approval of others versus gaining their respect, I would have to choose approval. T or F

13. I seem to need everyone's approval before I can make an important decision.   T or F

14. I am strongly motivated by the praise and approval I get from others.   T or F

15. I am always deeply concerned about what others think of me in nearly every area of my life.   T or F

16. I get very defensive when criticism is directed at me.   T or F

17. I need to have everyone like me, even though I don't really like everyone.   T or F

18. I would do almost anything to avoid the disapproval of people who are important to me.   T or F

19. It only takes one person's criticism or disapproval in a group to upset me even if everyone else is giving me praise.   T or F

20. I need the approval of others in order to feel loved.   T or F

How to Score and Interpret Your Answers

First, total the number of times you circled "true." Here is what your total score means:

♦ *If your score is between 15 and 20:* You are addicted to the approval of others and to avoiding their disapproval. And, because you think you need *everyone's* approval, your craving can never be truly satisfied. Your approval addiction is a major cause of your Disease to Please problems and requires your immediate efforts to change.

♦ *If your score is between 10 and 14:* You may not be an approval addict yet, but you certainly have an overly strong concern with what others think of you. Your desire for approval, which could easily develop into an addiction, is a problem that warrants your immediate attention since it plays a significant role in your people-pleasing patterns.

♦ *If your score is between 5 and 9:* Your approval needs are moderate and not addictive . . . at least not yet. However, even at this level, your desire for approval and concern about how others think of you still predispose you to people-pleasing problems. While your approval needs are not as important as other causes of your Disease to Please, you should still keep a watchful eye on them.

♦ *If your score is 4 or less:* Your approval needs are unusually low for someone with people-pleasing problems. Review your answers and be sure that you have answered every question carefully and candidly. *Denial is the enemy of self-awareness.*

In addition to interpreting your total score, it is helpful to look at your responses to individual items. The total score addresses your *overall* tendencies to need the approval of others and to be highly sensitive to their disapproval or criticism. But your responses to individual items can be significant and revealing. Look over the statements again. Pay particular attention to those that are most applicable to your own thinking.

The Thin Ice of Approval Addiction

There is nothing wrong or unhealthy about valuing the approval of others, especially those you love and respect. Wanting to be liked by others is a perfectly natural human desire. But, if your preference for being liked and approved of becomes mandatory, or if the consequences of disapproval seem monumental and catastrophic, you've crossed over into dangerous psychological territory where the ice can get very thin.

As the quiz statements illustrate, if you are an approval addict, you believe that being liked and gaining others' approval are absolutely essential to your emotional well-being. You do not merely *want* to be liked; you *need* to be. For you, approval is not simply desirable; it is *imperative,* like oxygen.

Like any other addict, you seem to consume whatever approval and displays of liking you receive. There is no storage or banking of approval in your psychological economy. However much approval and liking you may gain today, it simply won't last; you will feel the craving for approval again tomorrow. Just because people liked you yesterday, your insecurity (which is only enhanced by this addiction) will propel you to earn their esteem and approval all over again today.

Criticism is enormously upsetting because of the inflated significance you attach to it. To approval addicts, criticism is always highly personal. In part, this is because people-pleasers as a group, and approval addicts in particular, cannot clearly distinguish who they *are* from what they *do*— between their essence as a person and their behavior.

If you are an approval addict, when your actions or work products are criticized, you respond emotionally as though your worth as a human being has been entirely invalidated and devalued. It is no wonder, then, that you become defensive and/or distraught in response to any critical remarks directed your way.

Since approval is vital in order for an addict to feel happy and worthwhile, disapproval must be avoided at nearly any cost. For most approval addicts, the avoidance of disapproval becomes a strong motivation because it occurs more often than do expressions of approval and liking.

If you think about it for a moment, in everyday experience, nobody receives evidence that they are liked and approved of constantly. Open displays of approval and esteem occur just periodically even toward the most popular people.

Probably most of the time, social interactions are simply neutral or mildly civil or polite. More open expressions of approval are frequently left to inference. If someone constantly asks others for reassurance that he or she is liked and approved of, that individual is branded "insecure," "annoying," and worse.

▶ *Nobody gets approval all the time from everybody. Approval is so addictive precisely because it is available only some of the time.*

Hardwired versus Learned Habits

In order to develop an effective strategy for changing your own people-pleasing habits, you first need to understand the basic mechanisms that control all behavior.

Human behavior can be divided broadly into two basic categories. The first is *innate* behavior that is built into our hardwiring—encrypted into the biological and genetic code that is our birthright. Assuming normal development, innate behavior emerges in all of us without instruction from anyone. Babies, for example, will roll over, sit up, crawl, and eventually stand up and walk without anybody teaching them how or what to do. So, innate behavior does not require learning.

The second category of behavior consists of that which is *acquired* or *learned.* People-pleasing is acquired behavior that is developed through a process in which other people play major roles—either as role models whom you try to imitate or emulate and/or as providers of important rewards.

▶ *Nobody is* **born** *a people-pleaser. Importantly, since people-pleasing is a learned behavior, it can be unlearned; or, perhaps more accurately for our purposes, it can be relearned in ways that are more effective and less costly emotionally and physically.*

How People-Pleasers Learn

The first or most basic form of learning is called *role modeling.* This means learning by copying or imitating what significant other people in your environment are doing. Like most people with the Disease to Please, one or both of your own parents may have served as role models from whom you learned your people-pleasing habits through imitation. It is important to recognize that your own children may well be learning people-pleasing habits by imitating you.

The second learning process entails learning behavior because it gains rewards *or* because it avoids or stops something unpleasant or painful. When given immediately after a desired behavior occurs, reward or positive reinforcement increases the likelihood that the same behavior will occur again in the future. Most of us are quite familiar with the concept of learning through reward. We instinctively praise our children and reward our pets when they act in ways that we want to encourage.

The concept of negative reinforcement, however, is generally less familiar to most people by name. Nevertheless, habits learned through negative reinforcement can be even stronger than those learned through straightforward reward. And, every people-pleaser has been trained through negative reinforcement although she may not recognize the formal term.

Behavior is learned through *negative reinforcement* because it works to avoid or *stop* an unpleasant or painful sensation or experience. The negative reinforcement (or negative reward) lies in the avoidance of something bad, rather than in gaining something good. However, just as with positive reinforcement, behavior that is learned through negative reinforcement also will be more likely to occur again in the future.

Your people-pleasing habits were learned through both positive *and* negative reinforcement. When people-pleasing behavior earns approval through praise, appreciation, acceptance, affection, or love, the habit is positively reinforced or rewarded. However, when your people-pleasing habits result in avoiding or stopping disapproval in the form of criticism, rejection, withholding of affection, punishment, or abandonment, your behavior is negatively reinforced.

How You Got Hooked on Approval

Approval from significant others is a powerful source of reward for nearly every human being. From infancy on, our behavior is highly influenced and shaped by the approval we receive. Our biological and genetic wiring along with our deepest social programming propels us to seek the praise and approval of other people—especially those whom we deem most important by virtue of the rewards they control (e.g., love, social status, school grades, salaries, etc.).

▶ *People-pleasers get hooked because their behavior earns them the approval they crave.*

Pleasing other people makes you feel good because, over time, it has become associated with approval. When something makes you feel good, you will tend to do more of it in order to sustain the good feelings.

Almost all people-pleasers, like Marilyn, initially learn that making others happy by doing what they want is a direct avenue to gaining their all-important approval. Approval is the currency of positive reinforcement that most directly rewards and maintains people-pleasing.

If the wish to please others were contained within set boundaries, it would be a highly desirable personal attribute. Set boundaries, for example, might involve limiting the group of others that you please to immediate family and closest friends. It would also include being capable of saying "yes" or "no" on a highly selective basis to the people beyond your inner circle. The problem is that because people-pleasing behavior is met with approval, people-pleasers have a strong tendency to expand their efforts to please others beyond reasonable boundaries and limitations. The reward value of approval to people-pleasers makes them victims of their own success at making those around them happy. Understandably the beneficiaries of people-pleaser's efforts, like satisfied customers, come back for more and more. Thus the weight of demands from others grows. At the same time, the people-pleaser includes an ever increasing number of people whom the pleaser can strive to make happy.

▶ *People-pleasers become plagued by the Disease to Please because they cannot and do not say, "no."*

After all, it is saying, "yes"—either verbally or through compliant actions—that the people-pleaser has come to associate with getting the reward of approval. The Disease to Please, as we have said, is not just a problem of *nice* people who may go overboard by trying to make too many others happy, or by doing too much for those they seek to please. At some point, people-pleasing stops being a matter of choice. Instead, it takes on the problematic characteristics of a deeply ingrained habit and, ultimately, of a compulsive, addictive pattern of behavior.

How Addiction Works: A Tale of Two Pigeons

As an approval addict, you think in broad overgeneralized ways about needing to be liked by everyone. And, like an eager puppy, you would be happy to receive approval from everyone all of the time. In reality, however, approval addicts (like everyone else in the real world) only get the approval they so ardently seek *some* of the time, from *some* of the people. Ironically, it is precisely this partial or occasional reinforcement that maintains your addiction to approval.

Contrary to intuition, addiction is actually created when behavior is rewarded only *some* rather than all the time. Addiction develops when rewards are random and unpredictable. This type of reinforcement or reward is called a "gambling schedule" because of the similarity to the way a slot machine pays a hopeful gambler—on a random, occasional, or intermittent basis.

In a parallel way, if you are an approval addict with the Disease to Please, you are really hooked by the *chance* or hope that approval *might* be forthcoming each time you do something nice for another person, even though you do not actually receive praise each and every time. In fact, you rarely, if ever, feel certain that approval will be given. Certainty, security, and consistency of reward are simply *not* part of the addictive experience, as the example that follows illustrates.

The best demonstration of how random, partial reinforcement works is a laboratory experiment designed to study the nature of addiction. It is a classic psychological study that will give you remarkable insight into your own approval addiction.

In this experiment, there are two pigeons, both of which have been deprived of food for a while in order to motivate them with hunger. Pigeon 1 is put in a specially designed cage called a "Skinner Box," named after the famous behavioral psychologist B. F. Skinner. In the Skinner Box, there is a lever that the pigeon can depress with its beak. Below the lever is a food trough for holding pellets of pigeon food.

After Pigeon 1 explores its cage for a moment or so, it hits the lever with its beak. When the lever is depressed, a pellet of pigeon food appears in the trough, which is eaten by the hungry pigeon. Rewarded by food, the bird pushes the lever again, and it is given another pellet. This one-press, one-pellet arrangement continues. After just a few minutes, the pigeon has developed what psychologists call a strong lever-pressing habit.

Pigeon 1's lever-pressing habit is maintained on a 100 percent schedule, *continuous reinforcement*. This means that each and every time the bird presses the lever, a pellet of food is delivered.

Now, Pigeon 2 enters the second cage. For a few minutes, things proceed just as they did for the first bird. Each time Pigeon 2 presses the lever it receives a pellet of food. However, once the lever-pressing habit is firmly established, life changes for the second bird, and what ultimately happens isn't pretty.

Instead of continuing to reward Pigeon 2 with food every time it presses the lever, the experimenter shifts to a *randomized or partial reward schedule*. This means that the pigeon might press the lever four or five times with no pellets of food, only to receive a pellet on the sixth press. Then, Pigeon 2 might press 20 times with no reward, but receives the pellet on the 21st press and again on the 22nd press. But, after the 22nd, the bird might press many more times before another pellet is offered.

The key to the second bird's situation is that it is only rewarded for pressing the lever some of the time. The pigeon cannot predict or anticipate exactly when the next pellet is coming, since the rewards are given randomly.

The final step of the experiment is to clock how long each pigeon will persist in pressing the lever without any reward at all. The food is cut off for both pigeons. For our purposes, we are interested in finding out which bird will press the lever for the longest time in the absence of any reinforcement. For a bird in a Skinner Box, pressing the lever without any reinforcement represents *addictive behavior*. Which pigeon do you think will press the lever for the longest time?

Without getting any food, Pigeon 1 presses the lever for only a short time, probably less than a minute. Having received continuous reward previously, the first bird stops pressing the lever soon after the reward stops. The pigeon, in effect, figures out that there is no point in pressing if there are no more rewards. So it merely walks away from the lever, presumably happy and well nourished.

But Pigeon 2 is very different. The hapless bird presses the lever over and over again, with no reward, until *eventually it collapses from fatigue*. The bird is a true lever-pressing addict. It appears to be wholly unable to cease the behavior even though the lever pressing is unrewarding and exhausting.

In human terms, the second bird persists in a self-defeating habit because it is addicted to the hope or chance that the pellet might appear again on the next press of the lever, or the next, or the next. . . .

In the same way, your addiction to approval is fed by the "fix" you receive from periodic—not continuous—expressions of appreciation, gratitude, or affection from others.

> ▶ *Nobody gets approval all of the time and that is precisely what makes it so addictive.*

Are You a Pigeon for Other People's Approval?

The pigeon illustration is the classic addiction paradigm in behavioral psychology. The example has powerful implications for how your own disposition to do nice things for others has deteriorated into a compulsive addictive pattern over which you seem to have little choice and even less control.

The explanation for an addictive, compulsive habit lies in the pattern and nature of reinforcement that people-pleasing habits elicit over time. Understanding the power of random, intermittent reward is key.

In a figurative sense, you have become a "pigeon" for the approval of others. But your lever is more akin to that pulled by a gambler throwing money into a slot machine. The parallel between slot machines and Skinner Box levers is so close, in fact, that the term "gambling schedule" is widely used as a tag for intermittent reinforcement.

Visualize yourself standing at a slot machine, dropping in quarter after quarter, and pulling the lever time after time without reward. Every so often, however, a jackpot comes up on the spin. The quarters come clinking down and you experience the gambler's high, "the big fix" of winning.

Now, the fact is that you lose far more money in unsuccessful spins than you ever realize in jackpots. The periodic and unpredictable payoff hooks you on playing the slot game as you look and hope for more frequent and bigger payoffs. While you're hoping and playing, your wallet is growing lighter all the time.

The desire for more approval, more often, and from more people builds in the same way. But the reality of life is that a great deal of the things you do for others goes unacknowledged or unappreciated. This is especially true of family members and closest friends who have come to expect and may even take for granted many of the things that you do for them. It may be that your actions *are* appreciated. The approval and appreciation simply remain unexpressed, at least each and every time you extend yourself.

You are addicted to a gambling schedule of approval. Instead of the clinking of coins, you receive the "Every-now-and-then-somebody-really-appreciates-what-I-do-for-them" payoff. And, because approval seems meted out only some of the time, you will want to broaden the base of people whom you seek to please. You do this in an attempt to increase the frequency of the approval that, of course, you continue to crave and on which you still thrive.

It is as if you have decided to play four slot machines simultaneously because it is more rewarding to hear the bell and the clink of coins on what *seems* to be a more frequent basis. You will more than likely continue to lose more money than you ever win back. And you will become harried and tired just trying to keep all the machines pumped with coins continuously. In the short term, you may *feel* temporarily happier because the payoffs come more often. Over time, the joy of winning is replaced by the monotony of compulsively stuffing the machines with quarters. Eventually, you are drained, exhausted, and quite possibly broke.

For people-pleasers, the analogy to playing multiple slot machines is that you reach beyond your inner circle and do exceptionally *nice* things for more and more people. In this way, it *seems* that your chances of getting more frequently expressed approval and appreciation are increased.

But, as the circle widens, the pressure to please increases, until you remain mired in a quicksand of other people's needs, depleted, exhausted, and even resentful.

You then feel entirely out of control in an oppressive cycle that your own good intentions combined with your inability to say "no" have created. What was once a source of pleasure and satisfaction, meeting others' needs and gaining their approval, eventually becomes an overwhelming and even debilitating source of stress.

As the circle of explicitly or implicitly demanding others continues to expand, you can become alienated from those closest to you including immediate family and dearest friends. You can ultimately be left entirely out of touch with your own needs except insofar as they entail the need to please others.

▶ *The Disease to Please finally and fully takes on the mantle of addiction when your motivations flip from seeking approval to avoiding disapproval.*

Psychologists distinguish a benign habit from a harmful addiction when the primary reason for continuing the behavior is no longer to gain good feelings but, rather, to avoid the negative feelings associated with stopping the behavior or withdrawing from the habit.

How Far Will You Go to Avoid Disapproval?

Samantha, an attractive woman in her mid-fifties, was married for seven years and had one son. Divorced in her early thirties, she has never remarried.

Samantha grew up as an "army brat." Her father, a career officer, moved the family from base to base with every new posting, while her mother was the "perfect officer's wife." Samantha, an only child, recalls her childhood with sadness.

"I never stayed at the same school for more than four years, usually less. Samantha explains. "I was always a very good student—my parents demanded high performance—but I never felt like I really fit in

with the kids. All I ever wanted was to have everyone like me. I remember the pain of not being asked to join a club or of not being invited to a party, and the joy of being included every now and then. I think that's why it's so important to me today to be liked and to have lots of friends."

"I know my father was terribly disappointed that I wasn't a boy. So I never felt that I could make him happy. I guess that's why earning his approval became so all-important to me."

"If I got high grades, or if I was 'charming and pretty' at one of their parties, or if I just stayed in my room and left them alone, I was called 'a good girl' and they would tell me they loved me."

"But, if I did something wrong—and that could be not cleaning my room, or not smiling right when the general came over for drinks— they wouldn't even speak to me, sometimes for days. It was real mental torture to grow up with them."

Samantha married Phil as a way to leave her parents. During their courtship, Phil was romantic and kind. Samantha believed that she was selecting a husband who would be totally different from her critical, cold father.

Very soon after their wedding, however, Phil changed. He soon became, in Samantha's words, "demanding, rejecting, and mean . . . just like my father."

"As soon as he became my husband, he acted like he owned me. He wanted to control every aspect of my life. The sick part is that I let him. He told me what to wear, how to act, and what to feel. He constantly criticized my mothering skills and told me our son would grow up to hate me."

"His cruelty and control felt like life with my parents all over again. I just wanted him to be proud of me, and I was willing to do anything to get his approval. I never felt that he loved me as a person," Samantha muses.

Samantha knocked herself out trying to please her withholding, hostile husband. Her people-pleasing compliance was the only survival mechanism she knew to cope with the twin threats of disapproval and abandonment. Ultimately, Phil left anyway.

"By the time he left me for another woman, my self-esteem was ten feet below the ground. I didn't even know who I was anymore. I lived to make him happy. But, there was just no pleasing him."

"It took me several years to feel slightly more secure about my mothering. But I still feel threatened whenever my son spends time with his father, which is rare. My son is a grown man now, and I have to be *very careful not to let him manipulate and control me the way his father did."*

"Every man I've dated since has figured out how much I need approval. My son knows it too. I can see that I just hand over the strings to the other person in a relationship, and I behave like a good little puppet," she says of herself derisively.

"What's really ridiculous is that I'm literally still trying to get my father's approval. It's just absurd. He's 83 years old and as critical and withholding as ever. I keep hoping he'll let me know that he really loves me before he dies. But, he'll never really give me his approval because I'm his daughter, and all he ever wanted was a son. No wonder I never feel good enough."

Pressing Your Own Lever

When you knock yourself out trying to get approval from someone who seems impossible to satisfy, you become stuck in the same downward cycle as the hapless pigeon 2 we saw earlier. Samantha's story is a case in point.

The good news is that Samantha is making great progress today. In therapy, Samantha is learning to correct her self-defeating thinking and habits of trying to be liked by everyone. She now understands how her addiction to approval made her a prime target for controlling men who quickly discovered the ease with which she could be manipulated and emotionally tormented.

Samantha is currently dating a few different men, but has a good relationship with herself for the first time in her life.

"I finally realize, at this age, that it isn't the most important thing for others to like me, especially if what I have to do to please them keeps me from knowing and liking myself. I know now that it's not even possible for everybody to like me or give me their approval, and I truly feel okay about that."

As an afterthought, she adds, "Now that I have my own approval, I feel better about myself than I've ever felt before."

Behavioral Adjustment: Breaking Your Approval Addiction

Just because you may have an addiction to approval doesn't mean that you're doomed to remain helplessly hooked. Even if you're addicted, you can break your people-pleasing habits. Here are some important steps that will help you change starting right *now:*

- It is impossible for you (or anyone else) to get *everyone's* approval, *all of the time.* So you might as well just stop knocking yourself out trying to do the impossible.

- If you keep habitually trying to gain everyone's approval, you'll wind up depleted, exhausted, and demoralized just like the hooked second pigeon. Pigeons have very small brains; humans don't.

- Trying to make everyone like you will only deepen your sense of inadequacy. It will never make you feel better about yourself.

- Having others' approval may make you feel good, especially if the others are people you like and respect. But, you don't *need* the approval of others to validate your worth as a human being.

- Some people may never like or approve of you simply because of their own problems and not because of who you are or what you do.

- The most important, effective, and lasting source of approval is the acceptance you give to yourself. Develop a clear sense of your own judgments and values and govern yourself accordingly.

- Exercise *choice* in the place of compulsive habits. Be intentional about what you do and why you are doing it.

CHAPTER 8

Why Can't You Get Your Parents' Approval?

I f approval is the drug, as we saw in the last chapter, then parents—however unwittingly—are often the pushers.

In particular, when parents use love as a conditional reward, they set the stage for their children to become approval addicts and, consequently, people-pleasers. When their child's behavior or appearance is pleasing to them, these parents label the child as "good," and presumably worthy of love; but when the child does not please them, love is withdrawn. This is called conditional parental love, and it can be devastating to children.

Viewed in this way, the approval seeking and the people-pleasing it spawns are coping skills developed by the child to deal with an otherwise frightening and uncontrollable emotional environment.

To a very young child, parents are all-powerful beings that control nearly everything that matters including, prominently, love and protection. From the earliest consciousness of an infant, children learn to associate their parents' smiling faces and approving sounds with displays of love and feelings of security and safety.

The problem arises when the child perceives that love must be earned and that it *depends on* being "good" and on pleasing the parents. The child reasons then that if she or he fails to please the parents, love will no longer be given. In a child's simplistic world, once love is withdrawn it may be gone forever. This can bring on an awesome fear of abandonment.

In the mind of a young child, there is no meaningful distinction between who she or he *is* as a person and what he or she *does* in the form of behavior. Consequently, in a family where love is meted out on a conditional basis, that child's sense of worthiness as a person becomes enmeshed with the way he or she behaves.

In this psycho-logic, *doing* something "bad" is equated with *being* "bad;" and, *doing* something "good" is the same as *being* "good." The consequences of growing up in this conditional emotional environment are that the child connects pleasing others with being "good," which means being deserving and worthy of love. Conversely, being "bad" means that others disapprove of you. Disapproval, in turn, means that you are no longer loved because you are unworthy. When you are unworthy of love, people leave you alone—you are abandoned, unsafe, and miserable.

You can appreciate the emotional stakes the child faces when parental love is conditional. Approval, which signals the presence of love, takes on huge significance in the child's mind. When the child gains signs of the parents' approval by pleasing them, the child feels loved, worthwhile, and happy. Approval indicates that, at least for the time being, the child is safe from abandonment.

Disapproval, on the other hand, becomes downright dangerous. If these parents disapprove, they disavow the child's worthiness and security. While approval signals love and safety, even a hint of disapproval threatens abandonment, danger, and fear.

> ► *When children are loved unconditionally, they are taught a very important message. They come to understand the distinction between their value as people and the correctness or incorrectness of their behavior.*

In an environment of unconditional love when a child misbehaves, the parents' words and actions say, "We love *you*, but we don't like what you did."

The implicit contract in unconditional love is that parents promise to love their child simply because she or he is theirs. Praise and approval are meted out in order to influence the child's behavioral choices. Approval is still a reward and reinforcement. But, because approval for behavior is separated from the child's worthiness and being deserving of love, it does not become the all-important signal of safety that it takes on in families that give love conditionally. Nor does disapproval or criticism set off mental alarms warning of impending danger and abandonment.

Children, such as Samantha whom we met in the previous chapter, often carry their fears of disapproval and abandonment throughout their lives. As adults, they are finely tuned to the slightest hints of disapproval from others. The emotional baggage of their childhood still makes grown-up approval addicts respond to criticism with intense anxiety.

Quick to yield control to others, these people-pleasers will do nearly anything to reduce the painful fear of abandonment that is triggered by criticism, disapproval, or, even a clue that they are not liked. With their pleasing skills finely honed over a lifetime, they scramble to placate disapproval in order to make themselves feel safe—or safer—once more.

Adult Children of Alcoholic Parents

Significant numbers of people-pleasers are adult children of alcoholic parents. In their case, people-pleasing as a means to gaining approval develops in response to parental behavior that is inconsistent, confusing, and often frightening because it is controlled by alcohol.

From a young child's perspective, parents who are heavy drinkers change their moods and behavior like chameleons. For example, one minute their father can be warm and loving. But, an hour and several drinks later, that same father can be cold and withholding or irrationally angry and explosive.

During the morning and afternoon, the alcoholic mother might remain sober and do a good job caring for her children's needs. But, late in the afternoon as she anticipates her husband's return from work, she might start sipping. By dinner, which often doesn't quite make it to the table, she may be passed out and emotionally unavailable to her children. Or, she might cry inconsolably as she bemoans her hard life and unhappiness.

The alcohol abuser's world is a confusing and burdensome place for children. It is frightening, too, because parents—those all-powerful adults that are supposed to be in charge and take care of the kids—are barely able to take care of themselves. The parents are out of control of their drinking, while the children feel just plain out of control.

At the same time, these children feel enormously responsible for trying to "fix" their parents. Even if they are too young to articulate their reasoning clearly, the children still look for the causes of their parents' abusive drinking, often even blaming themselves. For example, the children might believe that if their parents weren't so unhappy, disappointed, or angry with each other and/or with the kids, they wouldn't be as likely to head for the bottle to drown their problems.

In an attempt to impose order on chaos, children of parents with drinking problems try to maintain control by being "good" and doing "nice" things in order to make their parents happy. If their mother or father is pleased and approving, the children reason that perhaps the desire to drink will diminish or at least the consequences of intoxication on the children won't be as bad.

Ever hopeful and overly responsible, children of alcoholic parents try to please their parents and earn their approval so that "the bad thing"—the drinking and the abusive behavior that often accompanies intoxication—will stop. When the drinking fails to stop, the children blame themselves for not being good enough.

If being good won't stop the drinking, the children hope that at least by staying out of trouble they won't become the target of the drinker's irrational anger. Avoiding disapproval and criticism by keeping a low profile and not drawing parental attention become the safest means of childhood survival in alcoholic families.

> ▶ *As adults, the children of alcoholic parents frequently maintain their fear of criticism and disapproval. Now grown, their people-pleasing behavior is still driven by a deep memory of anger and painful verbal and/or physical abuse associated with their parent's alcohol-fueled disapproval.*

Childhood Rejection and Approval Addiction

Approval addiction doesn't necessarily or always stem from deficient parenting. In some cases, traumatic social experiences in childhood and/or adolescence can create an excessive need for approval from loving parents that carries over into a more generalized approval addiction in adulthood.

Nearly all of us can recall at least a few painful moments from those years in which our tender, developing egos were bruised by intentional or even unintentional slights, insults, or exclusions. If rejection is a predominant theme in your childhood history, those hurts may well have left their imprint on your personality in the form of an extreme sensitivity to and need for approval from and acceptance by others as an adult.

There are many versions of exclusion that can intensify the need for approval. Samantha, for example, moved around from school to school due to her father's military career. Anyone who has ever been the new kid in a school or class—even once—can relate to the social challenges posed by multiple school changes. Samantha's adaptation, role-modeled by her socially appropriate and adept mother, was to become a people-pleaser as a way to gain entry to new friendship circles.

Since children can be cruel, a physical disability, impairment, or deformity can form the basis—however unwarranted—for social rejection or ostracism. Similarly, race, gender, sexual preference, or other aspects of identity can involve painful social alienation by other children.

In such cases, the unconditional love and wise counsel of affectionate parents can serve as a lifeline to which the ostracized, emotionally wounded child clings. Parental approval can become the only safe harbor in a sea of social rejection and negativity. For such people, the ongoing need for approval from parents as well as other authority figures throughout their adulthood can seem necessary to survival itself.

Simply falling short of "ideal" or stereotypically defined standards of beauty or athleticism can be enough to make children and especially adolescents unpopular and undesirable. These old but deep wounds can continue to hemorrhage even into adulthood.

One middle-aged male patient of mine, while now a successful attorney, nevertheless becomes intensely anxious and fearful of rejection whenever he meets with a group of two or more other men. He traces his anxiety to the pain and shame he felt as a young boy who was always the last one selected by other boys to be on sports teams.

Another patient, a tall, very attractive actress now in her forties, insists that she still feels the sting of rejection from being a "skinny, funny-looking, flat-chested teenager" that boys laughed at and popular girls rejected. For both of these individuals, gaining and maintaining approval and broad social acceptance as adults are central to their need to "even the score" by compensating for the intense social rejection pain of their growing-up years.

While all of us have endured some degree of rejection at one time or another, approval addicts still carry the wound.

Are You Still Trying to Meet Your Parents' Expectations?

Not all approval addicts come from troubled or dysfunctional families where there are rifts and conflict between the parents and their offspring. In some families, there is a tight bond between parent and child. The child, as an adult, still feels the tug to please the loved parent or parents. Often the adult child seeks to do so by making significant life choices in accordance with the parent's explicit or implicit wishes. Hooked on the approval of one or both parents, the adult child seeks to live up to what he or she perceives to be the parents' expectations in order to gain and maintain approval from them.

If you are still trying to live up to your parents' expectations as a way to gain approval, you were probably exposed to one of two causal scenarios. First, as a child, you may have been so extravagantly praised and adored by one or both parents that any other source of approval or appraisal pales in comparison. Nobody can make you feel as good about yourself, as important, as talented, or special as your parents.

As an adolescent and adult, then, you may have conformed to their expectations of what you should do with your life as a way of holding on to the kind of unequivocal approval and praise that only your mother and/or father could give. This excessive parental praise may have felt great as a child. But, as an adult, you will have a tendency to discount it on the very basis that it does come, after all, from your parents.

In the second scenario, like Samantha's case, your parents may have had perfectionist standards, and been demanding, withholding, and sparing in their doling out of approval. This parental style can create the sense that you are never quite good enough or that what you do is not quite up to their standards. And, like Samantha, you can get hooked on trying to get what has always been—and, in all likelihood, will continue to be—just out of reach: Your parents' *consistent* love.

Whatever the reason for continually striving for parental approval— because you got so much of it, or because it was withheld and given up only sparingly—the price you pay as an adult for living up to anyone else's expectations is too high.

▶ *Living up to others' expectations, even those of your parents, alienates you from your own desires and capacity for self-fulfillment. Using the criterion of what will make your parents happy as the compass point for directing your major life choices is a misguided strategy. Remember, you are living your own life, not theirs.*

While it may be desirable and preferable for you to make your parents pleased and proud, you should guard against doing so at the expense of your own fulfillment and happiness. Your parents' approval will not overcome or neutralize your own dissatisfaction. If you are not happy with the school you selected, or the career path you are following, or the partner you have wed, it's up to you to change it.

Gaining your parents' approval may be preferable and even desirable. But, it is not mandatory that you have it in order to feel good about yourself and satisfied with the life choices you make.

Behavioral Adjustment: Some Closing Advice on Dealing with Mom and Dad

♦ You may want to have your parents' approval, but you don't *need* it in order to be a happy, fulfilled person.

- You'll be happier if you accept your parents as they are rather than try to change them or make them more approving and accepting of you. They very likely won't change, and you run the risk of winding up feeling inadequate and even bad about yourself.

- You are not alive to fulfill your parents' expectations and needs. You're here to live your own life.

- Your own children have their own lives to live and are not here to fulfill your expectations or needs.

- If your parents don't approve of your life, you don't need to become upset or unhappy. It's more important that you respect and approve of yourself.

- If your parents didn't give you approval or unconditional love, the healthiest way to heal the wound is to love your own children the way you wish your parents had loved you.

CHAPTER 9

Love at All Costs

M any women, especially those with the Disease to Please, seem to find relationships with men problematic. All too often, these women use their people-pleasing habits—sometimes unconsciously—as silken handcuffs designed to prevent men from ever leaving them.

Some try to foster dependency in their partners in order to prevent abandonment. The basic premise is that if you can make a man *need* you because of all the nice and essential things you do for him, he will never leave you alone and miserable.

The strategy here actually turns on using the people-pleaser's own intense fear of abandonment as a benevolent manipulation. The woman knocks herself out taking care of her partner's every need, in order to prove to him how essential she is to his very existence. The people-pleaser erroneously reasons that if she succeeds in making him dependent enough that he cannot live without her, she will secure his staying with her.

▶ *The one central need she forgets to serve is his desire to be needed in return.*

Many people-pleasers who have used this approach sadly discover that manipulating a man into an excessively dependent position—no matter how *nice* and well-intended your motives—may actually push him into doing the very thing you most fear: abandoning you. Jennifer learned this lesson the hard way.

Jennifer was married to Ron for four years. During that time, Jennifer did everything and anything that Ron wanted. She announced on their honeymoon that her life would be devoted to "spoiling" her husband. In short, Jennifer channeled nearly all her own needs into making Ron need her. Her efforts were aimed at securing Ron's dependency so that her marriage, unlike that of her parents', would endure.

After their first year, Ron indeed had become spoiled. He came to expect that Jennifer would take care of him, but put out very little effort to reciprocate. By the second year, Ron lost interest sexually in Jennifer although he attributed his low sex drive to "stress and work pressures." Jennifer never complained. In fact, Ron was very active sexually, just not with Jennifer.

She decided to remain available to Ron if and when his sexual interest returned. She had no intention of making him feel more pressured or bad about himself because she wasn't being satisfied sexually. She was smarter than that, or so she thought.

Jennifer believed she knew the secret to staying married. She would make Ron so dependent on her that he simply would not and could not live without her.

But Jennifer learned otherwise when she returned one evening to find a letter on the bed and a half-empty closet with Ron's clothes and personal belongings cleaned out. The letter said that Ron wanted a divorce because he had fallen in love with another woman. He admitted that he lacked the courage to face Jennifer personally because he didn't want to see the hurt he was causing.

Ron wrote: "I know how much you have always done for me, and I should have been more appreciative. But what I felt instead was growing resentment, even anger, because I felt weak and needy. I never felt like you needed me, and that made me stop feeling like a man. You deserve a much better husband. Please don't blame yourself, Jen. You're the nicest person I've ever known."

As Jennifer found out, when you plant the seeds of unbalanced dependency in a relationship, you may harvest far more than you sow. The overly dependent partner—particularly if that is the man—is likely to develop feelings of resentment and anger because his excessive dependency makes him feel vulnerable and out of control. At the same time, his self-respect and sense of personal autonomy diminish.

Partners of people-pleasers, such as Ron, may not even recognize the intensity of their own anger. Instead, the partner who is made to feel dependent may strike back through withholding or other passive-aggressive means of punishment. Ron acted out his anger by withholding sexual interest and attention toward his wife and by cheating behind her back.

At the same time, if you are the people-pleaser in an unbalanced relationship like Jennifer, you will be forced to deny or suppress your own needs. Inevitably, even the nicest people will become frustrated and angry when their emotional and sexual needs are denied indefinitely.

Even worse, in fostering unbalanced dependency, you create conditions of love based on deficiency rather than on wholeness and strength. This, in turn, is a further breeding ground for lowered self-esteem, exploitation, and dissatisfaction.

▶ *In unhealthy relationships the feeling is, "I love you because I need you." In "healthy love" relationships the feeling is, "I need you because I love you." These are not mere subtleties of language, but critically different emotional postures.*

Healthy relationships that endure are balanced and interdependent. Balanced interdependence means that both partners are aware of and sensitive and responsive to the needs of the other.

The Balancing Act

There is yet another way in which imbalanced dependency needs can damage the relationships between men and the women who have the Disease to Please them.

Over the years I have treated many highly successful career women who have entrapped themselves in bad relationships with men by their self-imposed people-pleasing subservience. A large number of these women who are now at the pinnacle of their professions grew up in the 1950s and 1960s, in an era when femininity and sexual attractiveness still carried with them certain gender stereotypes such as submissiveness, dependency, passivity, and sensitivity.

Today many of these women, and even a significant number of younger women too, fear that the very traits that account for their success in the workplace—assertiveness, mental toughness, aggressiveness, competitiveness—become liabilities in their romantic relationships with men.

One of my patients, a 42-year-old single woman CEO of a large corpo-
ration, told me, "I really think that men consciously believe that they
can handle being with someone like me who represents financial suc-
cess, power, achievement, intelligence, and ability. But, once the rela-
tionship develops, these guys all seem to tell me the same thing. They
say that I'm so strong and independent that I don't need a man. What
they don't know is how many nights I cry myself to sleep, so lonely for a
man who is strong enough to understand that I have dependency
needs—needs to be loved and cherished—probably more than other
women! Why can't they get it?" she cried in frustration.

Many women like my patient, harbor misgivings about whether their
achievements might boomerang when it comes to relationships with men
and come back to haunt them. These women carry the double burden of a
fear of their own success and Disease to Please men. As a consequence of
this dangerous combination, they may engage in a range of self-defeating
behaviors that can sabotage either their careers or their personal relationships, and often both.

If you are both a high achiever and a people-pleaser, you may be trying
to reconcile two competing inner motives at considerable cost to your own
physical and emotional health.

Some people-pleasing women attempt to resolve the dilemma by split-
ting their personality traits into two discrete "sides." They may display their
competitive, assertive, and aggressive side at work. In their personal relationships with men, they may adopt an exaggerated "femininity," display-
ing passivity, submissiveness, and compliance. This masquerade, of course,
is no solution at all. Rather, it is a recipe for inner conflict, anxiety, identity
confusion, and lowered self-esteem.

An exceedingly unhealthy relationship dynamic can develop when a
high-achieving, people-pleasing woman participates with a controlling,
hostile man in her own mistreatment and emotional abuse. If you recognize remnants of the fear of success in your own thinking, you must
become aware of the damaging and dangerous patterns in your personal
relationships that the Disease to Please can spawn.

Helene, for example, is a wealthy, powerful corporate executive who
holds sway in the domains of her businesses, politics, and community
affairs. But, after many years of unhappiness and what she considers
failures in her personal relationships, Helene harbors the fear that
because she is strong, influential, and competent, she cannot expect
and does not deserve to be cherished and protected by a man she loves.

Her current companion, Bob, is ten years her junior. Bob is a middle management underachiever who blames his thwarted ambition and undistinguished performance on the affirmative action policies that have advanced "women and other minorities over more qualified white men."

However, Bob comes from a wealthy family and is counting on an eventual inheritance to "even the score." Bob is also very handsome, sophisticated, and charming. Helene believes that Bob is a man whom she "can take anyplace."

But behind closed doors when they are alone, Bob treats Helene abusively. He seems to relish the opportunity to dominate, demean, and devalue her verbally, emotionally, and sexually. Helene says that she knows that Bob might be taking out his frustration and hostility toward women on her. Additionally, Helene defends Bob's behavior by "understanding" how difficult it is for a man to stand in her shadow.

In therapy, Helene uncovered the toxic assumptions that supported her self-defeating people-pleasing habits as well as the tacit acceptance of Bob's abuse. Helene realized that she needed to correct some of her own gender stereotypes. Helene believed that by demonstrating her people-pleasing behavior in her personal relationships with men, she was being more feminine and, therefore, more sexually attractive.

Interestingly, Helene had an established reputation in public as a prime mover in the women's movement and was an admired role model to younger women in business. She had a firm zero-tolerance policy in her corporation on sexual harassment. However, because of her Disease to Please, Helene was actually rewarding a man for treating her abusively behind closed doors.

Chipping Away at Your Identity

It is imperative that you recognize how dangerous and self-sabotaging your people-pleasing tendencies with men can become so that you can change the unhealthy dynamic of your relationships. Otherwise, the Disease to Please will serve as a veritable mating call to men who have a perverse need and desire to control nearly every aspect of your behavior. Worse yet, you will allow them to do so.

Nothing is out of bounds to a controlling man with a people-pleaser whom he can mold at will—from your appearance to your opinions, your performance in bed to your performance at work, your relationships with friends to your bonds with family. And, in no time, your ego and self-esteem will deteriorate from modeling clay into silly putty.

When he is done playing with you or you are done being played with (whichever comes first), you will have some serious reparative work to do on a self that you may hardly still recognize as your own.

Unless you repair the damage by curing the Disease to Please that produced it, you will limp away from the relationship with the brand of "damaged goods" on your ego. Then, issuing the familiar mating call, you will continue to present yourself as the people-pleasing victim to the next controlling man that recognizes your vulnerability to his power.

The controlling man will always keep you off-center and feeling anxious. Since he needs to change you to demonstrate his control, you can never feel comfortable or secure with the thought that he cares about the person that you truly are—or used to be before he started chipping away at your identity.

When they met, Gail was an ambitious, beautiful but still aspiring model/actress. At 50, Bruce was 25 years Gail's senior and a famous film director. Gail not only fell "in love" with Bruce, she was entirely in awe of his power and talent as well.

Bruce was accustomed to being in control of all his relationships, and Gail was happy to oblige his every request. In many ways, they seemed the perfect match. Gail used to joke with her friends that Bruce made her "a changed woman."

Bruce, who loved to create women in the image he desired, had never felt truly satisfied with any of his myriad partners. Gail had the Disease to Please with a specialization in men. Their "perfect" match was destined to turn toxic.

Soon after they met, as a one-month anniversary present, Bruce took Gail to an exclusive hair salon and told the hairdresser how to cut and style her hair. The color was changed from blonde to auburn at Bruce's direction.

While she was at the salon, Bruce "suggested" a make-over and insisted that her lipstick match the bright red polish he had selected for her fingers and toenails. But he warned Gail never to let her polish chip because he "hated that in a woman."

Bruce also generously insisted on buying Gail a new wardrobe. He loved to take her shopping so that he could select her clothes and shoes.

"As long as he pays for them, why shouldn't he choose my clothes and shoes?" Gail would ask. "After all, the person I most want to please by how I look is Bruce."

Bruce was somewhat reticent about marriage as he was still in the process of divorcing his third wife when he and Gail started dating. But

Bruce insisted that he still believed in "love and romance" and thought that, with Gail, he might "get it right the fourth time."

It was with an eye toward a possible marriage, he explained, that his suggestions for "polishing" Gail's appearance were made.

"I admit that I'm not very tolerant of 'flaws' in women," Bruce told Gail early in their relationship. Speaking of his previous wives, he told Gail, "What really hurt me was the way they all gave up trying to make me happy after we got married. Obviously, I got turned off sexually and the marriages had to end."

Gail promised Bruce that she would never stop trying to make him happy.

Bruce made sure that he and Gail worked out in his home gym with a private trainer for two hours every day. He tried to monitor everything that Gail ate or drank. He wouldn't permit her to drink any alcohol because it would make her look older and constantly reminded her that eating fat would make the "cellulite" on her thighs (which was nearly undetectable) get worse.

During the first several months or so of their relationship, Gail was actually flattered by Bruce's constant efforts to "improve" her appearance. But, after the first year, Gail admitted that she began to feel somewhat oppressed by Bruce's control. When Bruce went out of town without her to shoot a movie on location, she became acutely anxious fearing he would become attracted to another woman.

Gail relapsed into symptoms of an eating disorder she thought she had conquered in her late teens. When she felt particularly anxious, she would secretly binge on chocolate. Then, in her panic over gaining weight and fear of Bruce's disapproval and rejection, she would try to undo the damage by bulimic purging. Alternatively, she would overeat and then counter the calories with compulsive, excessive exercise sometimes spending four hours or more working out.

On their two-year anniversary, Bruce's "suggestions" grew more extreme. But, he held out the carrot of marriage and Gail munched on cue.

Bruce thought Gail's breasts were lovely but "a bit too small for that wedding gown." So, he took her to a plastic surgeon and selected the size implants that he believed would look best. But, Bruce's creation didn't stop there. Six months later, Bruce brought Gail back to the plastic surgeon to have her now substantial breasts "augmented" yet another half-size. Bruce also told her to get cheek implants to improve her facial bone structure and thought it would be a good idea for Gail to have her lipstick, eyebrows, and eyeliner permanently colored (with *a type of cosmetic staining process) so that she would "look beautiful in bed first thing in the morning." Despite considerable misgivings, Gail complied.*

Ironically, the more Bruce changed her, the less confident Gail became in her appearance. In her attempts to make Bruce happy, Gail lost control of her own identity. Her extreme dependence, cultivated by his excessive need for control, left her vulnerable to a paralyzing fear of abandonment that, ultimately, became a painful reality.

"The punch line of this sick joke," Gail concludes, "is that he left me anyway, no matter how much of myself I was willing to sacrifice just to make him happy. The saddest thing is that when I look in the mirror, I see Bruce's image of me instead of seeing myself. And, because I wasn't 'good enough' to keep him, I feel fatally flawed no matter how pretty other people think I am."

Gail's story, while extreme in proportion, illustrates a widespread and highly destructive pattern in certain relationships between men and people-pleasing women. It is no coincidence that women with the Disease to Please find themselves in relationships with controlling men who first wrest away their identities (albeit with the women's full cooperation and compliance) only to later criticize and eventually even discard them as uninteresting, overly dependent, and not sufficiently challenging.

As Gail unhappily learned, the rejection and abandonment that her people-pleasing compliance was designed to prevent can become a cruel and painful reality.

By changing yourself into *his* fantasy of who you should be, you actually make yourself less—rather than more—desirable to him. This is because his fantasy is merely an extension of himself. To paraphrase the inimitable Groucho Marx, the man doesn't want to belong to any club that would have him as a member.

One male patient of mine explained the pattern from his perspective.

"I used to love to get a woman hooked who just wanted to please me," he began. "Then, as soon as I knew she'd do *anything* to please me, I would reel her in and then let her out, watching her dangle on the hook of my control. For a while, I was just fascinated by how much control I had over her behavior.

"Then, one day, I realized that I'm sitting in the boat all alone. I don't want the kind of woman who will do anything to please me anymore. It's boring and lonely. I want a partner who can sit on the boat next to me and keep me company. I want us to please each other without losing all boundaries of our identity."

Another man explained, "I do like to be in control, but I really want someone who will push back. I like steak because it gives me something substantial to chew on. I don't want to eat pre-chewed baby food. That's how I wind up feeling about a woman who will give up her own substance just because she's trying to please me. There's nothing to chew on; there's no challenge there at all. I just get bored."

Whose Orgasm Is It Anyway?

Dina is sitting in my waiting room trembling and crying. When she comes in, she sits mute for several minutes. As she begins to talk, her tears choke off her words. It takes close to 30 minutes before Dina can even begin to tell me why she has come for therapy. What unfolds is a chilling story.

Dina says that her boyfriend, Paul, has kicked her out of his house where they have lived together for the past five years. He has told her that he cannot and will not marry her and that he has found someone else.

Five years ago, Dina, who is now 33, was introduced to Paul, a 38-year-old self-made multimillionaire. Dina describes him as "the most exciting man I had ever met." The moment she met Paul, Dina says she was hit by the proverbial thunderbolt. They went out on their first date and Dina simply never went home. She moved into Paul's very elegant home. After one week, they promised each other they would be together for the rest of their lives.

But, right from the outset, Paul told Dina that his biggest problem with women was that he got bored very easily, especially sexually.

"That scared me a bit because I never wanted to lose this man. But, I knew how to make a man happy in bed, and I was determined that Paul wouldn't ever get bored with me."

"I realize now how he was setting me up," she continued. "After we would make love, he would say, 'Promise me that I'll never be bored sexually.' And, of course, I would make the promise. Little did I realize what he meant," Dina says.

"The first six months with Paul were like a fantasy come true. I didn't fall in love with him because of his money. I would have loved him anyway, but the money just made it possible for us to go anywhere and do anything we wanted. I stopped working and he totally sup-ported me. Of course, that gave him even more control."

"But, after about six months, he started to get restless. He told me that he was getting bored with our sex life and that he needed some

variety. I thought he wanted to see other women, at first, and I was devastated. But, from my perspective now, that would have been better than what happened," Dina remarks.

"One night he told me that he wanted another woman in bed with us. I thought he was kidding until a woman actually walked into the bedroom naked and crawled into our bed. I freaked. That's not for me."

"But, Paul took me aside and told me that if I didn't go along with it, he'd get bored with me and end the relationship. That scared me to death, so I did what he wanted. But, I was very depressed afterwards."

Shortly after that, Paul took her to a private "sex club" and insisted that she have sex with other men so that he could watch. On other occasions, Paul would pay for call girls and male prostitutes to come to the house.

"I kept hoping that I would be enough—just me. It got so stressful that I developed serious sexual dysfunction problems. I couldn't have orgasms anymore at all, and sex became painful because of my anxiety. Of course, I wouldn't let Paul know because I was sure he would dump me on the spot. I was terrified that I would get AIDS and die. I felt like I would deserve it, too. I felt so ashamed and dirty," Dina says.

"The worst part is that I knew he was sick and that he was making me hate myself. I thought about killing myself a lot. And, I knew in my heart that Paul couldn't really love me or anyone. But, I felt so confused—so damaged and guilty. I couldn't imagine leaving Paul because who in the world would want me after I had done these things? So, it became a total trap. I felt like I had no options."

"I started drinking heavily and using drugs so that I wouldn't have to think about what I was doing or what I had done," Dina admits. "He turned me into a whore." Dina sobs.

"I kept telling myself that this was just some phase he was going through and that if I loved him enough and made him happy, he would change and listen to what I wanted."

"Then, I became physically ill. I couldn't get out of bed for a month. I think that was the only way I could stop doing this sick sexual stuff. When I started to recover, Paul wanted to do some totally kinky make-your-own-porno film to put on the Web! Can you imagine? My father and brothers use the Internet!"

"That really woke me up. I finally got up the nerve to say 'no' and suggested that we stop all this sexual experimentation. I told him I wanted to get married and start a family. Paul laughed in my face."

"I'll never forget the demeaning way he spoke to me. 'Marry you?'

Paul asked. 'You can't be serious. How could I marry someone who does the things you do sexually? Do you think I would have you as the mother of my children?' He was unbearably cruel," Dina weeps.
"Then he told me I was boring him. And he basically kicked me out."

After brief, intensive crisis therapy, Dina contacted her family in the Midwest. They were loving, supportive, and embraced Dina in her crisis. Dina knew that she needed to put a lot of geographical distance between herself and Paul as a first step toward getting better. And she knew she needed a lot of professional help. Most of all, Dina knew that she had to stop her Disease to Please men.

Paul's pathological control took a staggering psychological toll on Dina. She was treated for depression and panic disorder. The experience with Paul was almost like a shock therapy cure for Dina's Disease to Please. She finally understood how sacrificing herself to please a man—particularly someone as toxic as Paul—nearly destroyed her.

Three years after I treated her, I received a gratifying letter from Dina. She had married her high school sweetheart and was the mother of a baby girl. She wrote that the first word she intended to teach her daughter was an emphatic "no!"

As with the case of Gail, Dina's story is a dramatic illustration of a common and widespread problem among women with the Disease to Please.

> ▶ *In the arena of sexual behavior, when people-pleasing women get involved with controlling men, dangerous physical and psychological boundary violations can occur.*

Every woman needs to know where her personal boundaries are when it comes to sexual behavior, and she must consistently enforce them. When a controlling man gets into bed with a people-pleasing woman, he calls the shots. This means that the implicit—and often even explicit—expectation is that the people-pleaser will have sex when *he* wants to, in the position, style, and manner that *he* imposes, as frequently as *he* wants to or can, and with the sexual or birth control protection that *he* permits.

This arrangement is so unhealthy for the people-pleasing woman that even the "credit" for her orgasms is assumed or co-opted by the controlling and often self-deluded man. If the woman does not have an apparent orgasm, the controlling man interprets it as a personal failure on his part and as a negative reflection on his capability, talent, and prowess as a lover. If she does achieve orgasm, *he* takes the bows, lauding himself for his stellar sexual performance.

For this reason, the controlling man typically is far more concerned about the impact of the woman's failure to reach orgasm on *his* self-esteem than he is about *her* sexual pleasure and satisfaction. And, because the woman has the Disease to Please, she too sublimates the issue of her orgasmic pleasure to the needs of his delicate ego.

This bias in the couple's perception of sexual performance and satisfaction often disrupts the people-pleaser's sexual enjoyment, decreases her sexual desire, and disrupts her sexual functioning. The significance he attributes to her orgasms—or lack of orgasms—as literal biofeedback of his sexual adequacy can create anxiety, pressure, and self-consciousness in the woman. These emotional states, in turn, further hamper her ability to reach orgasm. Over time, a vicious sexual dysfunction cycle is established. The people-pleaser's mounting pressure to validate her controlling partner's competence continually interferes with her ability to reach orgasmic release.

To reduce *his* anxiety about being a good lover and to stroke *his* ego, the people-pleaser will forgo her real attainment of pleasure by choosing instead to simply fake her orgasms. Then because she will not assert her own needs, ask for help from her partner, or admit to "the big lie" about her orgasms, people-pleasers often develop nearly intractable sexual dysfunction problems.

Beyond the psychological traps people-pleasers lay for themselves with controlling men, learning to say "no" in the sexual arena can be a life and death matter.

While most women will not confront the kinds of sexual challenges that Paul posed to Dina, people-pleasing women regularly must deal with men that do not want to use a condom to have sex because it "doesn't feel good." Or, they will encounter various pressures to comply with sexual positions or acts that they do not wish to perform or with which they are uncomfortable.

When HIV exploded in the American gay population, fear combined with profound grief and bereavement cast a spotlight on the need to change high-risk sexual behavior. The gay community rallied behind an intensive and focused educational effort that involved, among other things, teaching people how to say "no," to insist on using condoms, and to stand fast to their own personally defined sexual boundaries.

That effort compellingly showed that by learning to stop people-pleasing in the sexual arena, lives were saved. In our contemporary culture where date rape, sexual harassment in the workplace, domestic violence, sexually transmitted diseases, and other personal and sexual boundary violations are commonplace, people-pleasing equates with high-risk behavior.

> ▶ *When it comes to sexual behavior and relationships with men,*
> *the Disease to Please can literally be a deadly serious issue.*

Memories of Abuse

It is both noteworthy and highly disturbing that many women with histories of domestic sexual abuse develop strong people-pleasing tendencies as adults.

The linkage produces highly confused feelings about being a nice, compliant woman especially when those defining traits suggest that her prescribed role is to please and satisfy the needs of a sexually dominant, controlling male.

Often, women who were abused as children or adolescents recall that their abusers (frequently family members) would instruct them to "be nice" and to quietly, without resistance, submit to the sexual demands. At the same time, there was generally an implicit or explicit threat that not being nice would result in getting hurt.

Sexual abuse in families typically continues over the span of several years without discovery. As part of "being nice," the victim is required to protect the abuser and his dirty secret. Consequently, the victim is instructed by the perpetrator to behave politely toward him in daily family life. The victim may even find herself motivated to please or appease the abuser so that he won't hurt her the next time he invades her bedroom and her body.

As a consequence, the victim's rage must be denied and repressed. Her rage is not exclusively or even mainly directed toward the sexually abusive parent or sibling. In addition, the victim harbors acute anger and resentment toward the adult who fails to protect or even believe her—usually the mother or stepmother. This rage, too, must be suppressed while the victim's people-pleasing skills develop and become refined under the roof of this dysfunctional family home.

Understandably the victim's emotional wiring is utterly crossed and tangled before she enters adulthood. She may feel guilty for being nice and for letting the abuser have his way with her; or, she may blame herself for not resisting.

She may feel that she wasn't nice or good enough. Otherwise, she erroneously reasons, the perpetrator would have stopped abusing her sooner or wouldn't have abused her in the first place. Perhaps, she may think had she been nicer, he might have loved her in an appropriate way instead of sexualizing and sullying the relationship.

The people-pleaser victim emerges from this dark childhood and adolescence with deep confusion over what she must do to earn love, affection, and acceptance from the world. She has contradictory, ambiguous memories about the feelings she associates with being *nice* and compliant.

On the one hand, she associates being nice with safety and protection from [further] harm—"Be nice and I won't hurt you while I force you to have sex with me." At the same time, being compliant is linked to being victimized in one of the worst kinds of female sexual exploitation.

If you were the victim of sexual abuse, changing your people-pleasing behavior especially as it relates to men is likely to be complex though certainly not impossible. You may find it helpful to examine how your personal memories link niceness, compliance, and submissiveness toward men with sexual exploitation and violation. But, being nice and giving men what they ask for or demand may also be considered in your mind an effective means of self-protection.

Integrating your sexual abuse history with your present people-pleasing habits will help you get to the root of your Disease to Please issues with men. Remember, awareness can open the door to change for the better.

Behavior Adjustment: Breaking People-Pleasing Habits in Relationships with Men

♦ There's nothing wrong with wanting to make a man you love happy or wanting to please him. Just be sure that you're not pleasing him by hurting yourself in the process.

♦ In healthy love the feeling is, "I need you because I love you." In unhealthy love based on deficiencies the feeling is, "I love you because I need you."

♦ No man is worth devaluing or demeaning yourself in any way.

♦ Any man who is threatened or feels diminished by your intelligence, achievements, success, or talent is *not* someone with whom you are likely to have a gratifying relationship anyway. Look elsewhere.

♦ If a man truly loves you, he will not try to make you over into somebody else. He will treasure the person that you are and nurture your own *self*-directed process of personal growth and *self*-improvement. Changing you away from your best self isn't loving; it's manipulative, coercive, and controlling.

♦ Know your sexual boundaries and honor them. Insist that any man who wants to share your body respects your boundaries. If sex doesn't feel loving, it isn't.

CHAPTER 10

Romantic Addiction

*A*t 34 Louisa, a pediatrician, is acutely aware of the sound of her biological clock and is ready to get married. Dick, 28, is a great-looking, sophisticated investment banker whose prior relationships have never lasted longer than a few months.

When they met, the relationship took off in high gear. By their third date, they were already discussing marriage and children—at least hypothetically.

But after three months of high-speed courtship, Dick panicked and inexplicably distanced himself.

"Let's face it," Louisa states, "he totally flaked. Suddenly, he 'forgot' about dates or cancelled our plans the last minute. Basically, he blew me off."

"I got up my nerve and went to his apartment. He admitted that he was scared to death and said that we had taken this relationship way too fast. I asked him to tell me what his concerns were so that I could help calm him down, but I wasn't ready for what he said."

"He explained that he wasn't feeling attracted enough to me. He told me that all his other girlfriends were beautiful. Dick actually said that he had hoped my 'brains and personality' would be enough, but that he was having serious doubts about whether he could remain faithful to me," Louisa wipes her tears and shakes her head.

"I'm used to overcoming obstacles," Louisa says. "So I got into my usual coping mode and decided to solve the problem by simply making myself more attractive. I dieted, exercised, changed my hair and make-up, and got new clothes. Everyone said I looked great," Louisa says.

After a month of separation, Dick called to beg Louisa's forgiveness.

"He told me he didn't mean a word of what he said about my looks. When he saw me, he told me he thought I was beautiful—that I not only looked great but that I had an 'inner-beauty' other women lacked. I believed him because I needed to. Dick explained that he said those mean things just to push me away because of his fears of commitment. Then he reassured me that he was truly in love and ready to get engaged . . . soon. He invited me to come home for Christmas to meet his family."

"I really expected to have a diamond ring under the tree," Louisa said. "But, as it turned out, I never even made it to his family's house. He bailed again on me three days before we were supposed to leave town. This time he told me I was too good for him—too smart, too serious, too down to earth. He topped it off by saying that I was 'too nice' and that I made him feel guilty because he wasn't as nice as me. What was I supposed to do about that?"

"So, I went home, alone, to my mother and cried my way through the holidays, swearing never to date a younger man again."

"He called me 10 days after the New Year. He sent me 50 red roses and again begged me to take him back. Dick told me that he cried like a baby on New Year's Eve because he had lost the only woman that ever mattered to him."

"I let him convince me because I was so miserable. I was like a strung out drug addict without him. I'm ashamed to admit it, but I guess he's kind of like a male 'trophy.' When things are good with us, I feel great about myself. He's young and gorgeous and I want to show him off to all my friends."

"When he says hurtful things, my ego is smashed. Nobody and nothing can make me feel as bad about myself as he can. And, no one can make me feel better again except him."

The couple got back together, this time for several months until Dick began to lose interest in Louisa sexually.

"Every time we get close, he starts to have an anxiety attack about commitment and breaks up with me. I realize that the problem is really with him—his ambivalence. I have to admit, this is killing my self-esteem. No matter how I look at it, I come to the conclusion that if he *loved me enough—if I were attractive, exciting, sexy enough—we'd be married already."*

"I think I've known for a long time that I need to get strong enough to leave him. After this roller-coaster ride, I don't trust him at all. When thing are going well between us, I'm the one who gets panicky now. I'm always waiting for the other shoe to drop. I start expecting him to reject me. Then, I begin to act clingy and insecure, which I know makes him want to take cover and run. We're really in a messed up cycle."

What Louisa is describing is the alternately painful and exhilarating cycle of romantic addiction. Make no mistake: no matter how romantic the trappings, how beautiful the apology flowers, how sincere the protestations, or how big the diamond ring, this pattern of alternating intimacy and rejection, closeness and distance, idealization and devaluation, is *not* healthy love. It is addictive behavior driven by the people-pleasing need to avoid abandonment, rejection, and disapproval.

By the time Louisa had become hooked on Dick, she might as well have become a drug addict and he her pusher. Their story fits the model of addiction to a tee. Louisa is behaving like Pigeon 2 trying to earn back Dick's love and acceptance that he doles out on a random, intermittent basis.

Louisa understands that she is more strongly motivated by her need to avoid the pain and assault to her self-esteem of Dick's disapproval and rejection than she is to regain his love. She has come to distrust his love anyway.

Don't Give Anyone Permission to Make You Feel Inferior

Eleanor Roosevelt wisely counseled, "No one can make you feel inferior without your permission." Unfortunately it cost Louisa much unhappiness, depression, anxiety, and withdrawal distress before she realized that *she* was giving Dick her permission to treat her poorly.

People-pleasers often err on the side of attributing more noble motives and intentions to people with whom they are involved in a romantic relationship than is actually the case. It is quite common for one partner in a relationship to project his or her personality traits, motives, or ways of looking at the world onto the other and to assume similarity of values.

In short, other people—even those you love—may not be as kind as you are. In fact, many people are often not kind or nice at all. Sadly, your Disease to Please makes you an easy mark for those who would seek to exploit or hurt you.

> ▶ *To adequately protect yourself, you need to see people as they are and not how they appear through trick rose-colored lenses that magnify their assets and minimize or block out their flaws.*

Louisa, for example, could not perceive Dick accurately until she could differentiate her ego from him. As long as she thought of him as *her* ideal, rather than as a separate human being, she could not hold him accountable for the way he treated her. Instead, her logical mind kept approaching a *psycho*-logical problem with the assumption that if Dick would merely quiet his fears and discuss the "real" reasons for his dissatisfaction, she would do her people-pleasing best to fix herself in order to become *his* "ideal" woman.

Because she is such a *nice* person, Louisa had a hard time admitting that Dick, the love of her life, was not. Each time that Dick rejected her, Louisa was blinded by what she labeled "love." More accurately, Louisa's perception was severely impaired by the acute withdrawal symptoms inflicted on her by her hardcore romantic addiction.

Finally, when Louisa was sufficiently insulted and outraged, she allowed herself to feel curative anger toward Dick. When she did, she could also see that she was not the one in need of major fixing; Dick was.

However, as Louisa learned in therapy, her Disease to Please fostered addictive behavior in the relationship. In pure people-pleasing form, Louisa literally pleaded with Dick to tell her exactly how she was inferior or lacking so that she could change herself, make him happy, and forestall his rejection and abandonment.

Louisa offered Dick her permission to be treated as inferior and then begged for more mistreatment the way a junkie might beg for drugs.

People-Pleasing and Collusion with Angry Partners

Romantic addiction is just one of several relationship patterns in which people-pleasers unwittingly set themselves up to be *nice* victims who are treated badly.

> ▶ *Many people with the Disease to Please find themselves in relationships with angry, aggressive partners. While the motives of people-pleasers may be unconscious or unintentional, this association is neither an accident nor a coincidence. People-pleasers*

are not *innocent victims but rather active accomplices of their angry and often abusive partners.*

Over time, this collusion between the two—the people-pleasing accomplice and the angry partner—becomes a very dangerous game.

If you are involved with an angry partner, you will probably be surprised to learn that your people-pleasing makes you at least an active contributor to your partner's hostility and aggression if not a willing participant. But, in all likelihood, you believe earnestly that your people-pleasing behavior is meant to avert anger, evade conflict, and derail confrontation.

In reality, though, your Disease to Please sets you up as the perfect accomplice of an angry, accusatory partner. As you may already suspect, your people-pleasing is not making any headway in lowering or reducing your partner's tendency to become angry and to instigate conflict. On the contrary, as you will see, your people-pleasing behavior makes your partner even angrier and more likely to confront you with hostility and aggression.

How You Collude in Your Own Mistreatment

There are at least four main ways in which you unwittingly collude with a hostile partner:

1. *You're Too Willing to Assume Blame.* First, people-pleasers are too willing to assume blame when a problem—any problem—occurs in their relationships. You probably believe that doing so is a way to avoid further anger or confrontation. However, the reality is that by assuming blame, you merely reinforce and justify the anger that is being directed or misdirected toward you.

Anger, by definition, is an accusation made in response to a perceived error, mistake, or misbehavior. In order for anger to be activated, someone must be *blamed* for the perceived misdeed. And, in true people-pleasing form, you give the accuser permission to blame you—exactly what he or she needs.

▶ *Assuming blame is not the same thing as accepting your share of responsibility for a problem.*

The latter presumes that if a problem occurs between two people, the responsibility will be attributed jointly and fairly. It may not be equally shared, but both parties will acknowledge some degree of responsibility for the problem between them.

Blame, on the other hand, is one-sided. The accuser disavows any responsibility and seeks instead to hold you not just responsible, but answerable and punishable for your actions that are clearly labeled as wrongdoing.

2. *You Use Passive-Aggressive Tactics.* The second major way in which you are complicit with your hostile partner is by denying or submerging your own anger and adopting instead *passive-aggressive* ways to respond. As its name implies, passive-aggressive behavior is hostile in nature by virtue of being passive. The submissiveness permits you to deny your aggressive side to both your partner and yourself and to maintain your self-concept as nice.

Examples of passive-aggressive behavior include pouting, sulking, and refusing to talk. Additionally, you might defer, procrastinate, or continually "forget" or be late for various obligations that involve your partner. Or you might withhold sex, affection, time, or attention from your partner. And you may do all these things without recognizing or being at all aware of your own retaliatory intentions.

Because of your intense discomfort with your own negative emotions, you have probably developed a fairly extensive repertoire of passive-aggressive responses to your hostile, overtly aggressive partner.

▶ *Passive-aggressive behavior is uniquely dangerous when it is directed toward a hostile partner.*

Passive-aggressive actions actually incite your partner to greater hostility. Your passivity combined with the denial of your own deeply buried aggression become intensely frustrating to your partner. Since hostility is bred from frustration, passive-aggressive behavior ultimately enrages your already angry partner even further.

This is not to say that you are responsible for causing your partner's anger or hostile behavior. Your partner's anger is your partner's responsibility. But, your passive-aggressive behavior makes you a participant in an interactive pattern of behavior that *enables* your partner to continually become angry with you.

3. *You Become a Passive Victim.* The third way in which you collude with your partner's hostility is by becoming a passive *victim* when your partner becomes actively angry. In doing so, you create and perpetuate a cycle in which you and your partner assume complementary roles.

▶ *In order to establish dominance through intimidation, threat, or aggression, your partner needs a victim to control. Ironically, even in this negative, unhealthy dynamic, you are still a people-pleaser fulfilling your partner's needs.*

It would be unhealthy and possibly more dangerous for you to adopt an aggressive stance toward your partner. But, by acting *assertively*—instead of passively or aggressively—you would be standing up for your rights not to be mistreated, used as a verbal (or physical) punching bag, or otherwise be on the receiving end of your partner's hostility and anger.

   4. *If Your Partner Is Always Right, You're Always Wrong.* The fourth way in which your Disease to Please makes you an accomplice to anger is by your tacit agreement to always be wrong.

Hostile people need to win every argument and to prove themselves right in order to rationalize and justify their anger. As the partner of such an individual, you will continually find yourself in the hot seat. In a win/lose scenario, only one side can be right; the other, by definition, must be wrong.

Because you want to gain approval and because you are conflict-averse, your tendency is to agree with your partner and to passively submit to his or her point of view.

▶ *To allow your partner to always be right, you must always be wrong.*

The determination that you are always wrong has little or nothing to do with the merits of your partner's argument, or with the reality of your guilt or innocence, or with your moral rectitude. It has only to do with your partner's need for dominance and control, with your partner's persistent demand to be right.

Submitting to the role of the "wrong one" will make you feel guilty whether you are really at fault or truly in the right. If, in fact, you are wrong, you will heap blame on yourself, thereby compounding the load already placed on you by your self-righteous, punitive partner.

If, on the other hand, you know or believe that you are right, you will blame yourself anyway for being too emotionally weak and wishy-washy to stand up for yourself.

▶ *Allowing yourself to be perpetually wrong—just so your partner can always be right—will damage your self-esteem.*

Finally, a partner who is constantly poised to pounce on anything that will make you wrong can create yet another problem: *perfectionism*. When you live in an oppressive psychological environment in which your performance is continually scrutinized, you will not feel free to take risks, be creative, or to try new challenges where success and perfection are not guaranteed. Thus, perfectionism stifles your personal growth and performance.

In addition, you may try to cover up your mistakes in order to avoid your partner's—or others'—disapproval and reprisals. Here again, your attempts to avert conflict are likely to backfire. When your mistakes are discovered anyway, as they almost always are, you will lose the respect and trust of others. Moreover, you will be doubly faulted—for the mistake *and* for the dishonesty in failing to disclose your error.

Mistakes are valuable because you can learn from them. If you are too fearful of others' disapproval to acknowledge your mistakes, you lose that learning opportunity.

You Can't Change Your Partner, but You Can Change Yourself

So what can you do if you have a hostile, angry, punitive partner? How can you stabilize someone who has you on an addictive emotional roller-coaster ride?

First recognize that you cannot change your partner directly. If you have been thinking that your kindness and giving nature will win the day, it's time to realize the futility and cost of your efforts and to stop expending them.

Your people-pleasing behavior is having the *opposite* effect of what you intend: It is only rewarding your partner's aggressive or unstable behavior.

So, instead of asking yourself how you can change your partner, start your self-inquiry with this thought: *Knowing that I cannot and will not change my partner, what can I do to change the situation for myself?*

This thought will empower you, whereas thinking about how to change your partner will only reinforce your sense of powerlessness, helplessness, victimization, anger, and depression. These negative feelings keep you stuck, mired in an analysis paralysis that is going nowhere but down.

If you are unhappy with your partner, you have very likely already considered the option of terminating the relationship or, at least, separating from him. It is a good idea now to revisit this option given your new understanding that you cannot and will not change your partner. But you can change your own behavior.

Certainly, if you decide to leave your partner and end the relationship, you may produce profound changes in your life. However, if you *only* leave this relationship but do not overcome the Disease to Please, your next relationship may well be a replica of this one.

Of course, you may elect to stay in your current relationship for good reasons of your own. Or you may simply not be ready to leave or give up on it or your partner altogether. But, whether you stay or leave, *you must stop participating in your own mistreatment.*

Remember, your partner's behavior—like that of everyone—is influenced by its consequences. This means that if you alter the way you respond to your partner, you will have a powerful impact on his behavior.

▶ *When you stop rewarding and colluding with your partner's mistreatment of you, his or her behavior will adjust to the changing circumstances and consequences.*

Keep in mind that if you reward a negative behavior (e.g., anger), you will increase the probability and frequency of it happening again in the future. If you cease rewarding the negative behavior, you will diminish the chances that it will occur again and reduce how often the behavior happens. Finally, if you reward a *different* behavior—a more *positive* action— you will increase the likelihood that the new behavior will replace the old negative one.

This formula has powerful implications for how you can change the negative pattern between you and your partner. You can no longer afford to cling to the self-deluding thought that you can fix or change your partner directly by simply being a nice people-pleasing person. Doing so, as you now know, will only make a bad situation worse.

To paraphrase writer Dennis Wholey, expecting your partner to treat you fairly because you are a nice person is like expecting the bull not to charge because you are a vegetarian.

You must recognize that your chronic people-pleasing behavior is the equivalent of waving a big red cape at an angry bull. You must either drop the cape and run for the door or change your strategy immediately.

▶ *To cure the Disease to Please, you only need to change* one *behavior, (or one thought, or one feeling) and the cycle will start to unravel like a ball of yarn when you pull on a single strand.*

There may be knots along the way, but you will learn the tools to untie them.

Behavior Adjustment: How to Protect Yourself from Romantic Addiction

♦ Don't give anyone the permission to make you feel inferior, unworthy, or undeserving.

♦ When you are too willing to assume the blame for everything that goes wrong in your relationship, you merely fuel and justify your partner's anger. Overassuming blame is different from assuming your appropriate share of the responsibility for what goes wrong.

♦ Passive-aggressive tactics are self-defeating, counter-productive, and dangerous, especially if you use them with a hostile partner.

♦ Victimization produces shame; empowerment produces dignity.

♦ If you allow your partner to *always* be right, you will *always* be wrong. That is just not true, is it?

Part Three

People-Pleasing Feelings

W e are now ready to address the third side of the Disease to Please triangle where our focus will be People-Pleasing Feelings. The driving motivation behind people-pleasing habits and thoughts lies in the escape from, or avoidance of, emotions and emotional experiences that are uncomfortable, difficult, and frightening.

The People-Pleasing Feelings with which we will be most concerned are negative emotions—that is the discomfort with and fear of anger, hostility, conflict, and confrontation. Before you can truly overcome the Disease to Please syndrome, you will need to conquer these intense fears by learning to manage conflict constructively and to control and express anger appropriately and effectively.

You may actually find yourself wanting to put this book down or skip this section altogether simply because the prospect of facing the fears of anger and conflict is so scary. Don't give in to this impulse. As with other types of avoidance reactions, your fears will only intensify each time you run away from facing them. In fact, people-pleasing habits and the self-defeating thoughts that support them are strengthened every time you use them to escape these negative, fearful feelings.

As you will learn in the next chapter, fearful feelings become a self-fulfilling prophecy precisely because they prevent you from ever having the opportunity to express anger or deal with conflict appropriately. You will never learn to fight fairly and effectively if you run at the slightest hint of conflict. Nor can you ever fix the problems in your relationships with other people if you lack the basic communication skills for expressing your negative feelings or responding to those of other people.

When I use the terms *negative* versus *positive* to describe a given emotion, my intention is to differentiate a feeling that is unpleasant, painful, or difficult to accept from one that is pleasant, comfortable, and easier to acknowledge and communicate.

With reference to emotions, *negative* and *positive* are not meant as value judgments. Anger is a negative emotion for many people because it feels unpleasant and is often difficult to express or communicate appropriately—but not because it is necessarily wrong or bad. You will learn that anger is a natural, normal and under appropriate circumstances, even a useful and adaptive emotion.

While our focus will remain largely on negative emotions, the third side of the triangle also contains positive feelings. At some earlier point in time, your people-pleasing no doubt felt rewarding and gratifying because of the pleasure you derived from fulfilling others' needs and making them happy and from the approval, praise, and gratitude it earned you. Pleasing others still may be rewarding to some extent, although most people-pleasers feel far too exhausted by their habit to enjoy it much anymore.

In your early life experiences, you learned that pleasing significant others was an effective way to gain their much-desired approval. Praise along with expressions and gestures of love and affection also comprise the positive emotional rewards gained from pleasing others. Choosing how to take care of others' needs (e.g., where to go, what to eat, etc.) may also afford you a measure of *control* that, in turn, can register as a positive feeling.

> ▶ *Somewhere along the learning curve, you also discovered that by being compliant, nice, and submissive to others you could effectively deter conflict, deflect others' anger, suppress your own anger, and avert confrontation.*

Once the connection between *going along* and *getting along*—between compliance and conflict avoidance is made, it can take a dangerous turn into an addictive, compulsive pattern of emotional avoidance.

Be assured that since you taught yourself to avoid anger, conflict, and confrontation you can also be taught how to handle these difficult emotional experiences effectively and constructively. This section will help you gain insight into how your people-pleasing habits actually intensify your fears, cripple your communication, impair your "people skills," and limit your range of emotional intelligence and know-how.

Only by mustering the courage to face your emotional fears can you learn to overcome them, as you will learn in this discussion of the last side of the triangle. You will then be ready for your personal journey to recovery from the Disease to Please.

CHAPTER 11

Once More, Without Feelings

You have very likely become so adept at people-pleasing that you lack experience when it comes to recognizing, accepting, and expressing your own anger. Moreover, you have probably used your people-pleasing tactics to buffer yourself from conflict or confrontation. As a result of this low exposure to the negative emotions you fear, your anxieties about them have become self-fulfilling prophecies.

You are similar to a person who never learned to swim because of an intense fear of water. This individual will avoid any situation in which he or she might have to be near, on, or in the water. Over time, with repetitive avoidance, the individual's lack of exposure to water will likely make the fear of drowning become self-fulfilling.

Should this water-phobic person accidentally fall into the deep end of a swimming pool, the wild anxiety would likely create deadly panic. The individual would flail, swallow water, and even lose consciousness. And, because fear and avoidance prevented him or her from learning to swim, the dreaded prophecy of drowning could become a lethal reality.

If this same person entered the pool's shallow end accompanied by a skilled and reassuring lifeguard, he or she could learn survival and swimming skills. With repeated opportunities to get into the water under controlled conditions, the fear would diminish and eventually likely disappear altogether.

The important point is that conquering the phobia comes *through exposure to the fear itself* in order to learn effective and appropriate responses. In our example, the water-phobic person can only overcome his mortal fear by getting into the water under safe conditions and thereby learn to swim. Continued or persistent avoidance would merely intensify the fear and strengthen the escape behavior through which the anxiety is evaded.

You avoid anger, conflict, and confrontation through repetitive people-pleasing. As a consequence, you have never given yourself a chance to learn effective ways to handle these difficult emotions. Now you have the opportunity to unlearn your fears and avoidance responses and to replace them with competent anger management and conflict resolution skills.

If you were asked, you might first identify positive feelings as your emotional motivation for people-pleasing. A deeper probe of your motivation would likely reveal that *fear* and *avoidance* of negative feelings are even more powerful in shaping your people-pleasing habits than positive emotional rewards.

Cognitive therapist Dr. David Burns has coined the term "emotophobia" to refer to an excessive or irrational fear of negative feelings.[7] In the case of people-pleasing, the specific fears encompass anger, conflict, aggression or hostility, and confrontation. Take the emotophobia quiz below to determine how large a role your fear of negative feelings plays in your people-pleasing problems.

Do You Have "Emotophobia?" Quiz

Read each statement and decide if it applies to you. If the statement is true, or mostly true, circle "T." Or, if it is false, or mostly false, circle "F."

1. I believe that nothing good can come from conflict.   T or F
2. I become very upset when I suspect that someone I care about is angry with me.   T or F
3. I would go to almost any length to avoid a confrontation.   T or F
4. I almost never complain or show my dissatisfaction to a person that is waiting on me in a store or restaurant, even when I know I am getting bad service, a poor product, or terrible food.   T or F
5. I think it is my responsibility to calm down people around me if they become agitated, angry, or aggressive.   T or F
6. I believe that I should not get angry or have conflict with the people I love.   T or F

7. When I become angry or hurt, I am far more likely to sulk, pout, or become silent than to express my feelings openly and directly.   T or F

8. I believe that conflict is nearly always a sign of serious problems in a relationship.   T or F

9. I am easily intimidated by another person's display of anger or hostility.   T or F

10. When I get angry and upset, I often develop physical problems such as headaches, stomach or back pain, skin rashes, or other stress-related symptoms.   T or F

11. I am apt to apologize to another person just to end a fight or stop the anger, whether I am solely to blame or not.   T or F

12. I believe that something bad or destructive is likely to result if anger and conflict are expressed in a personal relationship.   T or F

13. If someone blames me for a problem, I am more likely to just apologize and avoid any further discussion than run the risk of getting angry and having a more serious confrontation, even if I am not truly at fault.   T or F

14. I believe that it's best just to smile and cover up angry feelings than to express them and risk getting into a fight or conflict.   T or F

15. I would do just about anything to avoid an angry confrontation with anyone in my life.   T or F

16. I believe that I am usually to blame if someone gets angry with me. T or F

17. I think I would be a better person if I never felt angry or unhappy. T or F

18. My own anger frightens me.   T or F

19. Most problems between people who care about one another will just resolve in time and are better left without discussion.   T or F

20. I almost never disagree with or challenge another's opinion for fear that I might provoke a conflict of some kind.   T or F

How to Score and Interpret Your Answers

Total the number of times you circled "T" for true to obtain your score.

♦ *If your score is between 15 and 20:* You are clearly *emotophobic*—intensely and largely irrationally fearful—of anger, conflict, and confrontation. Your avoidance of conflict and suppression of anger are probably exacting a heavy toll on the quality of your relationships with others as well as on your physical and emotional health.

♦ *If your score is between 6 and 14:* Your fear of anger and avoidance of conflict—while not phobic in proportion—are definitely fueling your people-pleasing habits and very likely getting in the way of your ability to form and maintain healthy intimate relationships. In addition, because of suppressing anger, your physical and emotional health may be at risk.

♦ *If your score is 5 or less:* You are not having *major* difficulty acknowledging or expressing negative feelings. However, if you have the Disease to Please, you may be minimizing how uncomfortable anger and conflict are for you. One important reason for this is that your people-pleasing habits have made you so conflict-avoidant that you don't know how difficult anger and other negative feelings really are for you to handle. But, you can be sure that your discomfort will only get worse and become more of a problem if you continue to use people-pleasing as a way to avoid anger and conflict.

▶ **Chronic suppression of anger may be as damaging to health as volatile, explosive rage.**

Chronic conflict avoidance is not only symptomatic of weak, unstable relationships, it plays a large role in undermining the growth and healthy maintenance of relationships as well.

In order to overcome your people-pleasing problems, you will need to learn effective and healthy ways to express anger and to manage and resolve conflict constructively and effectively. The short-term gains you get by using people-pleasing in order to thwart conflict, avoid anger, and abort confrontation are far outweighed by the costs of never learning critical anger and conflict management skills that will make you and your relationships happier and healthier.

The Danger of Conflict Avoidance

Patricia, 48, is the first to admit that she behaves like a "doormat" around men.

"I just tiptoe around guys. I'm always walking on eggshells. I'm terrified of making them angry. My father had a terrible temper. When he

got drunk (which was every night), he would rant and rave and physically abuse my mother," Patricia explains.

To protect Patricia, her mother instructed her never to talk back or stand up to her father. She told Patricia, "Just do whatever he wants. Smile and say, 'Yes, sir.' Then, go into your room. I know it's hard when he says mean things. Remember, your father really loves you. It's just the alcohol talking."

So Patricia learned to be a people-pleaser, especially to men. Her father died before Patricia was 18, but her fear of anger—particularly male anger—stayed with her for a lifetime.

"The curious part is that I'm afraid of my husband's anger, but I've never even seen it! He never gets angry and we never fight. To tell you the truth," Patricia admits, "we don't really talk about anything deeply enough to have an argument. I just agree with everything he says and wants. That's my way of keeping the peace," she concludes.

Patricia acknowledges that after 25 years of marriage, she knows her husband doesn't have a bad temper. "If he hasn't blown up by now, it's probably not going to happen," she reasons. "But, I still can't seem to change my reactions. I never tell him if something he does is bothering me or making me unhappy. I tell myself that whatever it is, it's not worth having a fight," she muses.

When her husband joined her in some therapy sessions, Patricia learned some things about their relationship that she had never understood before. Alex, her husband, disclosed that he was becoming "too friendly" with a female colleague at work. He said that he loved Patricia and didn't want "anything to develop romantically" with the other woman.

"But I realize how lonely I have felt for so many years in our marriage," Alex told her. "I know that you try to be the best wife you can be. You do everything to try and please me. But, honey, you never show me or tell me who you really are and how you're truly feeling. You edit everything out because you're afraid I'll get mad. You have me confused with your father!"

Patricia now realizes that she nearly paid the highest price for conflict avoidance.

"I've been so fearful of conflict my whole life because of my parents," Patricia said. "I know I married Alex because he is so gentle and sweet. I'm sure it hurts him that I don't trust him enough to tell him just about anything. My automatic reaction is to do what I think he wants or needs—although obviously I haven't always been right—and then to leave him alone so that I don't make him mad."

Once Patricia gained awareness of all the ways she uses people-pleasing to suppress her own anger (and other negative feelings) and to control and deflect the anger of others, she could target these habits for change.

People-Pleasing and the "White Door" Escape Hatch

Many of my patients, like Patricia, who suffer from the Disease to Please, have learned to use the tag "white door behavior" to label their people-pleasing when it is used to avoid or derail anger and conflict. This phrase is a shorthand way to refer to conditioning or learning through negative reinforcement. As you will recall from Chapter 7, negative reinforcement refers to behavior that is rewarded when an unpleasant, negative, or painful experience stops. People-pleasing habits are *negatively reinforced* because they lower the anxiety of disapproval or rejection in fearful situations.

We will return briefly to the laboratory for a clear illustration of how negative reinforcement operates and contrasts with positive reward. In the lab, we will use a cage that is divided into two equal portions. Half the cage is painted all black—floors, walls, and ceiling—with the exception of a distinct white door in the common wall partitioning the sections. The white door swings opens into the white portion of the cage where everything is painted white—walls, floor, and ceiling. The door is white on both sides.

The subjects of the study are two white lab rats, each of which will first be placed in the black section of the cage one at a time. Our purpose is to train each rat to leave the black portion of the cage by pushing open the white door and to enter the white portion.

Rat 1 will be trained using positive reinforcement. To accomplish this, we first place a chunk of cheese in the farthest corner of the white section of the cage. Then we place the rat in the black section and watch what happens.

The rat explores the black section for a few moments. Eventually, he will discover by knocking or pushing into the white door that it swings open and gains him access into the white section. Catching the scent of the cheese, the rat will proceed through the doorway and promptly move to the far corner where he eats the cheese and, by all appearances, is a happy rat.

The training procedure is repeated a few more times until the behavior of going from the black to the white section through the white door has become fairly well-ingrained. The next step is to remove the cheese from the white section altogether. Now, we place the rat in the black section and observe how many times he will continue to exit the black section into the white portion in the absence of the positive reward he has learned to anticipate. The positive conditioning effects of the training does produce a rat who will continue to exit the black section via the white door for several trials even in the absence of reward. The rat has come to *associate* the white compartment with something that tastes nice and presumably makes him feel good. However, after 5 or 10 trials without the cheese, the rat appears to lose interest and stops exerting effort for no reward. Eventually, when placed in the black cage, Rat 1 will simply remain there. At this point, psychologists say that the white door exit response has been "extinguished."

Rat 2 will also be trained to leave the black compartment through the white door. However, this rat gets the negative reinforcement training. Accordingly, he is first placed in the black section of the cage and no cheese is put in the white section. There is nothing in the white section at all.

Now mild electric shocks are applied through the floorboards in the black section of the cage only. The shocks, while not strong enough to be acutely painful or dangerous, are nevertheless clearly unpleasant to the unhappy rat.

Illustrating his displeasure, the rat starts jumping around agitatedly, and begins urinating and shaking (as upset rats are wont to do). During his jumping around, one random but fortunate leap will thrust him into the white door which will swing open gaining the rat access to the white portion of the cage. Importantly there are no electric shocks in the white section.

While there is no cheese or other positive reward in the white section, the painful shocks do cease as soon as the rat jumps through the white door and lands in the white side of the cage. It is the *cessation of pain*—that constitutes the negative reinforcement.

The procedure is repeated a few times to ensure that the rat has "learned" the white door escape response. Rest assured, a rat with normal rat intelligence gets the drill in a matter of seconds after only a few trials.

Now, to measure the strength of the negative versus the positive reinforcement conditioning, the procedure is repeated with the shock grids turned off in the black section. We want to observe how long the second rat will keep jumping or running through the white door even though the reward of stopping the shock pain has been removed.

When the rat is put in the black cage *even without the shocks,* he leaps for the white door and escapes to the white section in almost no time flat. Further Rat 2 will continue to run for the white door time after time, with no shock present. The negative conditioning effect is so potent that the rat will continue to engage in the avoidance behavior of jumping through the white door even when there is no longer anything unpleasant to avoid besides presumably the memory or fear of the shock. The second rat's white door escape response will take a very, very long time to extinguish.

Your people-pleasing should be understood as a white door response that is conditioned through both negative and positive reinforcement. The short-term rewards (or positive reinforcement) that you derive from pleasing others include approval, praise, and gratitude from others, as well as self-gratification. These rewards are analogous to the rat's cheese.

The negative reinforcement—the avoidance of anger, conflict, confrontation, disapproval, rejection, or criticism—that sustains your Disease to Please problem is analogous to the cessation of Rat 2's unpleasant shock experience. Your use of people-pleasing to avoid fearful feelings is analogous to the rat's response of jumping through the white door.

> ▶ *The impact of negative reinforcement in maintaining your people-pleasing habits has been far stronger than that of any rewards or pleasure you may have derived.*

Your fear of anger and conflict is only one negative experience analogous to the electric shock in the black cage. Others include fear of rejection, fear of disapproval, fear of conflict or confrontation, and fear of hurting others. Just as Rat 2 continued to jump through the white door *even when the shock was turned off*, you continue to avoid these experiences, never sticking around long enough to determine if there might be a better, more beneficial, or effective way of responding.

Look at Patricia. She's been jumping through the white door to avoid her husband's anger throughout her married life, although she has never even witnessed him losing his temper once during that period. If she had controlled her impulse to escape, she might have learned sooner that Alex was starved for more intimacy and a more authentic emotional relationship with her.

People-pleasing behaviors—such as "Yes-saying," meeting others' needs, or acceptance of blame—provide a white-door escape hatch from these negative emotions.

You have been conditioned to use people-pleasing in order to avoid anger and conflict. You have also prevented yourself from ever having the opportunity to confront your fears. As a result, you have never been able to gain mastery over them by learning appropriate ways to handle anger and conflict.

Preemptive People-Pleasing

Going back to our example of Patricia, she has followed a flawed strategy of using her people-pleasing habits to prevent the expressions of anger and other negative emotions by both Alex and herself. In this way, she believes she has averted what would otherwise be damaging marital conflict.

Patricia engages in preemptive people-pleasing. Her behavior is preemptive in the sense that she tries to prevent people—especially men—from expressing their anger. Patricia proactively tries to anticipate and fulfill the needs and desires of men in her life in order to remove any reason for them to become angry with her before the fact.

Patricia's people-pleasing habits have been reinforced and strengthened because they provide escape from what she believes would otherwise be dangerous anger and destructive conflict. Eventually, in therapy, she could admit that her marriage had long ago grown stagnate. Without an effective communication vehicle for redressing complaints and unhappiness or for identifying and solving problems, the marriage had endured, but failed to flourish.

Patricia, like most people-pleasers, learned the avoidance value of people-pleasing as a young child. She was taught to jump through the "white door" by her mother's explicit instruction. During the years of her childhood and adolescence, until her father's death, she practiced people-pleasing avoidance behaviors to escape from his alcoholic rages and violence. Her strategy worked imperfectly, however, as she was still subjected to his verbal abuse. But as long as she was sweet, obliging, and did what he wanted, Patricia's father did not physically abuse her.

During her therapy, Patricia learned that she could respond differently to abusive treatment from men like her father than she did as a child. As an adult human being, Patricia can make choices that rats and children do not have the freedom to make.

If her marriage, hypothetically, were ever to become abusive, for example, Patricia would have the option of leaving. Or she could choose to stand up for her rights and not be an accomplice to her mistreatment. In other words, as an adult, she could assertively request or even demand that the abuse cease.

Patricia's case illustrates the profound impact that early conditioning experiences have on human behavior. Despite the fact that he was very different in disposition and behavior, Patricia still behaved as though her husband were just like her father with respect to anger and proneness to violent outbursts.

Although she never actually witnessed Alex's anger or temper, she convinced herself that she was staying one step ahead of it by making sure that his every need was met. As it turned out, one of Alex's most important needs—for the intimacy that comes from self-disclosure of all feelings, positive *and* negative—remained sorely unmet.

People-Pleasing Protection

Your people-pleasing has become ingrained as a habit because you believe that it works to protect you from anger and conflict. But people-pleasing can have just the opposite effect. Instead of pleasing others by always being nice, you may unintentionally be provoking the frustration and, eventually, the anger of those closest to you.

Like Patricia's husband, those with whom you use preemptive people-pleasing (i.e., you please them *before* they can hurt you) may feel stymied and irritated by your unwillingness and, therefore, their inability to discuss problems or any negative feelings with you. While you may think that your people-pleasing is protective and even beneficial to maintaining a close relationship, those who desire a more intimate relationship with you may resent your strategy. It may surprise you to learn that your preemptive people-pleasing can be viewed as manipulative, coercive, and controlling—albeit in disguised form—to those on the receiving end. To them, your persistent *niceness* and conflict avoidance can feel like a passive-aggressive method for keeping yourself away from them at a "safe" psychological distance.

However, if you stay far enough away from people so they can't reach out and strike you, you are also too far for them to be able to reach out and embrace you. In this way, your "safety zone" may turn out to be a lonely and even perilous place to stand.

People-pleasing may reduce your anxiety and fears in the short-term, just after you have used it to avoid an angry response or conflict. In the long-term, your fears of negative emotions will only intensify. Unless you learn how to replace your avoidance habits with effective and appropriate ways to express anger and deal with conflict, the Disease to Please will grow worse along with your fears.

▶ *People-pleasing as an avoidance strategy is only effective up to a point, after which it can actually precipitate anger and conflict.*

Like many fears, yours are likely grounded in some false conceptions. In *The Wizard of Oz*, the main characters were intimidated and fearful of "The Great and Powerful Oz" until they pulled back the curtain and discovered that he was just a little man creating a frightening illusion with smoke and noise.

The emotions you fear seem far more threatening and ominous because you have kept them hidden behind the curtain of people-pleasing. In the next chapter, we will begin to draw that curtain of fear and avoidance aside.

Emotional Adjustment on Avoiding Fearful Feelings

Keep these points in mind as you ready yourself to overcome your fears of anger, conflict, and confrontation and to learn to manage them effectively:

♦ Chronically suppressing your anger may be as harmful to your health as "blowing up" frequently.

♦ Using people-pleasing to escape anger and avoid conflict can turn your fears into self-fulfilling prophecies.

♦ You must be exposed to the experiences you fear in order to desensitize your anxiety and to develop effective skills for dealing with them.

♦ Preemptive people-pleasing to avoid negative emotions can unwittingly backfire and actually provoke anger and hostility due to its controlling, manipulative, and frustrating effects on others.

♦ If the expression of negative emotions is off limits in your relationships, the price you pay will be to sacrifice true intimacy, honesty, and authenticity with others.

CHAPTER 12

The Fear of Anger

You know that the Disease to Please has seized control of your life when you find yourself avoiding people because they might ask you to do favors for them. As a people-pleaser, you have been unable to say "no" to requests even when you are pressed for time, or truly lack the desire, energy, or interest to oblige these wishes.

There are several reasons you feel compelled to say "yes" when you want to say "no." You may fear that the person will be angry with you or stop liking you altogether if you turn down the request. You may worry about appearing selfish, lazy, or unkind.

Before you can even think of a plausible reason to say "no," the sheer force of habit from years of conditioning as a people-pleaser makes your "yes" response pop out automatically. The weight of *guilt*—your constant emotional companion—holds you back from denying the favor.

You conclude, as you always do, that it is just easier to say "yes" than to find your way through the maze of negative emotions that saying "no" seems to create. What you fail to realize, though, is that by doing the favor for which you have neither time nor desire you will generate feelings that are even more difficult and threatening.

After you have said "yes"—sometimes before you have even fulfilled the request—you are flooded with anger and resentment toward the person who so effectively manipulated your *niceness* and your inability to say "no."

To further compound the problem, you feel ashamed and guilty for harboring such feelings since they are off-limits to a people-pleaser.

Expressing your anger and resentment directly to the favor-seeker for taking advantage of your giving nature seems unimaginable. After all, you can't even say a simple "no." Besides, you correctly reason, the real issue resides with *you*. So you take the "safer" route and direct the anger, blame, and emotional turmoil on yourself for doing the favor you didn't want to do in the first place.

The irony is that you wind up trying to avoid certain friends and family members who ask favors of you because of your compulsion to please them! The truth is that you don't really want to avoid or isolate yourself from other people. Rather you are reacting to the fear of your own and others' anger and resentment, and from those menacing emotional companions, conflict and confrontation.

Anger Is a Matter of Degree

Like many people, you probably have a number of misconceptions about the nature of anger that contribute to and inflate your fears. First, you may equate anger, which is an emotional state, with aggression, which is a behavior.

Aggression includes a deliberate intent to hurt, harm, or injure another, or to do damage to an inanimate object. Your fear of anger is based on the expectation that it will always lead to aggressive action, expressed either unilaterally or in the form interpersonal conflict.

Under certain circumstances, anger may indeed lead to aggression. However, it does not necessarily or inevitably do so. Learning to manage angry feelings and to express them effectively and appropriately greatly reduces the probability that aggression will develop when anger is aroused.

The second misconception is that anger functions like an on/off switch. In this inaccurate and polarized view, you are either calm and cool, or riled up and enraged. When anger is in the "off" switch position, you are clear and rational without visible signs of being upset or internal cues of anger. Once switched to the "on" mode, however, negative emotions are fully flared and you are now both manifestly and inwardly angry, agitated, and upset.

> ▶ *The black and white view of anger is simply incorrect. Anger doesn't work only on a two-position on/off switch. Instead, anger develops incrementally, on an arousal scale.*

There is a great deal of individual variation, from one person to another, with respect to the speed with which anger escalates on the scale. Some people, known as "hot responders," have a short fuse on their anger. For these types, the escalation from zero (no anger) to 100 (raging anger) occurs very quickly and can even create the illusion of an on/off phenomenon. Nonetheless, even the hot responders develop anger incrementally across increasing levels of arousal.

For other individuals, known as "cool responders," anger increases more slowly along the scale. A cool responder ultimately can become every bit as enraged as the hot responding counterpart, but he or she just gets there in a slower, more deliberate fashion.

People also differ with respect to the frequency or incidence rate of their angry responses and on the type of incidents to which they respond with anger. The original research on Type A personalities uncovered a notably higher risk of cardiovascular disease that was believed to be associated with such characteristics as "hurry sickness" (i.e., feeling constantly pressured by doing too much in too little time), impatience, competitiveness, and free-floating anger and hostility.[8] Over time, however, this rich vein of research on stress has demonstrated unequivocally that the real core of cardiac-proneness is chronic hostility and frequent outbursts of volatile anger.

The Four Phases of Anger

The fear of anger is closely associated with another more pervasive and ambiguous fear: loss of control. The misconception is that when anger is triggered, you will become flooded and so overwhelmed with emotion that you will necessarily lose control of any ability to manage or master your feelings and their expression. Misconstruing anger as an emotional on/off mechanism fuels the idea that, once it begins, anger always results in a loss of control.

In fact, anger occurs in four discrete phases. The first phase is the *yellow alert* comprising the earliest psychological and physiological warning signs that you *might* become angry. Learning to manage anger requires you to become exquisitely sensitive to how you feel right *before* your own anger starts.

Of course, emotophobia has thus far prevented you from recognizing your own yellow alert signals. This is because, as a people-pleaser, you have been too invested in denying that you even have angry or negative feelings in the first place.

There are early signs and sensations of anger that you can learn to read as a forewarning that your anger might soon be triggered. You may also learn to read the yellow alert cues that another person's anger might be triggered. Feeling hurried, stressed, and pressured is a typical forerunner of irritability and anger. The sensations of water retention, bloating, or premenstrual tension for many women are classic physiological yellow alerts of mood swings, irritability, and anger.

In the workplace, an employee who is devalued, put down, or humiliated by a supervisor is a walking yellow alert of anger that can even rise to a level of lethal violence. Finally, if you are fatigued, depleted, and sleep-deprived, you should also be forewarned that your irritability and anger might well be on a short fuse.

The second phase of anger, *ignition,* occurs when your fuse is actually lit. Effective anger control depends on becoming acutely sensitive to your internal physiological and psychological cues so that you can identify the ignition phase as early as possible. Invoking the anger management strategies as soon as you become aware of ignition will help you attain greater and more immediate control than if you wait until your emotions are full-blown.

The third phase of anger is *escalation.* Obviously the goal of anger management is to prevent loss of control. Learning to regulate both the rate at which your anger escalates as well as the degree of intensity you permit—from mild irritation to fury—will help you achieve mastery over how you choose to express your emotions. Here again, it is important to note that escalation is still a matter of degree and not an all-or-nothing phenomenon. While you may feel your temper rising, you can still maintain control over how you choose to express your anger.

As with many physical illnesses, early detection and intervention are the keys to managing anger and keeping its expression appropriate and constructive. When your anger is at the low end of the intensity gradient, it is responsive to interruption, distraction, counteracting thoughts, and other management strategies. Therefore, once you attain emotional command, your anger may move so smoothly from ignition to resolution that the escalation stage is bypassed altogether.

▶ *Effective anger management means preventing the emotional intensity from escalating beyond the threshold where control is lost.*

The fourth phase is the *resolution* stage. This is the period for cooling down, regrouping, reflecting on what just happened, and attempting to repair whatever emotional damage may have been done to a relationship as a result of mishandled anger.

This is the phase of effective conflict resolution in which the aftermath of anger is used constructively to identify problems and pinpoint solutions. When conflict is truly resolved, future visits to the same argument are rendered unnecessary.

The distinctions between appropriate versus inappropriate expressions of anger and between constructive versus destructive conflict—and what this means for people-pleasers—are the subjects of this and the following chapters. For now, just becoming aware that anger is a matter of degree and not an on/off phenomenon is an important first step in developing control. And, understanding how it unfolds in phases is equally vital to gaining command of your anger.

When you correctly conceptualize anger in terms of phases and a gradient of intensity, your sense that anger *can be managed* will strengthen. It is by being without a way to break anger down into discrete, identifiable phases and degrees of arousal that you remain vulnerable to feeling flooded, overwhelmed, and out of control by the experience of anger.

Is Anger Always Bad?

The short answer is "no." Anger serves a real and important purpose.

Anger is a key component of your natural emotional apparatus that is built into your hardwiring as a human being. Your brain and body are designed with the capability to get angry as a protective feature. *Anger is the emotional reaction that signals that something is wrong and that you might get hurt.*

In a primal sense, anger plays an important role in your very survival. If you were incapable of feeling anger, you would be psychologically disabled and dangerously vulnerable to social predators and others who would take advantage of your passivity—or your niceness.

If your rights or boundaries were violated, or you were subjected to abuse, exploitation, or other mistreatment, feeling anger is entirely appropriate. However, like most people-pleasers, you probably feel guilty when you are angry, especially with those closest to you. But guilt implies some issue of moral culpability. Since there is no issue of right and wrong or good and bad with respect to merely *feeling* anger, your guilt is misplaced. As a human being, you are not held morally accountable for having emotions; rather your moral accountability lies in how you treat other people—in how you choose to express your feelings.

Further, by reacting with guilt when you feel angry, you only compound the problem by adding yet another negative emotion to the mix of feelings with which you are already struggling. Psychologically, guilt and depression are reflections of anger directed inward on yourself. Therefore, when you respond to your own anger with guilt and/or depression, you compound the issue because you are now feeling angry about feeling angry. This emotional exercise is a colossal waste of time.

Accepting your anger as a normal human emotion—rather than resisting or deflecting it by focusing on guilt, depression, or other obstructive feelings—is an important step toward sound anger management. The value and impact of anger depends on when, how, and why you express the feeling.

Whose Anger Are You Really Afraid Of?

One of the reasons you may feel so fearful of other people's anger is the underlying worry that your own anger might get triggered. Since your people-pleasing has probably made you a stranger to your own anger, the possibility of unleashing it is fraught with uncertainty and anxiety. The most threatening aspect is the potential *loss of control* entailed in the ignition of your anger.

Because you are a people-pleaser, your long-suppressed anger may be pushing for expression just below the surface of your passivity and submissiveness. If you ignore the issue of how to best express your anger and elect instead to only worry about others, you would just be replicating the chronic people-pleaser's solution to every problem: Think about the needs of others; put your own needs last.

Learning to effectively handle your anger requires a decision that you *will* express your anger—appropriately—in the first place. You may work hard to suppress your anger entirely. You may even get to the point of denying the presence of most or all of your negative feelings, anger included. But, as I have told you, suppressing and denying anger is unhealthy both physically and psychologically.

It may seem to you that the bigger and more problematic issue is how to deal with other people's anger rather than how to express your own. You may believe that anger is not a problem for you because you just don't "go there." This is like an agoraphobic (a person who is confined to her house because of an intense, irrational fear of being outside among people) saying that she has no problem with the outdoors because she doesn't "go there."

Chronically suppressing anger or using passive methods to express aggression is problematic. Overcontrolled anger is actually a major cause of explosive (think: "going postal") rage. While frequent and/or excessive eruptions of hostility endanger your cardiovascular system, chronic suppression of negative emotions can be bad for your health in other ways, too.

Research suggests that people who chronically suppress anger and other negative emotions run the risk of breaking down a critical function of their immune systems, thereby potentially compromising their ability to ward off cancer and other infectious or contagious diseases.

For our present purposes, learning to accept and express anger constructively and appropriately is a vital step to take on the road to curing the people-pleasing syndrome.

▶ *It is not your responsibility to control other people's anger. However, you are responsible to understand and control your contribution to a potentially angry conversation or confrontation. Your words—and how you say them—can help to incite, provoke, and escalate another's anger. On the other hand, your side of the interaction can help to calm and refocus the angry other person and aid in de-escalating a potentially destructive conflict or hostile confrontation.*

Denial and suppression will not make your anger diminish or disappear. Inevitably there will be situations in which you *feel* anger—even if you try to deny or suppress it. Then, your inability or unwillingness to effectively communicate that anger in a fashion that promotes problem solving and conflict resolution will leave you feeling endlessly frustrated, dissatisfied, and inadequate.

It is a psychological axiom that frustration leads to aggression. Over time, perpetually suppressed anger creates volcanic frustration. That frustration, in turn, can lead to an eruption of hostility. Ironically, by suppressing the anger you fear, you actually risk creating the explosive rage you most dread.

As Bill had to finally learn in the case that follows, by trying to avoid anger and conflict altogether you can even produce the catastrophic consequences you fear most.

Fear of Anger and the Commitment-Phobic Partner

Bill describes himself as "the product of a divorced home." His parents divorced when Bill was 15, but they fought viciously throughout all the years of their marriage as well as during and even after the divorce.

"What I remember most was the vicious fighting that went on since I was old enough to understand English," Bill recalls with sadness. "They used to hurl insults at each other. No one could make my father as angry as my mother did, and vice versa. I just hated to hear them fight."

Because of his unhappy childhood experiences, Bill was very cautious about making a commitment to get married. And he developed people-pleasing habits—especially in his relationships with women—as a way to protect himself from the kind of anger and conflict that he believed destroyed his parents' marriage. Like other people-pleasers, Bill felt that anger and arguments could only lead to ruinous outcomes.

Bill met Connie when he was 42 and she was 30, and neither had ever married. Connie came from a large, stable family, a fact that was a huge asset about her in Bill's mind.

After nearly two years of dating, Connie was eager to get married. Bill told her emphatically that he would never marry anyone unless they lived together first. The reason, in Bill's words, was "to make sure we get along well enough so that we never have to get divorced."

Connie, reluctantly, agreed to move into Bill's apartment. Connie doesn't share Bill's fear of conflict although she tries to keep her own anger suppressed because she understands Bill's enormous sensitivity to it. In her family, anger was expressed in healthy, appropriate ways that never resulted in permanent resentment or a rupture of any family ties.

"The only thing Bill and I ever fought about was when—or whether—to get married," Connie says.

Connie and Bill were in a trap, largely of his making. After six months of living together, with no proposal forthcoming from Bill, Connie broached the subject of marriage. But Bill refused to discuss marriage, stating that by his seemingly arbitrary schedule, they had not yet lived together "long enough to know."

Connie responded angrily, "I'd say that 2½ years is long enough to know whether you love me and want to marry me or not!"

Seeing Connie's flash of anger, Bill quickly retorted, "See, you're angry. That's exactly what I can't tolerate. If you get angry and yell at me, we'll wind up getting a divorce. I'm not getting married until we can get along."

This scene was replayed in growing intensity for two more years, with no progress toward marriage. Every few months, Connie's frustration would erupt into another challenge, "Are we getting married or not? I don't want to just live together. I never wanted to. I want marriage and a family. I don't want to play house! You're driving me nuts."

But, each time Bill remained stubbornly withholding of a commitment. His justification was that Connie had, in fact, once again become angry. As long as there was evidence of anger in the relationship, according to Bill's very flawed model, there was a risk of marital fighting and eventual divorce.

Connie would respond by saying that she was not an inherently angry person. She pointed out that the source of her anger was the frustration and rejection she felt as a result of Bill's unwillingness to get married.

Connie certainly didn't start out in the relationship yelling or screaming at Bill. But, over time, her growing frustration loosened her self-control. Eventually, she found herself screaming in desperation, "Give me an answer! You say you love me. We never really fight about anything but this. But you keep insisting we don't get along well enough for you to marry me. I can't take it anymore," Connie wept with frustration.

Finally, after two years, Connie packed up and moved out. At first, Bill was smug, insisting that he saved himself a divorce by "testing" the relationship to see if it was anger-proof.

But, after six weeks of separation, Bill realized he had lost the woman he loved the most in life. Connie refused to move back in without getting married, and she insisted that Bill needed therapy to get over his fear of anger and avoidance of all conflict.

The happy ending of this story is that Connie and Bill did marry and, by all reports, are now living "happily ever after" (although, occasionally, they have healthy anger and conflict). My most recent contact from them was the birth notice of their second baby.

The Roots of Fear of Anger

People-pleasers' fear of anger can develop for many different reasons. The deepest roots of the fear are buried in childhood trauma, as were Bill's in the case above. To a young child, a parent who displays a volatile temper or explosive anger can become terrifying.

All adults seem powerful to young children, if only by virtue of their larger size, louder voice, and superior authority. Because of their nearly total dependence, young children *need* adults to appear to be in control. The child needs adults to behave rationally and consistently and to provide feelings of safety and security.

When a parent or caregiver displays anger in an explosive and volatile manner, the child's fundamental sense of trust is undermined. The adult who has temper tantrums appears irrational, undependable, and scary.

Worse if the parent's anger also fuels aggression or physical violence, the child's world turns into a frightening place fraught with very real, potentially fatal danger. Instead of providing refuge from stress and fear, the child's home and family become the source of terror.

If alcohol and/or drugs are added to the fear-provoking scenario, adult anger becomes even more capricious, unpredictable, and irrational. Since alcohol and drugs disarm the user's self-control, the chances are far higher that aggression might be expressed with a fist or even a gun.

All too often the domestic drama—or tragedy—that a child in a violent home witnesses is a passive, nonprotective mother who is victimized by a raging, brutal father or boyfriend who is high on drugs or intoxicated on alcohol or both. The child, who may also be subjected to physical abuse, absorbs damning psychological messages about the danger and destructiveness of anger from this nightmarish scene of domestic terror.

Through role modeling or imitative learning, the child understands only two alternatives for how to handle anger, both of which are unhealthy and inappropriate. If the child looks to the mother, he or she sees anger suppressed into passivity that, in turn, is punished by violence. If the child looks to the father or adult male, he or she witnesses anger transformed into a fierce, bullying rage that is turned on the weakest victims, including the child.

There is literally nobody home who teaches the child how to express anger *safely*, in a firm, direct, and constructive manner; no one even tells the child that this is a possibility.

A tragic but often observed fact is that adult perpetrators of physical abuse were the victims of abuse themselves as children. Lacking a constructive role model and left with what they perceive to be only two choices, these abusers opt to be the victimizer rather than the passive victim. After an episode of violence, abusers typically feel remorseful and speak of the fear and lack of control they have of their own anger.

Alternatively, adult children of abusive parents may identify with the victims. As such, they develop overly compliant people-pleasing personalities to cover up their own underlying, much-feared anger.

Sometimes, adults with histories of childhood abuse assume interchanging roles in which they vary from one behavioral extreme to the other, playing victim on one occasion and abuser on another. Most of the time these mixed-role adults overcontrol, deny, and suppress their anger. Then, given enough stress and pressure, they flip periodically into episodes of uncontrolled rage.

Many, though not all, people who struggle with the Disease to Please report abusive family backgrounds. For them, the internal experience of anger as a two-gear emotion that is either fully "on" or totally "off" reflects the way they saw anger played out in domestic or family relationships where someone was the abuser and another the passive victim. And people-pleasers' fear of anger—their own as well as others—can drive them to new heights of *niceness*.

Can Anger Kill?

For some people-pleasers, the fear of anger is grounded in the belief that anger literally can kill.

You may not even realize how deep your own fear of anger is rooted. Perhaps, like my patient Arlene whose case follows, you may be *deathly* afraid of provoking anger in someone you love. Not because you fear being attacked physically or otherwise having your own safety threatened. Rather your fear is based on the belief that anger will produce dire, catastrophic, or even lethal health consequences for the *other* person.

> *Arlene, 33, and Gary, a 40-year-old physician, have been married for seven years. The couple decided to seek therapy because of a recent incident during which Arlene had a full-blown panic attack in the face of Gary's anger.*
>
> *Both agree, however, that the root of the problem lies in Arlene's intense fear of and aversion to anger rather than in Gary's actions that, by all accounts, did not seem unreasonable or inappropriate to the circumstances.*
>
> *The incident began when Gary overheard a telephone conversation that Arlene was having with her mother in which she was crying and apologizing for being a bad daughter.*
>
> *"My mother is great at making me feel guilty," Arlene describes. "And I fall for it and put myself through a lot of pain. It's an old, sick pattern with us."*
>
> *"When I hung up the telephone, there was Gary obviously angry with me," Arlene explains. He gets very upset when I let my mother manipulate me. Furthermore, I know he's right. I could feel myself getting very anxious and I begged him not to get mad."*
>
> *"That just frustrated him more. He told me that he was a grown man and to stop telling him not to be angry. He clearly looked angry and he was raising his voice somewhat. He wasn't out of control or anything. Gary is a very sweet and gentle man," Arlene explains. "I can't remember what else he said because the room started spinning. My heart was racing and I started perspiring and shaking."*

"I really thought that I was going to pass out. I was convinced I was having a heart attack or going crazy or something," Arlene describes. "When Gary saw what was happening, he stopped scolding me and made sure that I was all right. Gary knew that I was having a panic attack."

In the therapy session, I asked Arlene a standard diagnostic question: "Were you afraid that you might die during the panic attack?"

Arlene's answer was intriguing and provided the critical clue to understanding her intense fear of anger.

"No, but I was afraid that Gary was going to die because I had made him so angry . . ." she pauses, "just like my father," she recalls tearfully.

Arlene was 15 years old when her father died. Arlene describes her father as a "walking time bomb" because of his tense personality and abysmally poor health habits.

Most significantly, Arlene's father was a very hostile man. He had a volatile temper, fueled by alcohol, and was prone to episodes of explosive rage.

"My dad's temper was on a hair trigger," Arlene explains. "He was always angry with somebody. My mother was totally intimidated by his temper and she worried about his health. My sister and I would literally run and hide when my dad was drunk and raging angry. He never hit us, but his anger was pretty scary.

"I can recall my mother warning my dad that someday his anger would kill him. What I remember most was my mother constantly telling me, 'Don't upset your father. If you get him angry, he'll have a heart attack and die.' "

"The night my father died, we did have a big argument. I can't remember why, but he got furious with me for something. My dad was screaming and swearing and he turned all red in the face, and shook his fists at me," Arlene recalls.

"He said that he needed to get some cigarettes and slammed the front door as he left. That was the last time I saw him. He was killed in a fatal car accident," Arlene reports with a mixture of anger and sadness in her voice. "Fortunately, he hit an embankment and nobody else was hurt."

"The worst part is that I always thought my dad died of a heart attack behind the wheel," Arlene continued. "That's what my mother told everyone, including me. Last year just before my aunt died, she told me that my dad had already been drinking for hours before he left the house. He got killed—he killed himself—because he was a drunk *driver and lost control of his car. I guess my mother needed a cover story so she wouldn't have to admit he was drunk. I think she just started to believe her own lie."*

"After I found out the truth, I still felt guilty because I kept thinking he wouldn't have had so much to drink if I hadn't made him so angry. Believing my mother's story that he had a heart attack made all her warnings come true—that I killed my dad by making him so angry with me." Arlene reflects. "You know, it was really cruel of my mother to lay that guilt on me. My dad was angry with everyone, all the time. He was a bitter, hostile man who was angry with life," Arlene says. "My mother has been making me feel guilty ever since. I guess she needs to blame someone other than my dad or herself."

Then, Arlene had a breakthrough insight, "When I saw Gary start to get so angry and upset, all I could hear was my mother's voice," Arlene remembers. "All I could think about was that I had made Gary angry and that he was going to die and leave me. That's where the panic came from," Arlene concludes.

The panic incident helped Arlene to understand the root of her fear of anger. She had a lot to untangle in therapy, but this was the opening she needed to start to change her thinking and, eventually, to overcome her Disease to Please.

Arlene's fascinating case dramatically illustrates the toxic and fearsome power that can be attributed to anger in situations where an illness could be made worse by hostility, conflict, and the stress those emotions and behaviors can produce. Typical illnesses of this type include cardiovascular problems like heart attack and stroke, cancer, alcoholism, and bipolar (manic-depressive) illness, especially where there is a history of suicide or attempted suicide.

When an individual suffers from such an illness, the concern of family members and close friends is that upsetting the "patient" or causing him or her to become angry may result in grave harm. For example, if a person is prone to heart disease or stroke, the impact of an episode of explosive rage could literally be fatal.

In the case of an alcoholic, the concern is that anger could trigger a bout of particularly heavy drinking; or, if the alcoholic is recovering, anger might precipitate a relapse. If a manic-depressive gets enraged, it may signal the onset of a manic episode. Worse, if the anger were turned inward, the fear is that it could precipitate a suicidal depression or actual suicide attempt. Since cancer and AIDS patients are advised to minimize stress, the fear is that upsetting or making them angry could have detrimental consequences.

While there are definite links among anger, stress, and illness, the causal relationships are often more complex. In the case of cardiovascular illness, the relationship between anger or hostility and the incidence of disease appears direct. In the case of other illnesses, however, the impact of anger and stress is more complicated and indirect.

For our purposes, what matters is not the science but rather just the *belief* that anger will cause additional harm, obstruct recovery, or create a relapse. Like Arlene, your own fear of anger and the related people-pleasing avoidance behaviors it produces may be connected to a health concern for yourself or someone close to you. If, like Arlene, you have come to believe or suspect that anger can literally kill, then your already substantial people-pleasing fear of anger would understandably be magnified.

Arlene's guilt began to clear when she properly attributed the cause of her father's death to his own self-destructive personality and lifestyle. Her relationship with Gary grew healthier when Arlene began accepting anger as a normal and sometimes necessary component of emotional intimacy.

Keep in mind that anger in and of itself is not inherently dangerous or bad. What makes anger potentially unhealthy is how it is expressed.

Is It Good for You to Blow Off Steam?

There is a popular myth that "blowing off steam" is good for you once in a while. You have no doubt heard some version of this dangerous and erroneous belief. Typically people who exhibit explosive rage and inappropriate fits of temper spread this medical disinformation as a rationalization for their own misbehavior.

This mistaken concept holds that pressure builds up in the blood vessels due to withheld anger and that these vessels will rupture *unless* the anger is permitted an explosive expression now and then to dispel the strain on the vascular system.

Nothing could be further from the truth. *The real danger lies in manifesting explosive rage, not in controlling it.* Nobody benefits from a volatile exhibition of rage. The "exploder," in actuality, *can* suffer a stroke or cardiac arrest on the spot from the physiological assault that the rage imposes on his body.

If the exploder lives through the episodes of rage, ongoing and cumulative damage nevertheless accrues to his cardiovascular system. Despite all the gesticulation and volume on the part of the exploder as he tries to demand the attention of the target of his tirade, the latter typically just stops listening. Instead, the target loses respect for the raging speaker, while the speaker just loses "it."

Mixing explosive anger with discipline is a recipe for trouble. In the workplace, an employee on the receiving end of a supervisor's enraged tongue lashing is not likely to reinvent himself or herself as a model worker. Instead the employee will likely feel sabotaged, resentful, angry, and utterly disinclined to even try to do a better job next time. Or, the employee may respond to the intimidation of the supervisor's enraged threats, but his sapped morale is likely to undermine even his well-intended efforts at reform.

Employees subjected to a hostile work environment—which may be defined by a supervisor who loses control of his or her anger—may claim to suffer stress-related emotional and physical symptoms. In the current litigation climate, a policy of disciplining subordinates using aggressive, hostile outbursts (especially those that become personal) is a lawsuit waiting to happen.

It is simply not necessary to scream, turn red in the face, pound fists, use off-color language, or display temper by any other means in order to emphasize the seriousness or gravity of the message. In fact, it is downright counterproductive.

Instead of commanding attention, an immature exhibition of anger causes the focus to shift away from the content of the message to the overly emotional style of its delivery. Seriousness is undermined, not underlined, by a display of temper.

What to Say When You Need to Say You're Angry

▶ *To meet the criteria of being healthy and constructive, anger must be expressed clearly, firmly, and directly.*

The goal of your message is to exchange accurate information—in this case emotional feedback—that will lead to effective problem solving and conflict resolution. In effect, you tell another person that you feel angry now so that you will not have to become angry again over the same issues in the future.

To be constructive, you must assume responsibility for your anger; other people don't *make* you feel your emotions. Instead of saying, "You make me so angry when you do xyz," it is far more constructive to say, "When you do xyz, I feel upset and angry."

Blame and accusation play no role in the constructive expression of anger; nor do insults, threats, ultimatums, or manifestations of aggression. Voice volume should remain as modulated as possible. Firm, unwavering, clear, and direct statements command more respect and attention than screaming, bellowing, and using hostile threatening language, all of which are abusive.

Intimidation through words or actions is neither constructive nor healthy even though it may accomplish its intent by frightening the recipient. You would be far more effective and appropriate in conveying your feelings by saying something like, "I'm so angry that it is even difficult for me to talk to you right now," than by yelling, "I'm so angry that I could tear your lungs out."

Threatening gestures—including fist pounding, kicking, throwing, or brandishing objects—are not constructive and are, intimidating and possibly abusive. Any act of violence in the expression of anger—whether actually committed or just threatened and implied—is destructive and unacceptable.

A direct statement, "I became angry when you did xyz because I feel . . . /or, because I think . . ." appropriately conveys anger. The recipient of the communication is made aware that you are reacting with anger because you *say* that you are, not because you demonstrate your anger by means of physical or verbal intimidation.

There is a place in the healthy expression of anger to analyze the causes of a problem by asking the legitimate question, "Why did you do that?" This presumes that you are genuinely interested in and willing to listen to an explanation.

However, there is no constructive purpose to the rhetorical, "How could you do that?" or "Why on earth would you do something that stupid?" These questions merely flog the recipient verbally.

There are times when your purpose for expressing anger is to promote understanding of your own feelings. You may wish to talk about your anger to a friend, spouse, therapist, or other listener—who plays no causal or contributory role in your negative feelings—in order to help you better comprehend your reactions.

Problem solving and conflict resolution require closing the loop by expressing your feelings to the person with whom you feel angry. If you withhold the information that you are angry in the belief that you are protecting the relationship or the other person by avoiding conflict, you won't give that person the information necessary to treat you better or differently in the future.

> ► *Contrary to people-pleasing beliefs, anger and conflict are not necessarily destructive to relationships. On the contrary, constructive conflict can be an enormously healthy force in the maintenance of healthy close relationships.*

Emotional Adjustment: Overcoming Your Fear of Anger

♦ Anger does not work on an on/off switch. It develops on a graduated scale and goes through discrete phases. Understanding this can help you effectively manage and control your own anger.

♦ Anger can be appropriately expressed and healthy for you and your relationships. It is necessary and constructive to the maintenance of good relationships to express your anger clearly, firmly, and directly.

♦ Inappropriately expressed anger—such as volatile rage or violence— is obviously dangerous and undesirable. Anger (an emotional state) is not the same thing as aggression (a hostile behavior).

♦ Chronically suppressed anger damages your health; so does frequently and aggressively expressed anger and hostility. The notion that "blowing off steam" is good for you is a dangerous myth. Rage isn't good for anyone.

♦ You are not responsible for controlling the anger or temper in others; they are responsible for their own emotional reactions. The link between anger and illness is complex. You are not likely to cause serious physical harm to someone because you express your anger *appropriately.*

CHAPTER 13

Words Can Really Hurt You

I t has long been my sad observation that the scars left from actual physical abuse heal, while those imposed by psychological, emotion, or verbal abuse last a lifetime. While exposure to physical violence may be *one* cause of fear of conflict and anger, it is by no means the only one. Children that grow up in psychologically abusive environments—where vicious words and emotional maltreatment are used to intimidate and punish—can also find themselves burdened by an intense fear of anger throughout their lives.

Parents who engage in verbal and emotional abuse of one another, and/or of their children, inflict painful psychological wounds. While the wounds are invisible, they nevertheless cut deep. When hurtful, cruel, and devaluing things are said either *in* anger or because of it, psychological injury and fear of anger can result.

In some abusive families, scorn and emotional mistreatment are not confined to episodic outbreaks of anger but reflect instead continuous undercurrents of hostility that characterize dysfunctional family relationships. These insidious forms of abuse become debilitating over time, hampering relationships and creating fertile conditions for the growth of people-pleasing habits.

For example, a father who yells sarcastic, angry put-downs of his overweight, nonathletic son from the sidelines of a Little League baseball game can wreak more havoc on the boy's self-esteem than the absentee parent who fails to attend games altogether. Or the parent who accuses her adolescent daughter of promiscuity, calling her a whore or a slut every time the girl wears make-up or trendy clothes, can cripple the girl's developing self-concept by creating debilitating guilt, anxiety, and sexual confusion.

People-pleasers who have been subjected to emotional abuse in childhood and/or adulthood become acutely sensitive to the pain-inflicting potential of words. Most of the time the fear of verbal confrontation fuels the white door avoidance cycle discussed in Chapter 11. Those who have been verbally abused can also become verbally and emotionally abusive themselves.

Molly, 23, has a beautiful face and about 75 to 100 pounds of excess weight with which she perpetually struggles.

Molly tearfully recalls the verbal taunts and teasing of other children about her weight. She actually breaks down sobbing when she recounts the verbal abuse she endured from her siblings and parents, particularly about her eating habits and weight.

Every member of Molly's large family of five siblings, plus her parents, attack one another verbally. She describes the daily interaction at the dinner table growing up as always involving teasing and wordplay, but inevitably at someone's expense—usually hers. Molly says, "Nobody was spared, even my parents. Our family 'joke' was that dinner wasn't over until someone cried and left the room."

"I realize now that it was a bitterly hostile environment to grow up in," Molly reflects. "I even dread getting together with my family for the holidays because I know that the verbal barbs will start flying and things will get real ugly."

Molly says that whenever anger erupts in her family, as it frequently did while she was growing up, the fighting is brutal. She says that she had to learn to fight back verbally so that she could defend herself and "save face" with her siblings.

As an adult, Molly struggles to control her own hostile verbal tendencies. Sharp-tongued, Molly can get verbally vicious, especially if she is pushed to the point where she loses control of her temper. Then she can lash out verbally with cruel, sarcastic observations about other people's weak points.

"In my family, you had to learn to defend yourself by going on the offense verbally. I'm not proud of it but I know how much I can hurt people with my words," she explains.

"Most of the time, I'm a real people-pleaser because I'm afraid of what will be said if there's a confrontation. I always expect to get

insulted and rejected," Molly admits. "If I can make people need me and like me, then I think maybe they'll overlook my weight and accept me anyway."

"If I think someone is getting irritated or annoyed with me, I brace myself for 'fat' remarks. Then, if the other person actually gets angry, my fear of other people's anger kicks in and flips me into 'attack mode.' I strike first to hurt the other person so that he or she will shut up and not hurt me. Our family motto is 'a good offense is the best defense,' " Molly explains.

"When I go on the attack, I can say very hurtful things. Later, of course, I feel so guilty that I go overboard apologizing and trying to earn the person's forgiveness. So all my people-pleasing just gets worse."

In therapy, Molly has come to realize that her people-pleasing strategies for avoiding confrontation weren't working. Instead, Molly has developed her skills of anger and conflict management and has trained herself to keep her "first-strike" verbal hostility in check.

Finally, Molly now realizes that most people are not like her family and are not likely to launch personal verbal attacks on her. She has learned that even if someone does insult her, she can choose to respond differently and not become so upset.

Can "Total Honesty" Disguise Anger?

There is a particular form of emotional mistreatment practiced by people who hide their anger and aggressive motives in the guise of "total honesty." The claim, of course, is that *total* honesty is always "the best policy."

The problem here is with the concept of *total* not with the concept of *honesty.* Too frequently, mean-spirited, gratuitous, viciously critical, and otherwise devastating statements are made under the self-serving banner of "total honesty." When comments are designed to hurt and when they hold no productive value to the recipient, they reveal the speaker's anger, aggression, and jealousy more than his or her "totally honest" character. Arguably, being *totally* honest without any tact, and at the expense of another's feelings, might well be construed as more a flaw of character than an asset.

Understandably the recipient of an unsolicited, gratuitously hurtful, but supposedly candid communication often responds angrily or demonstrates hurt feelings. The speaker then compounds the pain by rhetorically asking, "What's wrong with you? I'm just being completely honest," implying that the response should have been appreciation or even gratitude.

One of my patients was diagnosed with breast cancer a few years ago. Since she had a serious family history, she was given the genetic screening test and the doctors determined that she was indeed in a high-risk group. She was advised to have a preventative double mastectomy as well as a full hysterectomy. This courageous woman had a wonderful support system of women friends. However, her husband told her that he was going to have "a lot of trouble" still seeing her as a woman and responding to her sexually after the surgery.

When the wife began to cry in response to this disclosure, her husband snapped, "Why are you so insecure? You know I love you; I'm just being totally honest. That's what you want, isn't it?"

People-pleasers, as a group, are not generally the perpetrators of this kind of thinly disguised and abusive mutation of honesty. Sadly, though, you may be on the receiving end of it.

As a group, people-pleasers sometimes feel like punching bags repeatedly being pummeled by 16-ounce "total honesty" gloves.

True honesty and integrity are the center pins of ethics and morality. But, as the vignette above illustrates, even honesty and integrity can be softened with tact and mitigated by empathy and sensitivity. Using the word *honesty* as a shield to rationalize cruelty is a corruption of moral intent. Kindness, too, is a moral value.

Teasing Is Hostile

Hostility can take other subtle forms of expression that are nonetheless destructive. In certain families such as Molly's, for example, teasing is considered a blood sport. During a tease-fest around the dinner table, a child might be given the incredibly confusing directive by a parent or sibling, "Don't take it personally, I'm only teasing;" or, "She doesn't really mean it, she's only kidding so don't be upset."

Teasing, by definition, *is* hostile. Whenever a joke or tease is made at another's expense some degree of anger and aggression are the undercurrents.

> ▶ *Telling a child or adult not to be hurt by teasing is as bewildering as telling her not to flinch or cry when someone slaps her in the face because the assaulter was "just having fun."*

Contrary to the myth that teasing helps children develop a tough skin, adults with the Disease to Please who were teased a lot as children—especially by their families—tend to be easily hurt by sarcasm and hypersensitive to jokes made at their expense.

If you are sensitive to teasing, you have no apologies to make. Permitting yourself to be the brunt of jokes or the target of hostile humor is neither admirable nor a sign of emotional health. When you laugh along with those who tease you, you not only devalue your own self-esteem you also reward the teasers for their hurtfulness or cruelty as well.

The old and patently false children's chant, "Sticks and stones may break my bones, but words will never hurt me," needs revision. In reality, broken bones can heal relatively quickly; but words can and do leave deep wounds that sometimes never heal.

If you think back to your childhood, you probably cannot describe a single stick or stone that may have crossed your path or even struck you. However, you no doubt remember with crystal clarity the words that caused you the most emotional pain, even if they were couched as "good hearted" or "well meaning" humor.

As a people-pleaser, your aversion to anger and confrontation is likely not grounded in a fear of being beaten up or injured by a weapon. Far more likely you are afraid of hostile and hurtful words. Learning the skills of anger management will allow you to embrace the potency of words and use them to de-escalate conflict and to guide a potential confrontation away from anger and toward constructive conflict resolution.

Angry Love and Other Mixed Messages

If you identify with some of the childhood or family practices just discussed, you likely feel not only fearful of anger but possibly ambivalent and confused about some of your positive feelings as well. This is understandable given how often abuse—physical, emotional, or verbal—is connected by words and actions to feelings of love and affection. When love and anger get mixed together, the result can be a painfully mixed message.

In the textbook cycle of abuse, after the harm is committed, a period of self-blame, remorse, apologizing, and begging for forgiveness by the abuser to the victim takes place. The apology phase includes many references to loving the victim.

Next there is a honeymoon phase in which the abuser romantically "courts" the victim, trying to win back her/his love. Here, again, the emphasis is on how much love the abuser has for the person he or she has so recently beaten or otherwise abused.

The confluence of love in the same cycle as abuse creates severe psychological strain for the victim. For example, when an abused wife says, "He loves me so much, that's why he hit me," she reflects her confusion. Again she reflects her confusion when she justifies his anger by accepting the blame, "Of course he hit me. I know he likes his steak rare and I overcooked it. I'm so stupid."

Victims of domestic abuse generally have histories of multiple, repeated incidents of being beaten or emotionally abused. This implies that the victim remains in the relationship over time. If you ask an abused woman to say why she stays, her answer will often be, "I just love him."

Abused children are often given "love" and "caring" as explanations for their mistreatment. "You know your Daddy loves you," a mother might offer as comfort to a child or teenager that has been abused physically or emotionally by the father. Or, worse, a sexual predator may tell his young victim that their so-called "intimacy" is a secret bond of love and affection.

▶ *When anger and affection are inappropriately combined, the mixed message is that love hurts; or, that if you're getting hurt, you're really being loved.*

If your history involves experiences where there was a curious or confusing mixture of love and aggression, it may well be that now you trust *neither* emotion. Intimacy for you may feel like the precursor of aggression and people-pleasing may be your way of avoiding both.

You may have had experiences, possibly as a victim of abuse, where aggression was followed by protestations of love and remorse. You may have stayed overly long in a relationship where making up by making love (commonly referred to as "make-up sex") was the best part of the otherwise destructive fighting.

Based on your unique individual history, your reaction to anger and conflict may be complex and not adequately described as just being afraid. You may feel excited and repelled at the same time by confrontation. Or you may be frightened or anxious because you feel so confused about how you feel.

The bottom line is that people-pleasing keeps taking you away from the opportunity to sort yourself out, to overcome your fears, or to relearn healthier responses.

Fear of Hurting Others

Meredith is an attractive, single professional woman with the Disease to Please. At 39, Meredith is trying to meet "the right man" so that she can get married and start a family. She dreams about all the things she will do to make everyone happy.

For the past six months, Meredith has been going out with Fred, a 40-year-old divorced father of two sons. Meredith says that she and Fred have a "nice enough" time together and that he is "kind and considerate."

"But," Meredith explains, "I just know that he's not 'the one.' I'm not really that attracted to him and I'm not sure we have very much in common. It bothers me because he seems to feel way more for me than I do for him, but I don't want to hurt him, so I just don't say anything."

Last November, with the holiday season approaching, Fred asked Meredith to go with him and his two sons to Cleveland to meet the family for the first time. Meredith felt panicky at the thought of meeting Fred's parents.

"It all seemed so serious and I wasn't in love with Fred," Meredith explains. "I couldn't say 'no,' but I didn't definitely agree to go home with him either."

"I couldn't bring myself to break up with him. Truthfully, I didn't want to be 'in between' relationships during the holidays either. It's so depressing to be alone at that time of year. Fred is such a sweet guy. I just knew that he would be totally devastated if I told him how I felt. I hated the thought of hurting him," Meredith tells me. "I dreaded the thought of going to visit his family. When I was honest with myself, I knew that the chances of my ever marrying Fred were nearly zero.

"In the back of my mind, I'd been planning to break up with him after the holidays anyway," Meredith admits.

Meredith kept postponing their discussion about the holiday trip. Finally, one night, after Fred's office Christmas party in early December, Meredith braced herself with alcohol and told Fred how she felt—or, didn't feel—about him.

"I wasn't ready for his reaction," Meredith said, "Fred did get mad. But he wasn't upset that I told him the truth. He was angry and hurt that I hadn't been direct and honest with him. Instead, I led him on and let him fall in love with me."

"Fred said he even told his parents and kids that he was bringing home the woman he was going to marry!"

"He told me that by trying not to hurt him, I actually wound up humiliating him instead," Meredith continued. "Fred told me that he's a big, grown man and that if I had been grown-up and honest with him as soon as I was clear about my feelings—which, to be frank, was after two or three weeks of dating—I could have spared both of us valuable time."

"Over the months we've been seeing each other, Fred actually asked me to tell him how I felt about him and the relationship several times. It was just easier for me to let him think what he wanted to than to own up to my real feelings."

"The day after the party, we talked again. What really got to me was what Fred said about how disrespectful my behavior was. He said that if I had just told him after a few months of dating that I wanted to stop seeing him, he might have been disappointed but I wouldn't have damaged his self-respect nor embarrassed him. He told me that he looked and felt like a 'ridiculous, clueless teenager with an unrealistic crush.'"

"I think he's right," Meredith concludes. *"I may not have been in love with Fred, but I like him a lot as a person and never intended to hurt his pride on top of breaking his heart. I feel pretty terrible about myself and about how I handled this whole affair."*

Meredith has learned an important life lesson from the experience with Fred, though it cost both of them a high price psychologically.

Knowing When to "Fold 'em"

As a general rule, people-pleasers greatly overestimate the likelihood that any given problem will escalate into an aggressive confrontation or deteriorate into an emotional crisis. Just as Meredith misread Fred, you are likely to believe that other people will respond negatively to you unless you follow all the self-imposed "rules" of the Disease to Please.

For example, many people-pleasers recoil at the idea of sending back a meal ordered in a restaurant even if the food is grossly unacceptable. What is the reason for this reticence to complain? It's because people-pleasers do not want the waiter or restaurant owner to become angry! Or they don't want to insult or hurt the feelings of the chef!

This fear of hurting someone's feelings or of provoking anger or disapproval drives your people-pleasing avoidance patterns. The distorted, exaggerated expectation that other people will respond angrily, emotionally, or aggressively is a major reason that you don't say "no," don't stand up for your rights, don't take care of your own needs, and don't do a host of other assertive, healthy actions.

In essence, you predict that others will become angry with you, or reject, disapprove, or abandon you if you fail to please them. Then on the basis of your prediction, you jump through the "white door" to avoid the negative emotions you most fear.

When the mere shadow of hostility or negative emotion appears, you automatically call on your people-pleasing avoidance strategies. But, by evading most conflicts, you rarely if ever have the opportunity to test the accuracy of your predictions or to develop appropriate ways to cope with negative emotions.

Psychologists refer to the erroneous link between thoughts and feelings as *emotional reasoning*. The fear of others' anger and hostility causes you to act as though the anger and hostility were real. In this way, you justify whatever people-pleasing contortions you put yourself through in order to disarm the aggression of others even when, in actuality, no angry emotions from others have actually been expressed.

Meredith displayed a particular form of emotional reasoning that is rampant among people-pleasers. It concerns situations where you might find yourself involved in a relationship in which you are unhappy, dissatisfied, or disinterested. However fervent your wish to terminate the association, your courage to do so seems to chronically elude you. Your reason, in classic Disease to Please form, is that you don't want to hurt the other person's feelings.

However if you poke a little deeper into your motivation, you will find a fear of conflict lurking right behind your desire *not* to hurt another's feelings. Your hidden fear is that if you terminate the relationship, the other person might become angry, not just hurt. Then you might face a dreaded confrontation.

This particular aversion of people-pleasers of being the one to "end it" seems most prevalent in dating or more serious romantic relationships. However, I have seen many instances of the same basic phenomenon in purported friendships.

In these cases, the alleged friend may have repeatedly hurt the people-pleaser. Yet the people-pleaser will not be the one to terminate the relationship—even if it has become emotionally abusive—on the grounds that doing so might hurt the feelings of the abusive friend!

Another variant of this aversion occurs in the workplace. Here again, the people-pleaser may have very good reasons to want to quit a job—sometimes citing instances of mistreatment, harassment, or exploitation by the employer. Still, to avoid an angry, disapproving, or "hurt" response from the employer, the people-pleaser remains on the job unable to muster the courage to resign.

Whatever the form of the relationship, this avoidance keeps the people-pleaser in a self-imposed trap while paying the heavy price of lost time and passed opportunity to find a more compatible romantic partner, friend, or employer.

As Meredith's story poignantly illustrates, the negative impact of this avoidance behavior falls on both parties involved. Staying in the relationship to spare Fred's feelings, Meredith wound up not only doing the very thing she sought to avoid (hurting and making Fred angry), she also hurt herself as well.

Emotional Adjustment: Words Can Really Hurt You

♦ Don't try to anger-proof your relationships. It is far better to build safe and trusting relationships in which anger, when appropriate, can be expressed without fear on either side.

♦ Staying overly long in a romantic relationship because you don't want to hurt the other person's feelings belies a lack of respect for both of you.

♦ You have an obligation to examine your motives, monitor your intentions, and understand and communicate your feelings, especially when they affect another person with whom you are intimate or close. Are you really trying to protect someone else's feelings, or are you avoiding the possibility of an angry confrontation that you feel unequipped to handle?

♦ If you truly are concerned with being kind to others, be accountable for your actions and your motives. Make good choices about the way you treat others.

♦ Words *can* really hurt you. Teasing *is* hostile, and total honesty in the service of thinly disguised hostility is not defensible on either moral or psychological grounds.

CHAPTER 14

How Far Would You Go to Avoid a Confrontation?

Most people-pleasers hold fast to the erroneous belief that all conflict is destructive. You are probably quite adept at avoiding even the scent of a confrontation for this reason. The idea that conflict could serve a productive or beneficial purpose is likely alien to you. Instead, all conflict and confrontation seem dangerous and scary, dark and destructive, and definitely experiences to be avoided at almost any cost.

The notion that conflict can be constructive and healthy for a relationship might seem like a contradiction in terms. When handled constructively, conflict *can* be good for a relationship.

Contrary to your intuition, happy couples are not very different from those who are dissatisfied and unhappy with respect to the presence or absence of conflict. In other words, *all* relationships—both good and bad—are characterized by the occurrence of conflict.

The key difference lies in *how* conflicts are handled. Happy couples resolve their conflicts; unhappy couples, as a general rule, do not. As a result, unhappy couples fight about the same issues over and over again. Happy couples use the occasion of conflict to increase their mutual understanding and to benefit the interests of the relationship while unhappy couples view conflict as a power struggle where only one side can win and the other, by definition, must lose.

Happy couples handle conflict *constructively* to advance the goals and needs of the relationship. Unhappy couples untie and erode the bond that should hold them together because of the wrenching effects of *destructive* conflict.

Let's examine a typical type of conflict that might come up as a married couple gets ready to go out on a Saturday night. The conflict here is one of preference—the wife has a craving for Chinese food; the husband wants to eat pasta. His first choice movie is a science fiction action film; hers is a romantic comedy.

Clearly, this couples' respective choices are in conflict at the outset. However, it is entirely possible for them to air their respective preferences and still smoothly resolve their differences without an angry word spoken.

They might flip a coin and allow the winner to choose either dinner *or* the movie, leaving the other choice to the loser. They might agree to flip the coin twice—once to select the restaurant and once to choose the movie. Alternatively, the wife could decide to forgo her first-choice desires on the grounds that she wants to make her husband happy. Alternatively, the husband could grant the wife's choices to be a good guy. Finally, they could agree to disagree, and devise a compromise solution: They could eat hamburgers and see a sexy suspense thriller, happy just to be together.

Now, consider a second couple that faces the same dinner-and-movie preference conflict. Instead of a cooperative resolution, this couple lets the issue escalate into an argument and, eventually, even into a full-blown, screaming fight. The dialogue might be something like this:

> *Wife:* "We always go where you want, and see the movies you want to see, which are stupid men films. It's just not fair. You're so selfish. I cook for you every night and now you won't even let me pick the restaurant. If you really loved me, you'd try to please me once in a while."
>
> *Husband:* "Oh, give me a break. You're the most controlling person I ever met. You boss everyone in the house around and I'm not going to let you control me! If you cared more about my feelings as a man instead of just a 'meal-ticket,' you would ease up and go to my movie! I'd rather stay home alone than go with you to a ridiculous 'chick flick.' In fact, if you insist on having it your way, let's forget about even going out!"

And so on. Faced with the same set of objective facts, the two couples take very different routes through conflict. Only one arrives at the goal of conflict resolution. The second couple is unlikely to reach any agreements other than to stay home and be angry. This is because the second couple's fight is really not about restaurants or movies. Instead, it is about power and control. As you can see, the argument reflects deep underlying strains and tension in the relationship.

The comparison between the two couples is useful for two reasons. First, it demonstrates that the presence of conflict is not necessarily the forerunner of an angry confrontation. Second, it illustrates how quickly a conflict can escalate into dangerous territory, especially when destructive tactics are used.

The first couple resolves the conflict in a friendly, cooperative fashion placing their priority on getting along, making one another happy, and preventing a potential argument that would diminish or spoil the quality of their time together.

The second couple, however, adopts a win-lose/winner-takes-all approach to the problem. The conflict over what to eat and which movie to watch quickly deteriorates into a power struggle, complete with personal accusations, threats, and coercion.

It may seem hard to believe that a married couple could launch a full-scale battle over something as seemingly mundane as the choice of restaurant or movie. Though if you've ever spent time in a dysfunctional relationship or been a witness to one, the second couple's fight will have a ring of authenticity to it, perhaps even more than the first couple's calm and cooperative exchange.

The Benefits of Constructive Conflict

Handled correctly, conflict can be extremely beneficial. Through the experience of conflict, people in a relationship, for example, can advance their mutual understanding by talking about the issues that are troubling them or causing them unhappiness and dissatisfaction.

When conflict progresses to the goal of *resolution,* new agreements that govern what is and is not acceptable or desirable in the future may be forged. In constructive conflict, participants move away from polarized positions to midpoint compromise solutions that better serve the needs and wishes of both or all parties involved. When conflict is *effectively* resolved, there is a much smaller chance that the same disagreement will arise or become a problem in the future.

Constructive conflict can be the occasion to reaffirm positive feelings and commitments. Constructive conflict does not permit the infliction of emotional injury on anyone, nor the disintegration or weakening of the basic bond that holds the relationship together. This appropriate handling of conflict increases the overall sense of trust, security, and respect that the individuals have for the relationship, for their partners, and for themselves.

When two or more individuals agree to follow the guidelines of constructive conflict and control the escalation of anger, they provide a safe context in which to raise differences and discuss contentious issues. In these ways, the individuals can continually improve the quality of their relationship by solving problems, resolving issues, and meeting one another's needs. In turn, these accomplishments create intimacy, emotional gratification, and greater happiness.

If conflict can yield such rich rewards, why do people with the Disease to Please find it so frightening and threatening? Why are people-pleasers willing to do almost anything to stay out of the path of conflict and confrontation?

The Cost of Conflict Avoidance

When anyone tells me that they never fight or have disagreements with their spouse or partner, I become dubious and concerned.

Conflict avoidance is not a psychological strength about which to boast. Instead it is a symptom of worrisome dysfunction in a relationship that chills intimacy and belies closeness and trust.

In any relationship, personal or work-related, conflict is inevitable. This is not to say that fighting and open confrontation are guaranteed; rather, that sooner or later differences of opinion, preference, style, and/or interest will arise. How those differences are expressed and whether they are effectively resolved determine if the conflict is constructive or destructive in nature.

Avoiding conflict through people-pleasing or other methods does not eliminate its presence. Conflict avoidance actually refers to efforts aimed at suppressing the communication related to or concerning a conflict. The conflict nevertheless persists despite elaborate efforts to avoid it.

Think of conflict as an elephant that has parked himself squarely in the middle of your living room. You can ignore the elephant by simply walking around him. You can avoid talking to or about him, but the elephant will still be there. You know it and so does the elephant.

When conflicts aren't resolved, they occur repeatedly and can become increasingly frustrating and damaging to the relationship. Often they turn into dangerous power struggles, as we saw in the example above.

▶ *If you won't acknowledge or engage in any conflict, your issues and problems have very little chance of getting solved.*

The ill feelings that unresolved problems generate will spread insidiously throughout your relationship. Eventually, the relationship itself, strained under the weight of recurrent and unresolved conflict may end . . . and end badly.

You probably believe that your people-pleasing works effectively to avoid most if not all conflict. While your strategy may protect you from destructive conflict and hostile confrontation, it is also preventing you from learning to resolve conflicts through constructive engagement and, therefore, from reaping the benefits of conflict resolution.

This is like trying to avoid a wreck by never climbing aboard a train or trying to avoid a plane crash by refusing to fly. These avoidance strategies may spare you trauma, but they will also keep you stuck in one place, restricting severely your opportunities to go anywhere.

Similarly, people-pleasing may assist you to avoid destructive conflict, but your relationships will not go anywhere either. Conflict and its healthy resolution are necessary for personal and relationship growth. If you want to move forward in your relationship, you've got to climb on board.

Your well-intended people-pleasing, by guarding against any and all conflict, may actually be harming the very people and relationships you have labored so hard to protect.

How Conflict Escalates

Over the 25 years that I have practiced clinical psychology, I have often observed a curious phenomenon among couples that come to therapy for help with relationship issues. This happens when a couple tries to reenact or to revisit an argument they had at home.

As the individuals engage with one another, the cycle of conflict almost inevitably escalates and tempers rise turning the so-called acting into another real-life fight. At an opportune moment, say five minutes or so after the argument began, I interrupt to ask a seemingly innocuous question: "What started this fight in the first place? What was the subject or issue about which you initially started arguing?

There is a pregnant pause for several beats. The embarrassed couple looks at one another and then at me. Next comes laughing followed by the admission that neither of them knows the answer to my question. What accounts for this collaborative amnesia about conflict?

The answer lies in understanding the mechanism by which conflicts escalate, get out of hand, and transform in content. The case below is illustrative:

George begins a session by reporting that he and his wife, Alice, had a serious argument during the week since their last appointment. I ask them both to re-create the disagreement for me in the office. After some initial hesitancy, George and Alice soon all but overlook my presence and start to engage in a heated argument once again.

The fight in question initially started when Alice, an attorney, came home late one night from the office to find that George had left the dinner dishes unwashed in the sink.

Alice reports that this "really burns" her, because she works just as hard as her husband and generally for much longer hours. She says that her understanding has always been that they would share in domestic and childrearing chores equally. She views George's act of leaving the dishes as clear evidence that he is violating the conditions of their agreement.

George, a municipal court judge, retorts that he prepared dinner for their two sons as well as for himself but simply forgot to wash the dishes.

"You're completely overreacting. I wasn't making any kind of a big statement with it, I just forgot about the damn dishes," George protests.

"Oh please," Alice shoots back. "You just forgot? Why do I have trouble believing that? And don't tell me that I'm 'overreacting.' You know how angry that makes me."

"Maybe I don't believe that you just 'forgot' about the dishes," Alice continues, "because you always do this kind of thing. You do something halfway and then bail. You say that you believe in sharing responsibilities, but somehow I always wind up with the bulk of them."

"It's a man/woman thing," Alice claims. "Because I'm the woman, I'm just supposed to do more work around the house. You left the dishes there for me intentionally because you know I can't stand going to bed with dirty dishes and you knew I would have to do them myself. I just think this is totally unfair. We both work hard. Why should I get stuck with the clean-up?"

"Well, why should I get stuck with the cooking?" George responds quickly. "I cook, you clean. Now, isn't that sharing?"

"You know, honey," Alice says, her voice again dripping with sarcasm, "you always make a great argument. Tell the truth, how many days a week do you cook—once? I do the grocery shopping, I cook almost every night, and I clean up more than half the time because you say you have work to do. Well so do I!

"I'm afraid, Your Honor," Alice continues provocatively, "that you're not quite the egalitarian you think you are, judge or no judge. You believe in your heart that even if a woman goes to Harvard Law School like I did, her place is still in the home. I really worry about the message this gives the boys about how they should treat the women in their lives."

At this, George recoils. "Whoa," he says, "don't go there. Don't accuse me of being a bad father on top of being a bad husband. I'm sure you don't want your performance as a wife and mother scrutinized, do you?" George questions aggressively. "Besides, the boys are eight and ten. Let's not worry about how they are going to treat their wives. That's absurd."

Now Alice is wounded. She gets teary and says, "Why do you insist on making me feel so guilty about the boys? You're just like my mother! Whatever conversation we're in winds up being about my not doing a good enough job as a mother to my kids. You're such a cruel bastard!"

Right about here comes my opportune moment: I interrupt to ask, "What started this argument in the first place?" The question is purely tactical on my part. I know what incident ignited this fight, but I also know that they probably won't remember.

George and Alice are both riled. He is angry; she says she feels sad and guilty in addition to angry. At that moment of nearly peak conflict escalation, the original cause of the fight is temporarily subject to short-term, transitory memory loss. Eventually they reconstruct that the dirty dinner dishes left in the kitchen sink lit the fuse of this conflict.

What this example illustrates is the tendency of conflict to escalate. The fight that George and Alice re-create shows that once begun, their conflicts seem to get out of control quickly and to enlarge into dangerous arenas of personal attack.

Levels of Conflict

Conflicts escalate in a very predictable way moving upward along three discrete levels that can be specified and described.[9] To be most effective, conflict resolution should take place at the level that best matches or describes the problem. George and Alice's example will help illuminate the model and bring it to life.

Conflicts usually begin at level 1: *conflict over or about behavior.* This level includes disagreements or differences over what people do and/or say (to psychologists, speaking is a form of behavior). George left the dinner dishes in the kitchen sink after cooking dinner; Alice came home and found the dirty dishes and became angry and agitated. This is the behavioral level of the couple's conflict.

Conflicts then escalate next to level 2: *conflict over or about values, principles, rules, and collective beliefs that characterize the relationship.* In a real sense, these principles control the relationship in much the same way that laws control or govern nations or that by-laws control corporations. These principles characterize the expectations people have of how others should treat them and how they, in turn, should treat others with whom they share relationships.

For George and Alice, the conflict escalates to this level as soon as she invokes the idea of fairness and their prior agreement to share domestic chores. The argument occurs because George considers his cooking and her cleaning up to meet the rule of sharing. However, Alice believes that George has manipulated her into doing the dishes because he may harbor hidden beliefs that women should do more housework than men.

George and Alice are fighting about egalitarian values, gender roles, fairness, and the division of household responsibilities. They are fighting over the principles, rules, values, and beliefs to which they subscribe as a couple. This means they are engaging in conflict at level 2.

However, as soon as the accusations turn personal, the conflict escalates to the most serious or dangerous level 3: *conflict over or about personality, states of mind, feelings, intentions, and motivation.* Conflict at this level concerns what each person infers about the other's personality traits, emotions, state of mind, and intentions. At level 3, a fight can become most damaging.

George labels Alice's feelings as an *overreaction,* implying that she is being too emotional. (This, by the way, is a common level 3 conflict between men and women.) In response, Alice questions George's true nature, suggesting that he is not a true egalitarian even if he is a judge. In so doing, Alice is implying that George is a hypocrite.

The argument gets really heated when it shifts to mutual recriminations about parenting. Alice accuses George of making her feel guilty, just like her own mother. She claims that he always brings arguments around to evaluations of how she is doing as a mother.

George, responding defensively, warns Alice not to "go there," and not to throw blame his way about being a bad father on top of being a bad husband. In anger, Alice calls George a "cruel bastard."

Things get very personal when they reach level 3. Important differences still distinguish the two types of conflict at this highly personal level. These distinguishing styles can exert a significant impact on the health and strength of the relationship.

Constructive conflict protects the partners from questioning one another's love, loyalty, or essential commitment to the relationship. Mutual respect is affirmed and the fundamental values that bind the partners together remain unquestioned and, therefore, uncontaminated by the argument.

In destructive conflict, on the other hand, dangerous toxic questions are raised about whether the partners remain sufficiently committed and/or in love with one another. Even basic respect, trust, and liking may be "on the table," open for discussion. Once doubt is raised with respect to these fundamental issues, the relationship suffers damage. Destructive conflict spreads quickly and dangerously, spilling over from its origin in behavior to mutual recriminations, condemnations, threats, and coercion.

Couples that handle their arguments constructively affirm their basic relationship either explicitly or implicitly (i.e., by virtue of leaving basic values unquestioned). As a result, conflicts are contained within safe boundaries, and partners can feel secure in expressing dissatisfaction or even transitory anger. The process of hammering out behavioral agreements, such as who does the dishes or how to deal with the in-laws, can actually enhance intimacy and deepen understanding.

Effective conflict resolution most often takes place at level 2. This means that new agreements about the rules of the relationship are forged. Old agreements can be refined and further specified, as in Alice and George's case. Agreements at level 2 often reduce the occurrence of future arguments because mutually agreed upon rules can be invoked to solve further potential problems.

Alice and George's basic issue had to do with defining equal division of responsibility. Eventually this couple adopted a turn-taking solution. Monday through Thursday, they alternated cooking and cleaning responsibility each doing both tasks two days per week. Friday to Sunday, they ate their meals out so that neither had to cook or clean. This agreement helped eliminate the occurrence of future conflicts about whose job it is to do the dishes or other household chores.

Obviously, Alice and George have several other issues that trouble their relationship in addition to the household chore problem. The chore issue was a trigger for many angry words. When it was eliminated, Alice felt satisfied that the resolution was equitable and that George, once again, was behaving in a judicious and fair manner.

George and Alice also had to work out some agreements on fair fighting. They learned the guidelines for constructive conflict and, by following them, found that their disagreements became far less difficult and damaging to their relationship.

How to Fight Constructively

Obviously, the *content* or *subject* of a disagreement bears on the likelihood that angry feelings and escalation of the conflict will take place. When a couple has a disagreement about whether or not they have a committed, monogamous relationship, it is likely to become emotional, possibly angry.

If a conflict concerns money, the probability that anger and/or escalation will occur is relatively high. If, on the other hand, the conflict concerns where to make dinner reservations, it is less likely—although, as we saw earlier, certainly not impossible—that an angry argument will ensue.

Notwithstanding the importance of subject matter in a disagreement, there are certain processes or ways of engaging that are common to virtually all conflicts—or potential conflicts—from the serious to the mundane.

▶ *Any conflict can be handled constructively or destructively, depending on how the people involved relate to one another. Similarly, any conflict about any subject can escalate to a highly personal and possibly damaging level.*

By understanding the differences between constructive and destructive tactics and gaining insight into the dynamics of how and why disagreements escalate, you will be far better equipped to manage both the process and the outcome of conflict. The more you learn and the more skillful you become at anger and conflict management, the less you will have to fear and the sooner you can break the people-pleasing pattern.

So, let's take a closer look at the key differences between constructive and destructive ways to fight.

More versus Less Information. The first distinction between constructive and destructive conflict concerns the amount of information that gets exchanged between the parties. In constructive conflict, the amount is increased. The occasion of a disagreement becomes the opportunity to talk it out.

In the ensuing discussion, information about feelings, thoughts, values, or attitudes might be aired. Individuals might disclose facts about their childhoods, their relationship with their parents, or other family dynamics. Business partners, for example, might voice their personal visions for the growth of the company or their fears of financial failure.

Whatever the nature of the relationship or the content of the conversation, more, not less, information is made available through verbal disclosure in a constructive conflict situation.

In contrast, destructive conflict bears the earmark of *decreased* information flow. This means that during the conflict, one or more parties withdraw from the discussion or withhold verbal input.

This would occur when one individual refuses to talk about a problem unilaterally, delays or procrastinates the discussion, hangs up the telephone, leaves the scene, disconnects from an online conversation, or imposes the "silent treatment." Whatever the choice of method—or combination of tactics—the indicator of destructiveness is that the overall amount of disclosed information decreases during, and as a result of, the conflict.

Flexible versus Rigid. The second distinction is that parties engaged in a constructive conflict maintain a fundamentally friendly and cooperative attitude toward one another. They remain flexible in their approach to problem solving, willing to negotiate and open to a compromise that will put the maintenance and the well-being of the relationship before their individual desires to win an argument or prevail in a disagreement at any cost.

In a destructive conflict, the parties maintain an adversarial stance. They view one another as competitors in a zero-sum win/lose situation in which only one party on *one* side of the conflict will prevail while the other party on the opposing side does not. Individual self-interest is put before the best interests of the relationship. Winning is all that matters.

Moreover, in a destructive conflict, the parties are rigid as opposed to flexible, interested in adhering stubbornly to their original polarized positions. Compromise and negotiation are, in effect, off the table.

Trust versus Mistrust. In constructive conflict, there is mutual trust and open disclosure; in destructive conflict, there is mutual distrust which permits only selective, cautious disclosure as well as secrecy and suspicion.

Friendly versus Hostile Persuasion. In constructive conflict, threats are never used; persuasion, discussion, or even impassioned argument may be employed to influence the opposite party in the place of coercion and manipulation. Strategies of threat, coercion, and manipulation are the hallmarks of destructive conflict.

Responsibility versus Blame. Constructive conflict allows no room for insults or personal attacks. Nor does it permit blaming. While it is not always necessary to determine why a given problem or conflict has arisen, there is often a benefit to analyzing the reasons. If such an analysis seems valuable, all parties to the discussion try to remain as neutral and objective as possible.

> ▶ *The main purpose of a constructive conflict is to learn from experience as a way to prevent future recurrences of the same issues, not to point the finger of blame that focuses attention only on the past.*

A secondary purpose of seeking the cause of a conflict is to enhance the mutual sense of understanding. Caution should be exercised, however, not to elicit rationalizations or excuses in the place of genuine introspection and insight.

In constructive conflict, the speaker takes responsibility for his or her feelings, thoughts, and behavior. In destructive conflict, blaming is the currency of exchange.

Contained versus Spreading Boundaries. The constructive discussion is contained within boundaries of the issue in question and does not drift to historical or previous problems. In other words, there is no "loading on" of additional blame from past conflicts nor mention of preceding behaviors to bolster an argument. Both parties implicitly or explicitly agree to "stay on point."

Affirming versus Undermining Basic Relationship Values. Constructive conflict permits no mention or questioning of the basic foundation on which the relationship rests. In a constructive marital conflict, neither spouse raises doubt about the presence or degree of commitment or fidelity nor whether there is mutual love and respect. Inherently threatening words—such as separation or divorce—have no place in a constructive marital argument.

Similarly, constructive conflict prohibits questioning the fundamental principles of other types of relationships as well. In a conflict between coworkers or between supervisor and employee, doubts of loyalty, honesty, dedication, or continued employment are avoided since constructive conflict presumes that maintenance of the relationship into the future is desirable. And, among friends and family, constructive conflicts validate rather than undermine the ties of love and loyalty that bind the relationships together.

Once the foundation of any relationship is called into question, the conflict turns destructive by definition. Preface phrases such as, "If you really loved me, you would xyz," "If you were really a good friend, you'd xyz," or "If you cared about this company, you would xyz," herald the flip from what may have been constructive into what has now become a destructive mode of fighting.

Resolution versus Repetition. Constructive conflicts, in summary, are safe and productive. They produce new agreements based on deeper mutual understanding. Constructive conflicts, unlike those that are destructive, reach an endpoint in the form of resolution.

Parties to the conflict generally experience a sense of empowerment, pride, and renewed confidence in their ability to weather problems and develop effective solutions that will eliminate or greatly reduce the need to have the *same* conflict again in the future. Parties to a constructive conflict enjoy the sense of personal as well as relationship growth and change.

In contrast, destructive conflicts are repetitive, unsafe, hurtful, and counterproductive. They are most often left unfinished and unresolved. The lack of closure produces residual hurt feelings, resentments, and stewing anger. The parties to a destructive conflict, lacking effective solutions or agreements, will very likely argue over the same or very similar issues in the very near future.

Instead of being confident and proud, people who have engaged destructively emerge feeling wounded, upset, immensely frustrated, angry, and dysfunctional. They feel mired in their unresolved issues, stagnated, and stuck in recurrent patterns of provocation, accusation, and blame. They feel alienated and estranged from one another instead of developing the closeness and intimacy that constructive conflict resolution generates.

Destructive conflict is such a negative experience, it can cause individuals—especially people-pleasers—to become conflict avoidant, developing a fear of fighting. Gun-shy about raising problems for discussion in the future, their relationships lack the vehicle for effectively redressing problems and for correcting what is broken.

Your fear of conflict may be connected to some experiences of destructive, hostile conflicts in the past. Your chronic conflict avoidance through people-pleasing has made even the prospect of disagreement seem fraught with peril.

Now you know that the rules of constructive conflict can be defined and specified. Your fears of conflict have been *learned*—acquired from painful, frustrating experience, poor instruction, and role modeling, and/or self-taught with the aid of flawed thinking that supports your Disease to Please.

The good and hopeful news is that if your fear of conflict and anger are learned, they can be *unlearned*. Overcoming your fear through acquiring good, solid conflict management skills, you can release yourself from the oppressive habits of compulsive people-pleasing and automatic White Door avoidance behavior.

Naturally, conflict is best managed when both parties understand and commit to the constructive guidelines. Once you have the knowledge and the skills you will gain from this book, you can share them with those people who are closest to you, and with whom fighting fairly and constructively is most important.

Even if you are the only one that engages constructively, you are still better off than if you avoid dealing with conflict altogether or if you lower your standards to a destructive level.

Emotional Adjustment: Overcoming Your Fear of Confrontation

Here are some important things to keep in mind as you work to overcome your fear of fighting and confrontation:

♦ In your close relationships, don't be afraid to fight constructively; instead, worry about too strong a tendency to bury or avoid conflict as a symptom of relationship trouble.

♦ A certain degree of conflict is inevitable between people, especially in a close relationship. Constructive conflict is healthy and beneficial to relationships.

♦ You really cannot avoid conflict altogether nor make your relationships conflict-proof. (Remember: the elephant *is* there.) However, instead of avoiding conflict, you can learn to abort an escalating cycle before it reaches destructive proportions. With effective conflict *resolution*, you won't merely repeat the same conflict over and over again.

♦ As a people-pleaser, you learned to be afraid of anger, fighting, and conflict; you can unlearn your fears and relearn effective ways to cope with anger and resolve conflict.

♦ Your fear of anger and conflict makes you overestimate the chances that others will become angry or confrontational with you if you were to express your anger, however appropriately. This is a form of emotional reasoning—because you *feel* that something might be true you begin acting as though it were already an established fact.

CHAPTER 15

Small Steps, Big Changes

Y ou have now completed your step-by-step tour around the three sides of the Disease to Please triangle. You should have a good sense by now of the toll your people-pleasing habits take on the quality of your life.

You have put your own needs on a back burner for so long that the pot is stewing with frustration, resentment, and anger. You may secretly rail against others for manipulating your generous nature or blame yourself for letting them.

Each day has become a struggle in which you feel the need to prove your value by all the things you do for others just as you did yesterday and just as you will do again tomorrow. While you're stuck in a self-defeating cycle, there is a way out:

▶ *You must set your intention to truly change.*

The deal I propose is simply this: You provide the motivation, I will give you the tools and skills you need to reclaim control over your life. You don't need to know *how* to cure the Disease to Please; that part is my job. You need only decide that you are committed to doing so. As long as your mind remains open to the exciting prospect of change, I will provide the means to move you forward on your own personal process of recovery.

I realize that at first, the idea of overcoming a problem that is as deeply ingrained though disruptive to your life as your people-pleasing syndrome may seem too daunting a task. I assure you that you are up for the challenge. (Just remember *all* the things you do and the energy you expend each day to meet other people's needs.)

What matters most is your decision to become healthier in the ways you behave and in how you think and feel about yourself and other people. You know now that people-pleasing is not the path to satisfaction or happiness.

As the millions of people who have conquered their addictions and other unhealthy compulsive habits know, *recovery takes place one step at a time, one day at a time.*

While you've been traveling around the Disease to Please triangle, you have been reading, thinking, and talking to others about your people-pleasing issues. As we followed the triangular path together, I signposted many times along the way that when you change just *one* thought, *one* behavior, or *one* feeling, you will interrupt the people-pleasing cycle and set in motion the empowering process of change.

By taking small steps, big and encouraging changes *will* happen. Soon, you will watch yourself finally untangle your thoughts, free yourself from fears, and *regain control* of your behavioral choices as you recover from the Disease to Please.

The 21-Day Action Plan
for Curing the Disease to Please

A User's Guide to the 21-Day Action Plan

You are now ready to launch your personal change process. This section contains a training program laid out over 21 days that will help you begin to cure your Disease to Please. As I have told you, don't worry about why or how the program works. All you need to do is follow the daily plan and you will acquire the skills you need to turn around your people-pleasing habits and reach your goal of complete recovery.

Think of yourself as a kind of psychological athlete in training who works closely with her coach or trainer. The trainer understands why and how the exercises work. Her job is to show the athlete which exercises to do and how to do them correctly. Most important, the trainer's job is to keep the athlete on track, motivated to stick with the program one step at a time, one day at a time.

Please think of me as your own personal trainer. If you follow the program, you will reach your goal. I have developed and used every one of these techniques with great success for many years with my patients who have suffered from the Disease to Please. I *know* that if you stick with it, the program will certainly help you, too.

Changing your long-standing patterns will require patience, perseverance, and practice. Don't set yourself up for failure by expecting perfection or overnight mastery of the new relationship skills and personal tools you will learn. There is plenty of room for error and lots of time—the rest of your life—to continually improve with practice.

Naturally, since you have spent most of your life developing and refining your people-pleasing tendencies, you should not expect to achieve a total cure in three weeks. Think of 21 days as a minimum guideline. You may set your own pace and allow a longer time—say, two or three days—to accomplish what I present in one day.

In keeping with the "small steps" approach, remember *not* to read ahead. Read, and do, one day at a time. Don't overload yourself. It *should* take you a minimum of 21 days to complete the whole program.

The important thing is not how fast you can get the program done but rather that you proceed at a pace that feels right and comfortable for you. Racing through the program or stopping short of completion so that you can free yourself to take care of other people again is exactly the kind of behavior and thinking you need to correct.

This is *your* time. You earned it . . . a long time ago. Now, use it to help yourself get over your depleting and exhausting people-pleasing habits, thoughts, and feelings. It is important that you read and complete each step of the plan, one step at a time, in order of presentation.

It isn't necessary for you to undergo a comprehensive rewiring of your entire personality structure in order to cure the Disease to Please. No matter what the causes of your own syndrome, the journey to recovery remains largely the same for all people-pleasers: *small steps* and directed, strategic change.

You need only replace *one* flawed idea with a new, accurate thought; or *one* automatic knee jerk "yes" with an assertive "no;" or *one* conflict avoidance response with a positive problem-solving experience to start you on your journey to recovery.

The 21-Day Action Plan that follows, day-by-day, step-by-step, will lead you away from the Disease to Please cycle and into a far happier, healthier way of living. While the plan yields impressive results, there really is no magic or mystery to it. It is common sense and it is based on sound, effective principles of psychology and behavior change.

Once your journey of personal change begins, it will gain momentum on its own. With each step you take away from your self-imposed servitude to others, you will develop an increasing and exciting sense of empowerment over your own life.

The Choice to Care

I want to assure you that the 21-Day Action Plan is entirely consistent with your values and needs to remain a kind, loving, good, and generous person. (But it's okay *not* to be nice all the time!) When you complete the 21-

Day Plan, you will not become a selfish or self-centered person who is hardened and unkind to other people. Now, *that* would be a major personality overhaul in the wrong direction.

I want you to like the person you are *more* at the end of the next 21 days, not less than you do now. In fact, I really want you to be more like the giving person that you want to be. But, I want you to be in charge of the choices you make.

As you are about to learn, the more desirable alternative to being a people-pleaser is to be a person who makes a very intentional *choice to care*—a choice of when, how, and to whom you give your finite time and resources. This way, you will be certain to reserve adequate amounts of time and energy for your own needs that, incidentally, will be moved way up your ladder of priorities.

When you substitute the choice to care about others in place of your compulsive compliance with the needs and requests of others, you will finally reclaim control over your life. Making choices instead of knee jerk reactions will afford you the ability to do the things that you most *want* to do, instead of doing everything that everyone asks of you or that you merely anticipate that people need.

> ▶ *Curing the Disease to Please does not mean that you must sacrifice or change your giving nature nor your desire to bring happiness to many people. But, it does mean forgoing the compulsion to gain everyone's approval or to be nice to everyone all the time.*

When you complete the 21-Day Action Plan, you will have the necessary skills and the genuine freedom to make good choices. Instead of being controlled by your people-pleasing compulsion, you will be in control of your desire, intentions, and efforts to please others balanced against the parallel need to take good care of yourself.

What You Will Need to Begin

The most important things that you need, of course, are this book and your commitment and motivation. In addition, you will need:

- ◆ A few pads of lined paper
- ◆ Pencils or pens
- ◆ Post-it notes
- ◆ A manila folder to hold your papers

- A journal of blank paper
- A supportive friend and/or family member to assist you as needed (preferable, but not absolutely mandatory)

So, now you're ready to start. Get your mind in just the right place by taking a moment to reflect on these wise words:

"If I am not for myself, who will be for me?
  If I am only for myself, what am I?
  If not now, when?"

Hillel, twelfth century

Don't Say "Yes" When You Want to Say "No"

The first skill you will tackle today is the all-important ability to say "no."

There are five steps necessary to break your automatic "yes-saying" habit. You will be learning and practicing these steps over the next several days.

When you are faced with any request, invitation, or other type of demand from another person, you will replace your ingrained habit of immediately saying "yes" with the following sequence of actions:

Step 1: Delay giving an immediate response by "buying time."

Step 2: Identify your options.

Step 3: Forecast the likely consequences of each option.

Step 4: Select the best option.

Step 5: Respond to the request/invitation/demand firmly and directly by exercising your choice to:

- ♦ say "no" or
- ♦ offer a counterproposal or
- ♦ say "yes"

Now, one step at a time, you will learn the skill of identifying your options of how to respond to requests from others, and of how to selectively choose, taking into account your own best interests as well as the needs of the person making the request.

Buying Time to Respond

In order to break your habit of giving an automatic "yes" response to requests from others, you need to *delay* your answer in order to think through your options carefully. The old adage to think before you speak— or, in this case, agree—is wise psychological advice.

> ▶ *Once you learn to insert time between an invitation, demand, or request and your reply, your sense of control will immediately increase.*

Telephone Requests. Whenever possible after a request has been made, even before you actually "buy time," you should try to take a brief break from the conversation. For example, as soon as a person with whom you are speaking on the telephone has asked you to do something or go someplace, your immediate response should be something such as:

- ◆ "May I put you on 'hold' for a moment?" or
- ◆ "Could I ask you to hold the line for a minute?" or
- ◆ "I need to put the phone down for a minute or so," or
- ◆ "May I call you back in a few minutes?"

This simple action alone interrupts the cycle of automatic "yes-saying." After your caller is holding the line, or waiting for your call back, select a phrase from the list that follows, "Phrases to Buy Time." When you resume the conversation (or return the call), you will respond by using one of the phrases to "buy time."

Phrases to "Buy Time"

1. "Let me get back to you with an answer after I check my calendar (or schedule, appointment book, etc.)"
2. "I need a little time to think about that. I'll call you back later/tomorrow/in a few days/later in the week."

3. "I might have a conflict. I'll check and get back to you with an answer as soon as I can."

4. "I need a bit of time to check on some things, but I'll call you back with an answer just as soon as I know. Tell me the best times to reach you."

5. "I can't give you an answer right now. But I'll get back to you very soon."

6. "I'm not sure if I will have the time [to do the request], so I'll have to let you know about it tomorrow/later/next week."

The time you "buy" will allow you to examine your options, forecast the consequences of saying "no" versus saying "yes," and select the response that takes *your* best interests into account.

Requests in Face-to-Face Conversations. Unlike telephones, people don't come equipped with hold buttons. Nevertheless, if possible, it is also preferable to take a brief break after a person makes a request of you in a face-to-face setting so that you don't automatically slip into your old patterns.

Ideally, in a face-to-face setting, your first response to a request from another person should be to excuse yourself from the scene for a few minutes to interrupt your automatic "yes" response. This is the "live" equivalent of putting a telephone caller on hold.

If possible, after the request has been made but before you reply, excuse yourself for a few minutes. You can say that you need to use the bathroom, make a telephone call, get some coffee, or get something out of your office or car. The point is to remove yourself physically so that you can gain control over your automatic impulse to comply.

If it is not possible or too awkward to physically leave for a few minutes, no matter. The brief interlude that excusing yourself provides is desirable but not mandatory.

Respond with a Phrase to Buy Time. In any event, whether you have put a caller on hold, excused yourself from a conversation, or found yourself unable to physically leave the scene, the next thing you need to do is the critical first step of the five: Tell the person making the request that you need some time before you can answer their request.

Review the list of phrases to buy time. Each phrase will effectively gain you some decision time before you actually answer the request. Make several copies of the list so that you can keep them near all the telephones you use at home and at work as well as in your wallet or purse.

Rehearse the Phrases to Buy Time. These phrases will probably seem foreign to you. For that reason, you will need to practice saying them over and over until you can say them naturally and easily. Repetition will increase your comfort level. Practice and rehearse the phrases out loud as you would when learning a foreign language.

Be a careful critic of your tone and inflection—you want to sound firm and pleasant. You do not want to sound wishy-washy or as though you don't really feel entitled to "buy time." You don't want to sound angry and aggressive either. If possible or desirable for you, enlist the aid of a supportive friend or family member who can give you feedback.

When you say each phrase, keep in mind that you are not *asking* for time; you are informing the other person that you will be *taking* a little time to reflect before you respond. Take care not to raise your vocal inflection at the end of a declarative sentence as though you were asking a question.

> ▶ *You have every right to think before you commit yourself to doing anything.*

Your intention is simply to gain the time you need to make a good choice instead of giving your usual knee-jerk people-pleasing "yes" that you are likely to regret right after the word leaves your lips.

Select at least two phrases from the list and commit them to memory. Add more of your own if you wish. The more you practice saying each of the phrases, the more comfortable you will be when you need to use them. Say each phrase a minimum of five times, at least three different times this day until you sound firm, direct, and comfortable about "buying time." Try smiling as you rehearse; this will help to keep your tone pleasant but still assertive.

Summary of Day 1

- ♦ Make copies of the "Phrases to Buy Time." Put them near every telephone you use; keep one in your purse or wallet so that it can be available for use on a cellular phone or in a face-to-face situation (be sure to refer to the list discreetly).

- ♦ Say each of the six phrases several times out loud.

- ♦ Practice saying the phrases at three different times during the day. Be sure that you are sounding direct and firm, not apologetic or angry.

- ♦ *Stop here today.* Read Day 2 tomorrow and follow this *one-day-at-a-time* routine.

The Broken Record Technique

Yesterday, you learned the necessary phrases to buy time when a request is made of you. Today you will build on those skills by learning how to handle resistance so that you don't capitulate to pressure and wind up saying "yes" when you really want to say "no."

How to Handle Resistance with the Broken Record Technique

After you "buy time," the person making the request may try to insist that an immediate response is required. Or, since you have nearly always complied in the past, the requester may simply repeat the request two or three times expecting you to comply as usual.

The way to handle resistance is to use the "Broken Record" technique. Acknowledge that you have clearly heard and understood the request *and* the resistance by accurately empathizing with and paraphrasing back the person's emotional reaction. Then, *repeat your phrase* to buy time—just like a broken record. The key to this technique is to avoid responding to the actual content of the resistance attempt. If you do so, you may well lose control of the conversation.

The script that follows shows you how to put the steps together using the Broken Record technique to successfully fend off the pressure to comply.

Friend: [on telephone] "I need to ask you for a big favor. Can you come over this weekend and help me set up for the big charity luncheon? I could really use your help."

You: "Can I ask you to please hold the line for a minute?"

Friend: "Sure."

You: [*put friend on hold; consult* **Phrases to Buy Time** *strategically placed near your telephone*] "Hi, I'm back. Well, I might have a conflict so I'll have to check on it. I'll call you in a few days to let you know."

Friend: "Oh, I can't wait a few days. Can't you tell me now? I really need to know if I can count on you as always."

You: "I understand that you're anxious for an answer. But, I might have a conflict that I have to check, so I'll get back to you as soon as I can—probably within the next few days."

Friend: "Well, even if you can only come for a few hours, it would still help. I can count on you for that, can't I?"

You: [*with a smile even though you're on the telephone*] "I know how much you want me to help you out. But I might have a conflict that I have to check. I'll get back to you with an answer in a day or two. I promise."

You will find the Broken Record technique very powerful. Make sure that you accurately empathize with and paraphrase back the feelings you hear in the requester's resistance. Be careful *not* to respond directly or to engage in the content of the requester's resistance attempts. Then, immediately return to the same declarative sentence to buy time to respond. If you *stay* on your simple message, the requester will not succeed in pressuring you to respond.

Practicing What to Say When You Might *Want to Say "No"*

Buying time is the critical first step in learning to say "no." Naturally, you will need to follow through with your promise to provide an answer to the person who has made the request. You will learn how to do that over the next few days of training. For now, it is important to practice buying time and to handle resistance so that you can think over your response

Identify two people who make demands on your time on a regular basis who feel burdensome to you. The people can be family members, friends, people associated with work, or representatives of organizations. Create two lifelike examples of these people making requests/demands of you. Practice resisting the impulse to comply immediately by buying time and using the Broken Record.

▶ *Your goal is to remain firm in your declaration that you will need to take a little time before you can provide an answer to the request.*

Keep your intention clear to yourself and it will become clear to the requester. Remember, acknowledge that you hear the pressure, but stay on your "buying time" message like a broken record.

For variety, select two or more different "buying time" phrases to practice. You can either practice with the help of a friend or family member who can play the role of the other person making the demand on your time, or practice by yourself saying both roles out loud. If you have someone to practice with, ask her or him to improvise the script in order to really create pressure on you to respond *now*. The more practice you have resisting pressure in role playing, the more successful and confident you will be when the time comes to buy time when a real request is made of you.

Summary of Day 2

♦ Review the sample script using the Broken Record technique to handle pressure and resistance.

♦ Identify two people who make demands on your time and to whom you would like to say "no" sometimes. Practice with them in mind.

♦ Use the Broken Record technique to acknowledge pressure to respond *now*, but stay on your message that you need some time before you give an answer.

♦ Don't worry if you feel somewhat awkward or artificial at first. These are new ways of responding for you and it will take some time and practice for you to gain comfort with them. The more you practice, the better prepared you will feel when it is time to do the real thing.

The Counteroffer

Now that you have learned how to buy time, you next need to learn what to do with the time you have gained.

Identify Your Options

You have become accustomed to thinking that there is only one option—saying "yes"—when someone needs you or asks you to do something for them. In fact, you have two other options.

Obviously, you could say "no." This simple response lies at the core of curing your people-pleasing problems. You must learn to say "no" when that is really your choice.

However, there will be occasions when you're not sure whether you want to say "no" definitively, or make a counteroffer or negotiated compromise instead. For example, if a friend asks you to spend four hours volunteering at an event, you might respond by saying that you can't do four hours but you can spend one or two.

Be careful not to fall into the trap of using this third option too often or too much. You should reserve the counteroffer for situations where you *really* do not wish to give a definitive "no." Your reason for not saying a flat "no" should be because complying with the request is really something you want to do—or, at least, wouldn't mind doing, but you need to modify the demand to meet *your* conditions and best interests.

Don't use the counteroffer option as an *excuse* not to say "no" or because you are worried that the person will be angry, hurt, or disappointed if you do. You will learn how to handle those concerns when you learn how to say "no." You do not have to have a counteroffer. This third option is exactly that—*optional.*

Forecast the Likely Consequences of Each Option

You will need some paper and pen or pencil for this next step. For each request, you should have at least two, possibly three, pieces of paper depending on whether you have devised a counteroffer.

Yesterday, you identified two people or organizations who make demands on your time. Select one and create a realistic example of that person making a specific request of you on the telephone.

At the top of one sheet of paper, write the words, "If I say yes:" On the second page, write the words, "If I say no:" On the third page, if you have a counteroffer, write, "If I say [your counteroffer]:"

Now, under each heading, make a list of the reasons in favor of each alternative (pros) and a list of the reasons against each (cons). As you analyze the pros and cons, your focus should be on how each optional response would affect you emotionally, physically, financially, or in any other ways you can anticipate.

The important thing is to think about how your response will affect *you* not the person making the request. If you are only thinking about the other person's needs, you're back to your old people-pleasing habits. *Your* needs are the first priority in this exercise.

If you were to comply with the request, how are you likely to feel before, during, and after you do what is necessary to fulfill the request? Then forecast the likely consequences if you say "no." Finally, if you have developed a third response, forecast the likely consequences of implementing a compromise or negotiated solution.

Breaking out of the people-pleasing cycle does not require you to say "no" to every request from others. On the contrary, your purpose is simply to become deliberate and intentional about your responses. *In order to make good choices, you must learn to think through your options, ideally during the time that you "buy."*

Select the Best Option

Review your reasons for saying "yes," for saying "no," and as appropriate, for making a counteroffer, keeping in mind that your overriding goal is to learn how to consider your own needs and be selective in your responses to others.

Because this training exercise is designed to help you break your people-pleasing habits, saying "yes" ought to be your least desirable alternative. It may be easiest because it is familiar. There is an old saying that a horse will go back to a burning barn because it is familiar. In other words, familiarity does not always mean safety.

The outcome of a real analysis might lead you to say "yes" some of the time or to a negotiated compromise. That is fine as long as you are making a conscious choice to do something because you want to, not because you compulsively agree.

Now, select the best option for each request. Circle the option you choose in red ink.

Summary of Day 3

♦ Identify your options to a hypothetical request from one of the people you identified as being demanding on your time. You should have two, possibly three, options for responding: Saying "yes," saying "no," or offering a counterproposal or compromise.

♦ Make a list of the pros and cons for each response. Focus on how you will feel if you agree and then must spend your time and energy fulfilling the request.

♦ Beware of your tendency to avoid saying "no" for people-pleasing reasons. Remember, you are trying to unlearn your automatic habits and replace them with good choices.

♦ Select the best option taking into account your needs as well as those of the person making the request, keeping the latter's needs secondary to your own.

What to Say If You Want to Say "No": The Sandwich Technique

Today you will learn the single most important skill necessary to break the people-pleasing cycle: how to say "no" to requests from others.

Respond to Requests Firmly and Directly

You have the option to say "no" to any request, no matter how intense the pressure you feel. But you must put your choice into action.

Let's return to the example we began on Day 1. Assume that you have fielded a request effectively and bought yourself time to consider your options. Upon consideration, you decide to say "no." You will now need to recontact (or return to the "live" conversation with) the person who made the request. Here are three simple responses to convey that your answer is a firm but pleasant "no":

1. "I called to get back to you about your request/invitation the other day. It turns out that I won't be able to do that for you, but I want to thank you for thinking of me."

2. "Thank you again for that nice invitation. But I just won't be able to accept it this time. It turns out that I *do* have a conflict."

3. "I'm calling to get back to you about your request from last Tuesday. Actually, I'm sorry to say that I won't be able to do that. But thanks so much for thinking of me."

It's okay to offer a brief apology, but long explanations will get you into trouble. As soon as you start overexplaining or apologizing excessively, you will be revealing a vulnerability that the requester can exploit. But, don't worry—you still know how to resist pressure with the Broken Record.

The Sandwich Technique. One highly effective way to say "no" is to "sandwich" your negative response in between two complimentary or positive statements. This provides some cushion or buffer for your denial of the request or invitation. For example:

♦ "I want to get back to you about that very nice invitation/request from the other day. I'm sorry to say that I won't be able to accept this time. I hope you'll think of me again."

♦ "You are a wonderful friend but I'm calling to tell you that I won't be able to do the favor you asked the other day. If I could I would, and I know that you understand."

♦ "It was very flattering to be asked to [do something with/for you]. However, I won't be able to do it. Thanks very much for asking. It meant a lot to me."

When you use the sandwich technique, be sure that you mean every word you say. Don't give the message that you want to be asked again if you don't mean it. If you mean what you are saying, then the sandwich technique is quite effective.

You need only decide which way you want to say "no"—a brief declarative statement or sandwiched between two positives. There isn't really one "right" way to say "no;" many approaches are effective. The only "wrong" way is if the "no" turns into a "yes" without your intention or consent. The choice of which approach to use depends on your relationship with the person making the request, your personal comfort level, and the particular situation at hand.

Using the script you began on Day 1, add the recontact and "saying no" message after the "buying time" phrase and Broken Record. Next, you should practice saying the full sequence of responses out loud several times. Develop a style that feels most comfortable for you.

You want to sound relaxed, direct, and firm with the message. Don't think of this as delivering bad news. It's actually very positive news for you:

You're reclaiming control over your time. Steer clear of whining, apologizing, or being overly dramatic in your response. Don't overestimate the impact of your saying "no." The requester will cope; people say "no" all the time. He or she will simply have to ask somebody else for a change. You not only have every right but even the obligation to be selective with your time and energy.

Don't expect the other person to be angry with you. If you do, you will sound defensive when you give your response. Expect the other person to accept your "no" answer and to accord you the respect you deserve. If you signal that you feel guilty or worried about saying "no," you will give the requester an opening to manipulate and pressure you into compliance.

Deliver your message with a smile on your face, even if you're on the telephone. Use a mirror to practice. If you are smiling, you won't sound defensive or offensively hostile like you're expecting a fight.

Chances are that you've got plenty of earned "credit" with the person making the request. It is highly unlikely that anyone will become angry because you are saying "no." The other person might be surprised or disappointed, but she/he will get over it. You are not indispensable; no one is.

Resist Pressure to Comply. Of course, the person making the request may try to talk you out of your "no" answer. But you know what to do. Return to the Broken Record technique: Acknowledge that you have heard the effort to talk you out of saying "no," but do *not* debate. Try to accurately paraphrase back how the other person is feeling. Then return to your simple declarative sentence. No sandwiches this time.

Here are some examples of putting it all together.

> *You:* "I wanted to get back to you about your request the other day. I do have a conflict and I won't be able to do it."
>
> *Friend:* "Really? I was counting on you. You always help me out."
>
> *You:* "I understand you feel disappointed. But I have a conflict and I won't be able to do it."
>
> *Friend:* "Gee, are you absolutely sure? I just don't know what I'm going to do without you."
>
> *You:* "I understand you're a bit concerned, but I do have a conflict and I won't be able to do it. I'm sure you'll find someone who can help."

Be sure that you do not get into a discussion. If you start to argue back, or help her/him figure out what to do without you, you will lose vital ground. The point of the broken record is to acknowledge the emotion you hear and the effort being made. Then, simply return to the same declarative sentence, and say "no" again like a broken record.

Your "no" must be unequivocal and final. If you really wanted to offer a compromise or counteroffer, you would have done so at the outset. If you decided to say "no," stay on your message and stick with your game plan. If you know what you intend to do, no one will be able to talk you out of your answer.

Completing Your Script. You should now have completed one exercise. Your finished script should include the following components:

1. Requester asks you to do something.
2. You put him/her on hold if it is a telephone call; or excuse yourself for a few minutes if it is face to face. Your purpose is to consult your list of **Phrases to Buy Time** discreetly and set your intention on delaying your final response.
3. You return to the conversation and buy time.
4. The requester resists and tries to pressure you to respond immediately.
5. You reply with the Broken Record technique and stand your ground. You state again firmly and directly that you must delay your response for a brief time. (Repeat the resistance and your response once or twice for practice.)
6. You call back or see the person again to deliver your answer to the request. You say "no" firmly and directly. If you choose, you can sandwich your "no" response between two positive statements to cushion the impact.
7. The requester resists and tries to pressure you into compliance.
8. You respond with the Broken Record technique. Repeat the resistance and response at least twice.
9. You successfully communicate "**NO.**"
10. Congratulate yourself. You *can* overcome your Disease to Please.

Summary of Day 4

♦ You have learned three different simple sentences that indicate that you are not going to fulfill the request, accept the invitation, or comply with the demand.

♦ Use the Sandwich Technique if you prefer to couch your negative response between two positive statements. But, be sure that you mean what you say if you indicate that you're sorry or that you really want to be asked again.

♦ Remember, you should rehearse as much as you can. The more you repeat the "buying time" and "no" responses and the Broken Record response to pressure, the more comfortable and adept you will become at using them.

♦ It's okay to say "no."

The Reverse Sandwich Technique

Today you will learn to make a counteroffer, your third option for responding to a request, invitation, or other demand on your time and energy. Check your motives carefully to be sure that the compromise you offer is an affirmative response—something that you want or prefer to do instead of the original request—rather than a way of squirming out of saying "no" when that's your first choice.

> ▶ *If you use the counteroffer to avoid saying "no," you are not curing your people-pleasing problems.*

It is important that you frame only *one* counterproposal. Don't get into a bargaining stance with the requester. This is a slippery slope for a people-pleaser, and you can easily slide right back into your automatic compliance behavior.

When You Want to Make a Counteroffer

So far, a friend has made a request. You have followed the steps as outlined:

1. You put the person "on hold" or excuse yourself briefly from a face-to-face setting, if possible.
2. You return to the conversation and "buy time" to respond.

3. You resist pressure with the Broken Record technique.

4. You recontact the requester with your response. This time, you will propose your counteroffer of *what you want to do* or what you are able to do, instead of the request as initially proposed. State your proposal *as simply as possible*. Again, don't offer a lot of excuses, explanations, or apologies.

The counteroffer is a kind of negotiated compromise. But, since you are a newcomer to this, you will be offering only one counterproposal per request, on a kind of take-it-or-leave-it basis. This will not be a back-and-forth, give-and-take negotiation. You are the one naming the terms here; the requester will be put in the position either to accept your counterproposal or to accept "no" as the alternative. *This way, you maintain the control.*

The Reverse Sandwich Technique

To present your counterproposal you will use the *Reverse Sandwich* technique. This time you will "sandwich" your positive message—the counterproposal of what you are willing to do—between two negative messages.

The first negative is to inform the requester that you will not be able to fulfill or accept the original request as proposed. But, the good news—the sandwich filling—is that you are willing to do your counterproposal. The top of the sandwich is the take-it-or-leave-it message which you will present *not* as an ultimatum, but rather as a simple point of information. If the requester will not or cannot accept your counteroffer as is, then you must retreat to a firm flat "no" after all. Do not make or imply threats or coercion. Be friendly but assertive.

It is important that you do not engage in any negotiation. This is new territory for you. Don't allow yourself to be drawn into a bargaining posture where there's a chance that your old people-pleasing habits will take over and you'll find yourself saying "yes" when you want to say something else.

Here is the way the *Reverse Sandwich Counteroffer* sounds when you put it all together. Note that the Reverse Sandwich is followed by some resistance responses from the friend that, in turn, you deflect with your well-practiced and effective Broken Record:

> *You:* "I'm calling to get back to you about your request. Unfortunately, I won't be able to help you all day. But, I can come for one hour in the morning. If that won't work, I'm afraid I just can't make it at all."
>
> *Friend:* "Gee. I'm so disappointed. I was really counting on you. Is an hour all you can really spare? Are you sure?"

You: "I know you'd like me to help all day, but I can only make it for an hour in the morning. If that won't work, I just won't be able to help out this time at all."

Or

You: "I'm getting back to you with an answer to your request. I can't do what you're asking. But I can do [counteroffer]. I hope that will work out because otherwise I won't be able to be there at all."

Friend: "Are you absolutely sure? I was totally counting on you. You can't imagine how disappointed I am. Won't you think about changing your mind? For me? You've never let me down before."

You: "I understand you feel disappointed. But this time, I just won't be able to do what you asked. I *am* offering to do [counterproposal], but that's all I can do.

Friend: "Well, to tell you the truth, if you can't do [original request], I think I'll just have to call someone else."

You: "Okay." [*Note:* At this point, *you must stop talking.* If you start making apologetic noises here, you will lose critical ground and start on the slippery slide back to your old people-pleasing habits. Your friend will be fine. She is already onto the plan of calling someone else. Say goodbye and get off the phone.]

Rehearse and Practice Your Counteroffer Script. Practice the entire script out loud from beginning to end at least five times. You should write two alternative endings: one where your counteroffer is accepted, and one where it is not and you have to revert to a "no" response.

Again, in the latter case, be sure that you do not start backpedaling. You are *not* going to comply with the request as made: We know you can do that. You're in training now *to change* your compliance habits.

If you have someone to role-play with you, ask the person to really lay on the guilt and pressure to make you change your mind and agree to the request. The more practice you have resisting pressure, the better you will be at doing so in reality.

Rehearse and Practice Your Saying "No" Script(s). After you have practiced the counterproposal scripts (the one where the counteroffer is accepted and the one where it is not accepted, respectively), resume practicing your Saying "No" script several times again.

Don't forget in any version to always "buy time" at the front end so that you can fully evaluate your options and *make good choices* that fully take your interests and needs into account.

Summary of Day 5

♦ Don't use the counteroffer option as a way to wiggle out of saying "no."

♦ Use the *Reverse* Sandwich to wrap your counterproposal between two negative messages. State that you cannot fulfill the request as made; present your counterproposal; then indicate that if the counteroffer isn't acceptable, you will have to say "no" after all.

♦ Present the top sandwich slice as a piece of information and *not* as an ultimatum or actual take-it-or-leave-it threat. You're merely saying that this [counteroffer] is what you can do; if that won't work for the other person, you'll just have to say "no" this time. Remember, you're making an offer.

♦ Don't get drawn into negotiations and bargaining. Use the Broken Record technique to empathize with and paraphrase back your friend's feelings as accurately as possible and to acknowledge her/his efforts to convince you to do something other than your counterproposal. Remember not to engage in an exchange over content. Simply reflect back the emotion you hear underneath or behind the content. Then return to the message that you can *only* do your counterproposal or nothing at all.

♦ *Practice, practice, practice.* The more comfortable you get with these key skills, the further along you will be toward curing your people-pleasing habits.

Rewriting the Ten Commandments of People-Pleasing

Today you will make a direct frontal attack on your People-Pleasing Mindsets.

Specifically, you will rewrite the sabotaging *shoulds* contained in "The Ten Commandments of People-Pleasing" from Chapter 2.

As a reminder, the Ten Commandments of People-Pleasing are listed below. Read them out loud, trying to sound as unreasonable and demanding as possible. Feel the weight of these self-imposed *shoulds* as well as the burdensome load of guilt and anger that drags behind them.

The Ten Commandments of People-Pleasing

1. I *should always* do what others want, expect, or need from me.
2. I *should* take care of everyone around me whether they ask for help or not.
3. I *should always* listen to everyone's problems and try my best to solve them.
4. I *should always* be nice and never hurt anyone's feelings.
5. I *should always* put other people first, before me.

6. I *should never* say "no" to anyone who needs or requests something of me.

7. I *should never* disappoint anyone or let others down in any way.

8. I *should always* be happy and upbeat and never show any negative feelings to others.

9. I *should always* try to please other people and make them happy.

10. I *should* try *never* to burden others with my own needs or problems.

Your goal is to rewrite the 10 statements, replacing each with a personalized corrective thought. Accurate thinking, you will recall, may include *preferences and desires,* but will not permit the unreasonable notion that things *should* be the way you say simply because you insist on it.

Start with the First Commandment and go in order, down to the Tenth. Rewrite each statement by replacing the *shoulds* with a corrective thought. For example,

Instead of: "I *should* always do what others want, need, or expect from me."

Replace with Your Corrected Thought: "If and when I want, I can *choose* to fulfill the wants, needs, or expectations of others who are important to me."

In this example, the categorical demand is softened in several ways. There are conditions of time and preference placed on the thought (i.e., "If and when I want"). Further, the key word *choose* is included. Emphasizing choice reminds you that you are in charge and in control. Further, while you may choose to fulfill certain needs of selected others *some* of the time, you are under no absolute obligation to do so. Finally, note the inclusion of the clause "others who are important to me," that further qualifies the conditions.

Alternatively, here is another way to modify the First Commandment using some negatives to cancel the demanding *should:*

♦ *Instead of:* "I *should always* do what others want, need, or expect from me."

♦ *Replace with Your Corrected Thought:* "I know that I don't always *have* to do what others want, need, or expect from me. I can *choose* to give to certain people when and if I want to do so."

There are many different ways to soften, moderate, and correct the Ten Commandments of People-Pleasing. *It is important for you to really con-*

sider how to correct your own thinking in a way that feels both liberating and curative. Each corrective thought should have your personal imprint.

Don't get stumped if the Commandments seem accurate at first glance. Naturally, because you have suffered from the Disease to Please for so long, many or all of the Commandments will feel familiar and might even appear correct or at least accurate reflections of your old way of thinking.

But you have learned that these mindsets are distorted, flawed, and incorrect for many reasons. Moreover, you now understand that holding on to these rules will perpetuate the syndrome you are committed to cure.

Your job now is to undo the People-Pleasing Mindsets and to replace them with healthier, corrective ways to think. Your recovery depends on breaking the bondage of self-imposed rules and sabotaging *shoulds.*

When you have finished all Ten Commandments, read your corrected statements out loud. Be sure that you haven't inadvertently slipped a people-pleasing *should* or *ought to* in there. Verify that all exaggerations or hyperboles such as "always," "never," "all the time," "none of the time," and so forth, have been expunged. Corrective thinking is flexible and rationale, not categorical and demanding.

When you are satisfied with the accuracy of your new and improved thinking, read the corrected statements out loud with conviction in your voice. Make a copy of the set of 10 corrected mindsets in your nicest handwriting in a journal or on a clean sheet of paper. Title the new list, "My New Mindset as a Recovered People-Pleaser." You can also place the list in a nice frame.

Make a few copies (either handwritten or photocopied) to put in key places at home or at work. You might put one list on your bathroom mirror so that you can read it over each morning and evening when you brush your teeth or wash your face. You can put a copy in your car or tape one to your computer. (Of course, you can also have the list typed into your computer's hard drive so that you can call it up whenever you need to review it.)

Summary of Day 6

♦ Read The Ten Commandments of People-Pleasing out loud, emphasizing the word *should* in a directive, oppressive, and demanding tone. Remember, this is how the *should* statements have sounded in your internal self-talk all these years that you have been a compulsive people-pleaser.

♦ Write a corrective thought to replace each of the Ten Commandments of People-Pleasing.

- Review your corrective thoughts to be sure that they are rational, flexible, and above all, liberating. Use statements of preference, qualifiers of time, and moderate language. Try to include the word *choose* or choice as much as possible to emphasize your newly acquired sense of control.

- Make a clean handwritten copy titled, "My Corrective Thoughts As a Recovered People-Pleaser." The purpose of handwriting is to really make it personalized. Of course, you may also type your list into your computer.

- Make several copies of the list of corrective thoughts and put them in places where you will see them several times a day. Make a point to review them silently or aloud as much as possible.

Rewriting the Seven Deadly Shoulds

You have already been reprogramming your thinking by studying your corrective thoughts that you wrote yesterday. Try to become as aware as possible of any backsliding self-talk. In other words, if you find yourself thinking or saying a *should* statement from "The Ten Commandments of People Pleasing," do the following immediately:

♦ Write the word *should* on a Post-it note or self-sticking piece of paper. Draw a circle around the word and then draw a line diagonally through it in the style of a universal traffic sign. The message to yourself is: **No People-Pleasing Shoulds!**

♦ Put the Post-it note next to the telephone or any place else where you are likely to see it often.

♦ Immediately review your list of corrective thoughts. Focus on the corrective thought that is most applicable to the backsliding *should* that crept into your thinking.

As you progress in your training program, you will find yourself less and less likely to revert to old thought patterns. For now, you need to be patient. Expect yourself to need time to replace years of deeply ingrained thought patterns. Don't become discouraged when you realize you are thinking about old people-pleasing rules.

At first you may have lots of Post-it notes with the No Should messages. As you become more familiar with your corrective thoughts and as you work on replacing the demanding *shoulds* with them, the number of notes that you see around the house and office will decrease.

Correcting the Seven Deadly Shoulds

Following is the second list of toxic *should* thoughts from Chapter 2. Read the list over out loud using a demanding, oppressive tone and emphasizing the word *should* in a way that conveys a sense of entitlement.

The Seven Deadly Shoulds

1. Other people *should* appreciate and love me because of all the things I do for them.
2. Other people *should always* like and approve of me because of how hard I work to please them.
3. Other people *should never* reject or criticize me because I always try to live up to their desires and expectations.
4. Other people *should* be kind and caring to me in return because of how well I treat them.
5. Other people *should never* hurt me or treat me unfairly because I am so nice to them.
6. Other people *should never* leave or abandon me because of how much I make them need me.
7. Other people *should never* be angry with me because I would go to any length to avoid conflict, anger, or confrontation with them.

Now, starting with the first Deadly Should, write a corrective replacement thought that represents your new way of thinking as a recovered people-pleaser. Replacing the *shoulds* with statements of preference—what you would *like* to have happen rather than what you demand or expect—is an important correction.

You may use more than one sentence in formulating your corrective thought. Your goal is to develop seven new thoughts about your relationships with others that do not reflect the Disease to Please. Your corrective thoughts need to be flexible and moderate as opposed to rigid and extreme. Remember to modify exaggerated words and time frames such as *always* or *never.*

Coercive words like *should, ought,* and *must,* especially when applied to your expectation of others, set you up to feel angry, mistreated, and resentful. In contrast, your corrected thoughts will include more flexible and reasonable statements of your preferences or wishes in the place of insistent demands. The flexibility and moderation in your new thinking will increase your satisfaction in the relationships you have with others.

Here are some examples of corrective thoughts to replace The Seven Deadly Shoulds:

- *Instead of:* "Other people *should* appreciate and love me because of all the things I do for them."

- *Replace with Your Corrective Thought:* "I hope that other people love me for the person that I am rather than for what I do for them. When I choose to do nice things for others, I hope they appreciate my efforts."

- *Instead of:* "Other people *should always* like and approve of me because of how hard I work to please them."

- *Replace with Your Corrective Thought:* "I know that it isn't reasonable or even possible for other people to *always* like and approve of me. I would like the people whom I like and respect to reciprocate my feelings. But I want people to like me because of my values and because I treat others with kindness and respect and not because of how hard I work to please others. The most important approval that I need is my own."

As the second example illustrates, some of the Deadly Shoulds contain more than one thought. Therefore, the correction may also require a few or several sentences. You may use as many statements as you need to correct each of the seven Deadly Shoulds. In fact, the more complete your corrective thought, the more progress you will make in correcting your People-Pleasing Mindsets.

When you have completed all seven corrective thoughts, review them carefully and edit any remnants of people-pleasing toxic thinking. If you wish, ask a friend or family member who understands the program to review your corrected thoughts.

When you complete your list of seven corrective thoughts, make a clean handwritten list titled, "My New and Improved Guidelines About Others." Note that there is a big difference between the terms *guidelines* and *rules.* The former implies flexibility and suggestion; the latter implies rigidity and self-imposed constraints.

Put a copy of your new guidelines about others with your other corrected list from yesterday on the bathroom mirror, for example, so you can review it each morning and night. Carry another list with you or put one in your office so that you can review it again at midday or whenever you need to.

If you find yourself backsliding into Deadly *Should* thinking about others, make another **No People-Pleasing Shoulds!** sign and put it near a telephone, on the refrigerator, or in any other place where you will be reminded to rid your thoughts of people-pleasing rules.

Summary of Day 7

♦ Make a Post-it note or other self-adhering small sign each time you backslide into *should* thinking that reflects either "The Ten Commandments of People Pleasing" or "The Seven Deadly Shoulds."

♦ Read "The Seven Deadly Shoulds" out loud in an oppressive tone with emphasis on the *shoulds* and the sense of entitlement they imply. Note how coercive and rigid this thinking sounds.

♦ Replace the Deadly *Shoulds* with corrective thoughts that are flexible, moderate, and reflect preferences and wishes instead of demands.

♦ Make a nice handwritten copy titled, "My New and Improved Guidelines About Others." Put the copies in key places. Review your guidelines at least three times per day.

Taking Care of You

By definition, The Disease to Please has put your needs perennially behind those of others. As a recovered people-pleaser, things are going to be different—starting now.

▶ *The big attitude adjustment you will make today is this: Unless you take better care of yourself physically and psychologically, you won't be able to take good care of the people that matter most in your life.*

When was the last time you did something pleasurable just for yourself? Can you even remember what kinds of pleasurable things you like to do? If you are like most people-pleasers, taking the time away from serving others' needs to spend it exclusively on making yourself feel good is too dim and distant a memory to even recall. In fact, that memory might well be nonexistent.

Begin your personal journal (any bound book of plain or lined paper will do fine) by writing, "My Pleasurable Activities List" on the first page. Immediately under that title write, "I am committed to taking care of my own needs, both physically and psychologically, so that I will be happy and best able to care for the people that matter most in my life."

Next, make a list in your journal of at least 20 activities that you find (or think you would find) pleasurable. Reserve several subsequent pages to allow room for your list to grow. The activities should vary widely with respect to the amount of time and preparation they require. Some of your pleasurable activities might take only minutes to perform and even less time to prepare, while others may require several hours or even a few days to perform and necessitate considerable preparation.

Going outside to gaze appreciatively at the moon and stars and to smell the sweet night air, for example, are spontaneous acts that can be accomplished in a minute or two. Allowing a few extra minutes to read the comic strips or to work the crossword puzzle as part of your morning newspaper perusal takes no preparation. Soaking in a hot bubble bath in a scented candlelit bathroom may take as long as 30 to 45 delicious minutes but necessitates little preparation time other than perhaps buying the scented candles and bubble bath.

On the other extreme, spending a full day in a spa letting other people take care of you requires more time and some preparation such as scheduling and arranging for such details as child care or coverage of other responsibilities. Taking off on a weekend getaway requires still more time and preparation.

The point of your list is to construct a personalized menu of activities from which you can select. You should add to your list whenever you think of, or hear about, something that sounds fun, enjoyable, interesting, relaxing, exciting, or otherwise pleasurable.

The list can range from simple pleasures to extravagant indulgences, depending on your inclinations and budget. It is not necessary for you to engage in solitary activities. You certainly may share your pleasurable experiences with others. Indeed, there may be several of your pleasurable activities that require the participation of others.

The key is to make the primary choice yours. These activities are for your pleasure; if someone else participates and also derives enjoyment that is fine. Just be sure that you are not putting someone else's needs first and reverting to your old people-pleasing habits.

Do Two Pleasurable Activities Every Day

Refer to your personal pleasurable activities list. Select two activities and *do them today*. No excuses are allowed or acceptable. If you cannot find two activities on your list that are spontaneous and brief enough to include today, think of two more that will fit the agenda.

After today, you will continue to do a minimum of two pleasurable activities each day, for the remainder of the action plan. While you may repeat some activities, you will benefit more from striving for variety. Continue to add to your list as you discover or think of other ways to enjoy yourself.

After you've completed the 21-Day Action Plan, you will continue to do pleasurable things for yourself each day because you now know that *your* health, peace of mind, and happiness matter as much as anyone else's—maybe even more!

You may have noted that the root of the words *pleasurable* and *please* are the same. By thinking of, planning, and engaging in pleasurable activities each day, you will be honoring your new commitment to "please" yourself. In doing so, you will acknowledge the validity of your own needs, which you will no longer willingly subordinate to those of others.

Summary of Day 8

♦ Write your commitment to take care of your own needs physically and psychologically so that you can best care for the people that matter most in your life.

♦ Make a Pleasurable Activities List in your journal. Your minimum list should be 20 activities that vary widely with respect to time and preparation required. Add to your list often.

♦ Select two pleasurable activities and do them today.

♦ Do two pleasurable activities every day. You may repeat activities as desired, although you will benefit by striving for variety.

Talking Yourself Out
of Approval Addiction

Today you will be attacking another set of toxic thoughts that lie at the core of the people-pleasing syndrome: approval addiction.

In a very real sense, there are two sides of your personality—the old people-pleaser and the new recovered people-pleaser—that are at war with one another over a set of deeply held beliefs.

The people-pleaser, of course, believes that gaining the approval of virtually *everyone* is necessary in order to feel worthwhile. In a perpetual struggle to earn this universal approval, the people-pleaser attempts to do anything and everything possible to please others and make them happy.

The recovered people-pleaser realizes that it simply isn't possible to attain everyone's approval and knows that the most important and only truly essential approval to earn is one's own.

By giving voices to these two roles, you can take a good look at your inner self-talk. This way you can better "hear" the arguments from each side and objectively evaluate their respective merits. Uncovering the buried beliefs that underlie approval addiction by writing them down and saying them out loud has a potent impact on helping you overcome your old, flawed way of thinking.

When Someone Doesn't Like You

The first step in this exercise requires you to identify somebody in your life that you believe may not like or approve of you. This can be someone who has been critical of or has rejected you currently or in the past. You may lack hard evidence. All that matters is that you suspect or sense that the person does not like you. Write the person's name on the top of a piece of paper.

Next, write a paragraph or two in the voice or in the toxic mindset of the people-pleaser in you. Remember, because people-pleasing thoughts are based on an irrational and unattainable need to be liked and accepted by everyone, they are extreme, rigid, and illogical. The people-pleaser is *addicted to approval from everyone.*

When you think, write, and speak in the voice of the people-pleaser, your approval addiction creates feelings of deep inadequacy, rejection, and loss of self-esteem. This response is a direct result of the flawed, erroneous approval-addicted thinking.

When you have completed your writing in the voice of the people-pleaser, read what you have written out loud. Say the thoughts with as much conviction as you can. Try to really feel what this kind of thinking does to you.

Next, indicate on a scale of 1 to 10 how much it bothers or hurts you that the person you have identified doesn't like or approve of you. The scale's anchor points should reflect "not hurt at all" on the low or "1" end, to "devastated and deeply hurt" at the high or "10" end.

Now, assume the perspective of the recovered people-pleaser and write a few paragraphs in her voice. Develop a corrective mindset to the approval-addicted thinking of the people-pleaser. Your goal is to counter the people-pleaser's mindset and toxic thinking with reasoned, logical argument.

It may be helpful to think about how you might respond to a people-pleasing friend who was telling you how she felt about someone who didn't like her. This will allow you to use one of your greatest assets—your highly developed ability to take care of other people's feelings—to overcome and correct one of your biggest vulnerabilities. That vulnerability is the excessive, insatiable need for acceptance and approval of others that lies at the core of your Disease to Please mindsets.

The voice of the recovered people-pleaser reflects accurate thinking. Keep in mind that you should be attacking your addiction to approval—*not yourself.* When you come up with the counterarguments to people-pleasing thinking, be as kind and supportive to yourself as you would be to a friend who was distraught over the disapproval of someone else.

Be certain that your journal entry reflects your corrected thinking as a former approval addict. While you still may *prefer* to have the approval and positive regard of others, you don't *need* everyone's approval to feel worthwhile.

Here are some pointers to assist you:

♦ It isn't possible for *everyone* to like or approve of you. Don't try.

♦ It is actually manipulative to give of yourself to others as a way to "buy" their approval and affection. Better motives for giving of yourself are love, liking, and valuing the other person's company and friendship.

♦ Having the approval of others may be desirable or preferable, but it isn't absolutely necessary in order to validate your self-worth.

♦ Some people may dislike or disapprove of you because of their own biases, prejudices, or emotional problems. That's not your problem.

♦ The most important source of approval is your own.

When you have finished writing down the recovered people-pleaser's response, read what you have written out loud. Say the words with real conviction.

After you have read the recovered people-pleaser's response out loud two or three times, reevaluate how much it bothers you now that the person doesn't like you. Record your answer from 1 to 10 again.

You should notice a considerable reduction in the intensity of your negative feelings as a result of your corrected mindset.

Give Yourself Approval

The one source of approval that is critically important is your own. Using self-approval as a way to reward and motivate yourself is also a key skill to develop as a recovered people-pleaser.

As a general observation, while we reward children and pets for good behavior, we too often fail to reinforce the desirable actions of other adults as well as ourselves.

People-pleasers, you will recall, rarely feel pleased with themselves. This depletion of self-esteem is due, in part, to the unattainable, perfectionist standards they have used in the past to evaluate their own behavior. Now, as a recovered people-pleaser, you recognize the importance of sustaining your motivation with positive reinforcement. And you know that giving yourself approval is a powerful reward.

This evening, right before you go to sleep, take an extra few minutes to complete one or more of these sentences:

1. Today, I feel good about myself for doing . . .
2. Today, I approve of the way I . . .
3. Today, I am proud of myself because . . .

Be as specific as possible in your sentence completions. Also, be honest and accurate. There is no point to self-deception or vacuous self-affirmations. Since you are on a rapid path to changing your Disease to Please, there is much about what you are doing and how hard you are trying that is truly praiseworthy.

Summary of Day 9

♦ Identify someone who you believe doesn't like or approve of you. Write a few paragraphs from the perspective of your former people-pleasing mindset of approval addiction. Read these toxic thoughts out loud. Then rate how much it bothers you on a 10-point scale that the person doesn't like you.

♦ Next, write a few paragraphs of corrective thinking against approval addiction. Reevaluate your feelings. Notice the improvement when you let go of the need to have *everyone's* approval.

♦ Learn to give yourself approval. Complete an approval sentence (see above) tonight and every evening in your journal before you go to sleep. Reward yourself with approval for all the changes you are making toward curing the Disease to Please.

To Do or Not to Do, That Is the Question

Today you will begin learning the skill of effective delegation.
Since you now realize that your self-esteem and value as a person do not depend on how much you do for others, you can reduce your stress and free up more time for yourself by delegating some of the many things you do.

Your purpose in delegating is not to burden or exploit others. Rather, it is to rectify what has become a destabilizing imbalance in your relationships between how much you do for others and how much you allow others to do for you in return. Over time, that asymmetry has produced a crushing weight of responsibility on you. And the stress of this excessive workload poses a real threat to both your physical and emotional health.

▶ *It is no exaggeration to say, therefore, that the delegation skills you will learn are true lifesavers.*

Selecting Tasks to Delegate

Taking Inventory. In order to effectively delegate, you will first need to determine which tasks, chores, or projects you wish to turn over to other people. Think about how you have spent your time during the past month. Refer to your calendar, appointment book, day-runner, or any other aid to help reconstruct your memory. If the past month has been a vacation period, extend your time frame back to the previous month. The point is to provide a representative sample of your normal routine.

Using the past month as a window, make a list of all the tasks, projects, jobs, and chores that you performed. Be sure to include all the things that you did on a routine or regular basis. You don't need to repeat items that you did recurrently; simply indicate the repetitions parenthetically. For example, you might list "Make the bed (every day)," and "Change the bed linens (once per week)."

You should add to your list any additional jobs, projects, chores, or tasks that you anticipate doing in the present month and in the month ahead. You may also include jobs, projects, or chores that you would like to get done but have thus far procrastinated on since you have lacked the time to do them yourself.

Make your list as comprehensive as possible and number the items consecutively. Don't restrict your list in any way or think about delegation at this point. Merely write down all the things you typically do, anticipate doing, or would like to see get done.

Your list should encompass things associated with your work and home life as well as any social, childrearing, community, or other arena of activities that makes demands or requirements on your time. Your inventory should include mandatory chores or tasks as well as voluntary, enjoyable activities.

You should also include things you do only for yourself as well as those things you do for other people. Since you are a recently reformed people-pleaser, your list of chores, favors, and other tasks that you do for others is expected to be far longer than the list of things you do for yourself.

Collectively, then, you should have an inventory of all the routine or regular chores, jobs, and tasks that you currently do yourself along with the extra tasks you expect or wish to accomplish in the next 30 days or so.

Your ultimate goal is to off-load through delegation to others enough of the excessive things you currently do to noticeably lighten your burden. You also should aim for tilting the balance from less obligatory chores to more enjoyable activities. Remember, you are an intrinsically valuable human being and you amount to far more than the sum of the things you do for others.

You will begin by selecting a minimum of 10 percent of the chores/jobs on your list to delegate to someone else. For example, if your list includes 30 items, you will delegate a minimum of 3 to other people; if your list of special jobs numbers 50, you will off-load at least 5.

Naturally, you may elect to delegate more than 10 percent of your chores or jobs to others. As you continue your recovery, you will effectively decrease your workload by saying "no" to more requests and by setting reasonable, protective boundaries on the time and resources you are willing to give to others. And, because you will take care of yourself, you will necessarily have to reserve time and energy for your own pleasurable activities and gratification. As part of your recovery, you will continue to delegate more chores and other work to others.

Examine your list and total your items. Establish your target number for delegation as a minimum of 10 percent of your total. To make your selection, consider each item, one at a time.

For each chore or job on your list, ask yourself this key question: Is it truly *essential* that I do this myself?

This question is the litmus test. If, upon careful consideration, you determine that you *must* do a particular chore—that the chore cannot and should not be done by anyone else—the item belongs firmly in the "do not delegate" category.

Do not answer "yes" to this critical filter question if your only reason is because you cannot immediately think of someone to whom you might delegate the chore. Assume for the moment that you will find a suitable delegation candidate. Assume further that the person to whom you delegate can be trained or instructed to perform the task in question adequately.

With these caveats, circle the number of every item for which your answer to the key question is "no." The circled items represent possible chores or jobs to delegate. In other words, the only items that you may eliminate from delegation at this point are those that you believe are absolutely essential for you—and only you—to do.

Next, focus just on the items whose numbers you have circled—those that may be delegated. For each of these items, ask yourself these two filter questions:

♦ Do I enjoy doing this myself?

♦ Do I derive some important value, some sense of meaning or purpose from doing this myself?

For any item, if your answer is "yes" to one or both questions above, draw an X through the circled number. The crossed-out items should now be categorized as "do not delegate." You should still have some items remaining on your list that are circled without an X drawn through them. These circled items represent the jobs that you *may* choose to delegate.

If the number of circled items you have left to delegate is less than 10 percent of your total number of jobs and chores, you have likely been overly inclusive in your analysis of what is essential for you to do by yourself. This bias, of course, is a core aspect of the Disease to Please and requires correction.

To this end, reexamine your answers to the litmus test question: Is it *truly essential* that you do each task or chore yourself? Just because you have always done a particular chore does not mean that it is necessarily essential for only you to continue to do it.

Your answer to the litmus test question should not be "yes" if your only reason is because you feel nervous or uncomfortable about delegating. Almost every people-pleaser feels jittery about delegating (until she/he becomes a recovered people-pleaser). That is part of the syndrome. But, you will learn the necessary skills to delegate effectively tomorrow. Today, your goal is just to select tasks to delegate.

Examine your answers to the two filter questions again. According to the criteria you are using, the only items in your "do not delegate" category should be:

♦ Chores or jobs that are absolutely essential for you to do yourself; nobody else can or should do them;

♦ Chores or jobs that you truly enjoy doing yourself; or

♦ Chores or jobs from which you personally derive an important value or sense of purpose or meaning.

If you find that these criteria are applicable to more than 90 percent of all the chores or jobs on your list, you either have not made a truly comprehensive list or your analysis of whether you must do the work yourself is riddled with people-pleasing bugs in your program.

▶ *To cure the Disease to Please, you must commit to delegating to others at least 10 percent of the chores, jobs, tasks, or projects that you now do yourself. No excuses.*

Rank-Ordering Your Jobs to Delegate. Take a new piece of paper on which you will rank-order your possible chores and jobs to delegate according to this simple rule: Among the items still circled on your original list, select the one job or chore that you dislike doing the most. Make that the first item on your new list.

Continue ranking all your circled items according to the criterion of how much you dislike each; the first should be that job or chore that you dislike most, the second should be the one you dislike next most, and so on, until you have ranked all your delegation possibilities.

Calculate 10 percent of your original list as your target number of jobs to delegate to others. Draw a heavy line on the rank-ordered list under the first 10 percent.

Summary of Day 10

♦ Make an inventory list of all the chores, jobs, tasks, or projects that you typically do. Use the past month (or a representative month) as a "window" into your routine. Add jobs, chores, or projects that you anticipate doing in the coming month as well as things that you would like to accomplish or see get done but haven't yet committed to doing yourself.

♦ Using the litmus test and two filter questions, review each item on your list. Determine which items are not to be delegated and which are possibilities for delegation. Assume that you will find someone to whom you can delegate and that the person can be instructed to adequately perform the tasks.

♦ Put your list of possible delegated jobs in rank-order according to how much you dislike doing them yourself. You should have a final delegation list that represents at least 10 percent of your total number of jobs and chores on your initial inventory.

♦ Draw a heavy line under the first 10 percent on your rank-ordered list.

Tag, You're It

Today you will continue your training in delegation skills. Delegating tasks to others—instead of doing too much to please others—represents a major step toward your recovery. Because you have underused delegation in the past, you will have to practice today's scripts in order to build your competence and confidence.

Now that you have a list of jobs that you made yesterday to off-load onto others, to whom will you delegate?

Delegation Targets

As you consider delegation candidates, don't worry about whether the individuals know how to do the chores or jobs already. You should simply assume that, if necessary, you'll provide training, guidance, and/or supervision.

However, it is essential that you adopt a creative and flexible attitude as you look for people to whom you will delegate. There may be some minor obstacles to overcome as you downsize your own workload. But, as long as you maintain the will to delegate, be assured that you can find the way.

The only unacceptable alternative is to believe that there is nobody to whom you can delegate any of your chores or tasks. In your selection process yesterday, you eliminated chores for which you determined that your participation was absolutely essential. Therefore, for the tasks you selected to delegate, you *can* be replaced.

If you are committed to breaking the people-pleasing cycle, you must also be determined to delegate a minimum of 10 percent of your current workload to someone else. When you maintain a resolute stance, you *will* find a solution to the problem of locating delegation targets.

For example, you may decide to hire some people to whom you could then delegate chores and other work. Do a cost-benefit analysis of hiring help. As you do so, be sure to factor in the value of reduced stress, improved health, and enhanced quality of life that you will gain from the time liberated by delegation.

If you earn a salary or other income, compare the relative cost of doing chores yourself (based on your current market value) with the expense of hiring someone else to do them. For example, one former patient of mine is a high-priced attorney. Using the market value formulary, this woman finally gave herself permission to hire a cleaning crew when she realized that it was costing her $250 an hour to do her own housework.

Another creative solution is to use time and energy you pool together with a group of friends. For example, another of my patients contacted the group of parents that were already in her school car pool. She proposed that the group also "pool" their errands. Now, on every weekday, one of the car pool drivers spends an extra hour or two (maximum) doing errands for everyone else. Items such as dry cleaning and market or drug store purchases are dropped off along with the children in the car pool. With this method, each person spends only one day a week doing errands while benefiting from delegating errands to the other drivers on the other four days.

Of course, the most likely place to find delegation candidates is probably right under your own roof or among your closest friends. After all, the people closest to you are among those for whom you do too much. It is high time to restore the balance between what you do for them and what they do for you in return.

Keep in mind that people who truly love and care for you will want to support you. As was noted earlier: In healthy relationships, people need you because they love you; they don't love you because they need you.

If your family and friends truly care for you, they won't want to benefit from your exhaustion, stress, and unhappiness. By allowing the gross imbalance to persist between how much you do for others and how little they do for you, you are tacitly endorsing your own exploitation. In so doing, you not only victimize yourself, but you also inadvertently turn those you love into perpetrators of your mistreatment.

Assigning Targets to Tasks. Take out your 10 percent list of chores, tasks, jobs, or projects. This is your "For Delegation" list.

Next to every item on your list, indicate the name of the person or persons to whom you will delegate the task. You may use the same person for more than one job or more than one person for each job, as you see fit.

In the unlikely event that, after an exhaustive and creative search, you still cannot come up with a person to whom you can delegate one particular task, you may substitute that task for another from your original inventory. In other words, if you need to take back the responsibility for a chore from your delegation list, you must substitute another in its place so that your 10 percent criterion is still met.

Writing Delegation Scripts

For each task, you will prepare a delegation script. Write the sentences that you will say. For purposes of practice and rehearsal, write the likely responses of the target.

The basic elements of an effective delegation script are simple. But, the attitude you convey while making the delegation is critical. In other words, *how* you delegate is every bit as important as *what* you say.

▶ *You must be assertive and appear comfortable with delegating the task. It is imperative that you do not ask the target's permission to delegate.*

And you must not apologize for requesting help or assigning work, although you may certainly indicate that you are appreciative. The appropriate time to give praise, however, is after the job is completed.

Here are the six steps of effective delegation:

1. State your directions concerning the task you are delegating to the target. Your instructions should be as specific as possible; offer advice especially if this is the first time you have delegated a particular task.

2. Indicate the time frame/deadline for completion of the task.

3. Confirm that the target understands the directions.

4. Give the target the opportunity to ask questions; answer every question clearly and respectfully.

5. Respond to resistance with the Broken Record technique: Acknowledge the resistance and label the emotion you hear; then repeat your directions and time frame expectation.

6. Indicate your appreciation before the task is completed; offer expressions of praise and "thank you" after the work is done.

Following is a sample delegation script for a *recovered* people-pleaser (RPP) who is delegating the task of going to the supermarket to her teenage daughter. The RPP wants the daughter to use a shopping list and to unpack and put away the groceries in time for dinner.

Recovered People-Pleaser (RPP): "Honey, I need you to go to the market for some groceries. Here are the shopping list and some cash. Ask the produce man to help you select the fruit or vegetables. If you have any other questions or can't find something, be sure you ask anyone who works in the market to help you. They're very nice and they'll be glad to assist you.

"I'll be home if you need to call me about anything. Please bring the groceries home and put them away before 5 o'clock so I will have time to make dinner. Do you understand everything?"

Daughter: [Looks over list] "Okay. Can I get some things that I want for snacks?"

RPP: "Sure, a few things. But don't buy more than two or three bags or packages of snacks. Okay? Do you understand the list? Any other questions?"

Daughter: "Do I have to go now? I wanted to go over to Susie's house for a while to do some homework. Can't I go tonight after dinner or maybe tomorrow?"

RPP: "I understand that you're a bit bothered that your plans are changing. But I do need the groceries *today,* home and unpacked by 5 o'clock. If you get everything done before five, you can go to Susie's for an hour or so but just to do homework. I'm planning dinner for 7 o'clock so you need to be home by 6:45. Okay?"

Daughter: "Are you sure you really want me to get all this fruit and stuff? I'm not very good at picking produce. Maybe you should go to the market and get the kind of fruit and vegetables you want."

RPP: "I know this is a little new for you, but the produce man will be happy to help you pick everything. If you pay attention and ask him to explain, you'll learn how to pick fruit and vegetables as well as I can. Just get the things on the list and a few snacks, and remember that I need everything unpacked and put away by 5 o'clock. Anything else?"

Daughter: "No, I guess not."

RPP: "Thanks a lot, honey. I'll see you before five."

You should write a delegation script for each of your tasks to delegate. Keep the scripts quite short. If you find yourself overexplaining or repeating yourself—other than for purposes of the Broken Record—you are going overboard and undermining your credibility and authority to delegate.

▶ *Effective delegation is direct, brief, and to the point*

Practice your delegation instructions out loud at least three to five times. Pay close attention to your tone and inflection. Be sure that you eliminate apologies or any hint of guilt.

If the target senses that you feel the slightest bit wobbly about issuing directions, he or she may be encouraged to manipulate and resist your delegation efforts. But, even if such attempts to resist are made, you know how to stand your ground with the Broken Record technique.

Adjust Your Attitude About Delegating

Family members and other targets may balk at first when you delegate some new responsibilities to them. But, don't accept helplessness as an excuse. With instruction and supervision, even small children can help out with daily chores.

Whatever the arguments and resistance from others to your delegation instructions, you must not capitulate and regress to your old self-defeating people-pleasing habits. Do not allow yourself to be manipulated by passive-aggressive excuses such as, "I forgot that you asked me to do that," or by procrastination attempts such as, "I'll do it later."

▶ *Loosen up on your compulsive and perfectionist tendencies.*

For example, it really is not important that the towels or underwear are being folded differently than you would fold them; what *is* important is that someone else is doing the laundry and you are not.

You must steadfastly resist other maneuvers, however flattering their disguise. Your response to, "Can you show me how to do that again? You do it so much better than I do, are you sure it wouldn't be better if you just did it?" is an emphatic "No. Your way is just fine. The important thing is that you are doing it, and I really appreciate your efforts."

Resist your impatience and impulse to snatch the chore back to do it yourself. While doing the work yourself may seem easier or more efficient in the moment than training someone else or tolerating their mistakes, you will suffer in the long run by undermining your own delegation efforts.

If you reverse yourself and take back what you have delegated, you will be the big loser in the long run. Or, if you oversupervise and wind up doing the work yourself in the guise of showing someone else the "correct" way, you will merely defeat your purpose.

Finally, do not make the error of filling up the time you have liberated through delegation by doing still more chores and favors for others. Learning to delegate to others will help you recover only if you use the time and energy you have restored to take better care of yourself.

You may find it hard to believe and certainly paradoxical, but permitting yourself 20 minutes a day to do nothing but rest and relax may be the most productive time you have spent in years!

Use the precious time you have earned through effective delegation to feel satisfied with your successful efforts. Remember, even if you spent every waking moment doing things for others, you would still feel that you never do enough to feel truly satisfied. That is because the people-pleasing pit is indeed bottomless.

But, you can give yourself the gift of self-approval for spending time to take care of yourself. Don't worry that you are turning into a selfish person. You are not and no one thinks that about you. Besides, you are no doubt still doing plenty for other people. Taking care of your needs is simply good insurance that you will be healthier and happier when you choose to spend time doing things for the people you care about and love.

Summary of Day 11

♦ Identify targets for your delegated tasks. Be flexible and creative. If you have the will to delegate, you will find the people that are required.

♦ Write the target's name or identity next to each item on your 10 percent "For Delegation" list.

♦ Write a script, using the six steps of effective delegation. Keep the scripts brief and to the point. Do not ask *if* you can delegate; state politely but firmly that you are instructing the target to do something for you. Indicate your appreciation but resist all efforts to be manipulated back into people-pleasing and doing the chores yourself.

♦ Practice your scripts out loud. Eliminate all apologies or indications of guilt or discomfort.

It's Okay Not to Be Nice

Today you will begin work on changing a central, but problematic, word in your self-concept: the word *nice*.

The reality is that you probably don't yet fully believe that it is okay *not* to be nice all the time to everyone. The notion may still seem a bit threatening because you have identified for so long with the trait.

> ► *Your recovery depends, in part, on accepting that it really is okay* not *to be nice.*

In fact, you now know you have been paying a very high price for making *nice* the core of your self-concept.

Since your new and improved self-concept will not revolve around being nice, you need to develop a new vocabulary to describe who you are now. Today is your opportunity to replace *nice*—a weak, wishy-washy word—with some far more interesting, better descriptions.

All you need now is a little help from your friends.

The purpose of this exercise is to find out how others see you—and how you see yourself—when you explicitly eliminate the word *nice*. The data you collect will provide useful building blocks from which you can construct your new self-concept.

By thinking about yourself in new, different terms—that do not include *nice*—you will continue to make long strides toward recovery. And, by asking the people closest to you to describe your personality without using *nice*, you are subtly encouraging them to think of you in new ways, too.

What Are You If You're Not Nice?

Collecting Data from Others. On a separate piece of paper (not in your journal), make a list of five people's names, beginning with your own as number one. The list should include the four people whom you consider to be the closest to you emotionally. Since you will need to speak with them as soon as possible, make sure that the four people on your list can be reached at least by telephone.

Then, make a list of 10 words that you believe are accurate descriptors of who you are—without using the word *nice*. Naturally, since you have only been in training to recover for slightly less than two weeks, your list will still reflect some of your old self-concept. But, by deliberate exclusion, it will not include the word *nice*.

After you have written your 10 words, contact a person on your list. Read the following few sentences to him/her, and ask for 10 words that describe how that person sees you without permitting the word *nice*.

You should say something like: "I'm working hard on changing my people-pleasing habits. As part of my recovery, I need you to give me 10 words that you believe are accurate descriptions of my personality. You can use any words you want with one exception: you cannot use the word *nice*."

Write the words down on your paper under the following heading:

According to [name of person] these 10 words accurately describe my personality without using the word nice.

Continue collecting lists of 10 words from each of the remaining three people in the same manner. When you have finished, you will have 50 words (although there will likely be some overlap or repetition) that describe how you see yourself and how the four people who are closest to you describe your personality. The lists provide a rich inventory of descriptive words from which you may draw as you construct your new and improved self-concept.

Keep in mind that these four people have known you to be a consistent people-pleaser. In all likelihood, they have even been among the beneficiaries of your many giving efforts. Their words, therefore, will reflect their tendency to see you in a people-pleasing light.

Consider their descriptions carefully and think about which words you would choose to maintain in your new self-concept as a person who no longer suffers from the Disease to Please.

Notice, too, that one of your most important accomplishments today has been to notify these four people that you are recovering from the Disease to Please. Since you intend to carry through with your commitment to recover, this notice will serve to alert those closest to you that their relationships with you will be changing too. You will no longer make their needs more important than your own.

In all likelihood, you observed that no one, including you, was particularly stumped or blocked by making *nice* off limits on the lists. If *nice* were, in fact, so central and essential to your self-concept or to the way others see you, the task of making a list excluding *nice* would have been very difficult.

Composing Your Desired Self-Concept

Ask yourself, How do I want to think of myself now that I am a recovered people-pleaser? This time, you may write 10 words or descriptive phrases in your journal under the heading, My Ideal Self-Concept as a Recovered People-Pleaser.

You may include many of the same words from your initial list as well as those from the other people's lists if they fit into your ideal self-concept. But, you are under no obligation to include any words previously listed. The choice is up to you, with one exception. You should again omit *nice* from your ideal self-description. This final list represents ways of behaving, thinking, and feeling that you will strive to fulfill as part of your recovery.

The "Act-as-If" Cure

Starting today, you are to act as if you are the person described on your ideal self-concept list. Use the 10 words or phrases you have chosen for your ideal self-concept as prescriptions to guide your behavior, thoughts, and feelings.

The instruction to *act as if* you are your ideal self doesn't require you to do anything dramatic or to allocate extra time. It simply requires that you adopt the *act-as-if* mindset. You can begin today by assuming the mindset for a segment of the day—morning, afternoon, or evening. Increase the amount of time during which you assume the act-as-if mindset each subsequent day. Shortly, it will become second nature to simply *be* your ideal self.

▶ *The closer your ideal self-concept is to the way you actually behave, the more your self-esteem will benefit. The most direct way to build your self-esteem is to act-as-if you are your ideal self.*

The instruction to act as if you are your ideal self is not meant to ask you to lie or in any way represent yourself falsely. Instead, these should be personality traits or qualities of character toward which you strive as your "best self."

The purpose of devising and acting like your ideal self-concept is to define a desirable goal for self-improvement that is entirely within reach of attainment.

Summary of Day 12

♦ Make a list of 10 answers to the question Who Am I? without using the word *nice*.

♦ Collect 10 word descriptors from four people closest to you that describe your personality without using the word *nice*.

♦ Take note that you have informed each of the four individuals that you are working to recover from your people-pleasing habits.

♦ Review the lists as useful feedback about yourself and your relationship with others. Focus on accepting that it is okay not to be nice.

♦ Create a list of 10 words or descriptive phrases that comprise your ideal self-concept as a recovered people-pleaser without using *nice*.

♦ *Act-as-if* you *are* your ideal self for part of the day today and for increasingly longer periods of each day that follows.

The Anger Scale

Today you will begin developing your anger and conflict management skills. Because you have used people-pleasing as a way to avoid anger and conflict, your experience managing either your own or other people's anger is severely limited. Now, you will learn how to let yourself experience and express anger safely and appropriately, without losing control.

Developing Your Personalized Anger Scale

You will begin by developing a personalized anger scale. You will use the scale to rate the level of your anger as soon as you recognize that something or someone is disturbing you.

Using an anger rating scale is a highly effective way to maintain control. The very act of objectifying your feelings by analyzing and rating them immediately puts distance between your emotions and your impulses to act them out inappropriately.

Moreover, by using a scale to rate your anger, you also put your mind in charge. As soon as your mind is running things instead of your volatile emotions, your anger will be effectively managed and under control.

► *The challenge of anger management is to develop methods that interrupt the uncontrolled escalation of anger into realms of loss of control.*

Anger management should begin as soon as the pot begins to turn warm rather than waiting until it is threatening to boil over.

To make your own anger scale, draw a straight vertical line about an inch from the left side of a standard-size sheet of paper. Use the entire length of the sheet for your line.

Divide the line in half; mark the bottom "zero," the midpoint "50," and the top "100." Then indicate with somewhat smaller hatch marks the positions of 10, 20, 30, and on up the scale.

Next to 0, write "calm/not angry at all." Now, you are to provide a verbal label for each 10-point demarcation on the scale. You will need 10 words, ordered from low to high, which represent increasing levels of emotional intensity on your anger scale.

Below is a list of words, in no particular order, which can be used to describe various degrees of anger arousal. You may select your labels from the list below or provide words or phrases of your own.

You will note that the actual word *angry* appears on the list below only once. You may use *angry* to define any level on the scale that you wish, *but you may use the word only once.*

Sample Words to Use on Your Personalized Anger Scale

Infuriated	Hassled	Disappointed
Upset	Burned up	Irritated
Resentful	Boiling over	Frustrated
Exasperated	Fuming	Furious
Angry	Seething	Rage
Impatient	Blowing my top	Fury
Vexation	Blowing a fuse	Antagonized
Vexed	Displeased	Dissatisfied
Enragement	Annoyed	Bothered
Enraged	Irate	Disturbed
Vehement	Pissed off	Aggravated
Passionate	Ticked off	Infuriated
Provoked	Ferocious	Vicious

Rating Your Anger. You now have a personalized anger scale with 10 incremental reference points that are emotionally meaningful to you. Now, you will need some incidents of anger to rate in order to really develop proficiency with the scale.

You will need to search back through your memory. It doesn't matter if you have never actually expressed the anger to others. Your purpose now is simply to recall some instances when your anger registered someplace on the scale higher than 0.

Here are some questions designed to "jog" your memory of incidents from your past when you may have experienced some anger. You'll notice that the term *some degree of anger* is used in each as a broad reference to any and all emotions that would register on your personalized anger scale. Try to come up with an example from your memory that generally fits each question. Of course, if the question does not apply to you, skip it and move on to the next one.

When you have decided the rating for each incident, write a few identifying words (e.g., fight with father 1992; or argument with coworker over computer backup) to label each event. Then, place these brief descriptions at the appropriate numeric level on the anger scale. You should write your incidents to the right of your word labels at the appropriate scale rating level.

Events or Incidents that Made You Angry

1. Can you recall a time when you felt some degree of anger toward your mother?

2. Can you recall a time when you felt some degree of anger toward your father?

3. Can you recall a time when you felt some degree of anger toward a sibling?

4. Can you recall a time when you felt some degree of anger toward your spouse or lover/girlfriend/boyfriend?

5. Can you recall a time when you felt some degree of anger involving money or a financial transaction?

6. Can you recall a time when you felt some degree of anger involving a sexual situation?

7. Can you recall a time when you felt some degree of anger toward someone that you work or worked for, or someone who works or worked for you?

8. Can you recall a time when you felt some degree of anger toward a coworker or customer/client?

9. Can you recall a time when you felt some degree of anger toward a doctor?

10. Can you recall a time when you felt some degree of anger toward yourself?

Identify Your Set-Point for Action

Somewhere on your personalized scale is a point beyond which your anger threatens to escalate rapidly, erupt, or otherwise cross over into dangerous, out-of-control territory. Using your personal history and information, identify that point on the scale where you believe that your own anger threatens to escalate dangerously unless action is taken immediately to resolve the problem and reduce its intensity.

Danger does not mean physical or literal threat of injury. Your own danger point is the level at which you feel highly uncomfortable or concerned that your anger *may* go out of control.

There is considerable individual variability as to where this point is on the scale. For some people, the point is at 50; for others, loss of control isn't a possibility until their anger is at 75 or 80. Still others have a lower set-point for dangerous anger at 40 or 45.

The purpose is to personalize your own level of dangerous anger. Decide what level on the scale represents the intensity where you feel concerned about losing control. Then, take the number you select and subtract 10 points in order to give yourself a safety zone in which to act *before* you reach your danger point.

The danger level *minus* 10 points equals your set-point for action. Circle your set-point number with a blue marker; then circle your danger level in red. When any situation reaches the set-point, you will know that you must immediately move into problem solving and conflict resolution mode (which is covered in Day 19).

How to Use Your Anger Rating Scale. You now have had practice placing incidents from your past on your personalized anger rating scale. Starting today, you are going to pay attention to even the slightest ignition of anger. Remember, anything on the scale that is over 0 means that your anger, however mild, is ignited.

You are no longer going to deny, suppress, or try to avoid your own anger. And you will no longer use people-pleasing tactics just to prevent someone else from becoming angry with you. Unexpressed anger has a tendency to bubble and increase in intensity under the surface. All too often, suppressed anger increases to a dangerous point where it is no longer very manageable. Paradoxically, overcontrolled anger almost invariably produces out-of-control eruptions.

As of today, your new policy is to notice and become aware of your anger at the earliest point possible. This means that you want to keep a watchful eye on the low end of your anger scale where disturbances, frustrations, irritations, and annoyances register. You now understand that these are precursors to more escalated anger.

Make at least three copies of your anger scale (with all the labels and incident notations on it) to keep in your home, office, and in your wallet or purse. Work on developing an awareness of the earliest warning signs of your anger. Take particular note when you feel tired, stressed, in pain, premenstrual, or other conditions that could make you prone to becoming upset.

As soon as you begin to feel slightly anxious, out of sorts, irritated, or annoyed with someone or something, take out your rating scale. Determine that unless you can affirm that you feel calm/not angry at all (i.e., at zero), your anger may have ignited, albeit subtly.

If you cannot affirm that you are at zero, make a rating on your scale even if you cannot yet identify the source of your upset or annoyance. Once you are on the scale, you will need to keep a watchful eye on your level of anger. This simply means that you have an awareness that you are slightly or more than slightly upset and that your anger *may* escalate.

Once your awareness is awakened, you will notice movement up or down the scale. You must pay close attention if your anger is escalating near your set-point. Remember, once you hit the set-point, you have only 10 points to spare before things get potentially a lot hotter.

If you hit your set-point, you need to take action to lower your anger level through unilateral means or through an appropriate problem-solving interaction with another person. You will learn these skills over the next few days.

Summary of Day 13

♦ Make a personalized 100-point anger scale using words of your choice to reference each 10-point increment.

♦ Rate incidents from your personal life history using the questions above to jog your memory; place the incidents on the rating scale at the appropriate levels.

♦ Find your set-point for action, which is 10 points *lower* than your personal danger zone. Your danger zone is the point where you are at risk of losing control of your anger.

♦ Make copies of your personalized scale so you have it ready whenever you feel more emotionally aroused than "calm/not angry."

♦ By rating your anger and staying aware of its escalation and de-escalation, you will put your mind in charge and, therefore, be better able to manage and control your anger.

The Relaxation Breath

Today and tomorrow, you will learn two key exercises for anger management: the Relaxation Breath and Progressive Relaxation.

Select a place in your home or elsewhere where you can be quiet, alone, and comfortable. Preferably the area should have a place to lie down—such as a bed, couch, hammock, or reclining chair—but you may lie on the floor if you find it comfortable.

The Relaxation Breath will entail three to five minutes of deep, rhythmic breathing. Depending on your tastes and preferences, you may soften or dim the lights, play soft, slow instrumental music, or light scented or plain candles.

The idea is for you to easily create an environment that is conducive to relaxation. Don't do anything that requires much time or difficulty to set up since you will be doing this repeatedly over the next week or so and, thereafter, as you progress independently in your recovery.

When the space is ready, lie down and close your eyes. Take a slow, deep breath through your nose. Using the "one/one-thousand, two/one-thousand, three/on-thousand method," count to five seconds as you inhale through your nose.

At the top of your inhalation, hold your breath for one second. Then counting in the same manner, exhale slowly through your mouth for five seconds.

Repeat the inhaling breath through your nose counting to five seconds, hold your breath for one second, and exhale through your mouth for five seconds. As you continue this deep breathing, visualize the ocean at high tide. As you breath in, visualize a wave washing gently up the sandy shore. See the water appear to stop for just one second before it reverses direction and returns slowly back to sea.

The visualization of the wave washing ashore at high tide will help regulate your deep rhythmic breathing. Continue this exercise of deep rhythmic breathing in through your nose and out through your mouth for three to five minutes.

The Relaxation Breath is the basic breathing form for almost all forms of deep relaxation, self-hypnosis, meditation, and other methods of stress reduction. If all you do is practice the Relaxation Breath for five minutes, once a day, several days a week, you will benefit your overall physical and emotional health.

Do not *try* to relax; just let it happen. By definition, when you are trying hard at anything, you are not relaxing. Don't try to do the Relaxation Breath or other relaxation techniques flawlessly, correctly, or even very well. Again, once you are observing and judging your performance, you're really not relaxing anymore.

The Progressive Relaxation Exercise

After you have been doing the Relaxation Breath for three to five minutes, you may begin the second exercise known as Progressive Relaxation.

While you continue deep rhythmic breathing, focus your mind's eye, or concentration, on your right hand only. At the same time, say the following phrase out loud or meditate on it subvocally: "My right hand is growing heavy and warm."

After about 30 seconds or so, you will feel your right hand actually becoming heavier, sinking its weight into the bed or couch where you are lying. And, you will feel the heat intensifying in your right hand.

Next, shift your focus to your right arm and, as you continue breathing deeply, say the phrase: "My right arm is growing heavy and warm."

When you feel your right arm become heavy and warm (within 30 to 60 seconds), move the focus of concentration to your right shoulder. Continue breathing deeply, meditating on the "heavy and warm" phrase as you gradually shift your focus of concentration from one segment of your body to the next.

Notice how the warmth spreads throughout your body, radiating into your extremities, down to the tips of your fingers and toes. Continue shifting from one body segment to the next until you conclude with your left foot and toes.

Your purpose is to progressively relax every portion of your body. The entire exercise should take between five and fifteen minutes.

Over the next several days, you will be using the two relaxation exercises you have just learned in combination with other methods of anger management. You will also find them very effective for general anxiety and stress management.

Summary of Day 14

♦ Practice the Relaxation Breath for three to five minutes at least twice today. Don't try hard or attempt to evaluate yourself; just do it. Let relaxation happen.

♦ Then continuing the Relaxation Breath, move on to Progressive Relaxation. Practice the entire sequence of Progressive Relaxation beginning with your right hand, going all around your body and ending with your left foot.

♦ Today you can consider your relaxation exercises your two pleasurable activities.

Anger-Up

The goal of anger management is to teach you how to interrupt and de-escalate developing anger. One important way to do this is to apply self-induced relaxation to counteract aroused anger.

In order to practice reducing your anger, you will first need to learn to *make* yourself feel angry. By permitting yourself to become angry in a safe setting, you can learn how your thoughts and feelings operate to either intensify anger and make matters worse, or to de-escalate anger and calm things down. As you will see, "anger-up" thoughts and feelings magnify, exaggerate, and blow things out of proportion. "Anger-down" thoughts and feelings, in contrast, are rational, measured, and aimed at maintaining control.

Writing Visualization Scenarios to Arouse Anger

On Day 13, you recalled incidents from your past in which you felt angry. For each of the incidents you could recall, you rated the level of your anger on your personalized anger scale.

Now, select two incidents from your personal anger scale: One should be the incident that you rated highest on your scale; the second should reflect a somewhat lower or moderate degree of anger. If there are ties or more than one incident from which to choose, select the incidents for which you have the clearest or most distinct recall—perhaps the most recent incidents.

You will need to write a few paragraphs about each incident for use as anger-induction scenarios. Your goal should be to create two scenes that, when visualized in your mind, will allow you to actually feel angry. The scenes should trigger an emotional reaction much like what you felt in the actual incident.

Think of yourself as a method actor who needs to become very angry in order to effectively play a scene. Method actors draw on their actual life experiences to re-create emotional reactions from sensory memories. They do this through visualization and recall of the sensory cues associated with the feelings they are trying to re-create.

In your case, you will be using both incidents from your past to elicit feelings of anger. To do so, you will need to re-create in your mind the scene or setting that you most closely associate with the peak of your anger relative to each incident. In describing the physical setting of your anger experience, be sure to include whatever other sensory memories you can recall that will make your visualization vivid. Was it raining or windy? Was the sun shining? What noises could you hear? Were you or other people involved in yelling or crying?

Recall especially your internal physiological sensations of anger. Was your heart pounding hard and rapidly? Were your fists and jaw clenched? Were you perspiring? Can you re-create the tension in your body?

For this purpose, you don't need to rehash all the factual details of the argument or present the case of who was right and wrong. But, you do need to recall enough of each situation to enable you to return to the incident in your mind and to re-create the anger that you felt.

Add "Anger-Up" Thinking. Since your purpose is to elicit as much genuine anger as possible, you should intentionally include "anger-up" thoughts in your scenario. These are actually dysfunctional thoughts that serve only to increase the intensity of your anger. Anger-up thinking typifies the way you talk to yourself when you feel wronged or mistreated. Doing so will reinforce the angry feelings you are trying to re-create. By deliberately writing anger-up thoughts in your scenario, you will become sensitized to them and therefore better able to recognize their toxic effects when you next find yourself in an anger-provoking situation.

Here are some definitions and examples of anger-up thoughts:

♦ *Making Bad Situations Much Worse.* This kind of thinking makes catastrophes out of already bad or unfortunate situations. Using words like *awful, worst, devastating,* or *terrible* increases the intensity of your anger. Other typical "catastrophizing" thoughts include:

"I absolutely can't handle this. I hate the way he's yelling at me."

"This is the worst thing that's ever happened."

"This is terrible/horrible/awful/dreadful/horrifying!"

♦ *Sabotaging Shoulds.* This kind of thinking makes demands or imposes arbitrary rules on how you or others *should* behave (or, *ought, need to be, expected to be, have to be*). Demanding that people and situations be a certain way just sets you up to feel angry and upset—and justified with your anger—when your expectations aren't met. Examples include:

"People should never reject or criticize me because of all the nice things I do for them."

"He/she shouldn't treat me that way!"

"After everything I've done for them, they should be there for me when I need them."

♦ *Negative Labeling and/or Obscenities.* Obscene words and phrases increase anger, as do negatively charged labels assigned to people or situations. Examples include:

"That slimy creep!"

"This computer is a cheap piece of junk/crap!"

♦ *Magnification and Exaggeration.* This takes situations and inflates the significance, patterns, or tendencies far beyond the limit of what is factual. Words like *never* or *always* magnify and exaggerate perception and, therefore, increase responsive anger. Examples of this thinking are:

"He is never ready on time. Now my whole day will be wrecked!"

"She is always thinking only about herself."

"I will never forgive him for doing that to me."

♦ *Mind Reading, Assuming Facts, and One-Sided Thinking.* This is when you assume facts that support your anger without verifying that they are true or considering other possible explanations. Assigning blame all to one party or attributing negative motives without verifying the facts tends to increase the intensity of your anger. Examples include:

"This whole thing is his fault."

"I caused this terrible thing to happen. I'm entirely to blame."

"This guy is just trying to make me lose it."

Completing Your Scenarios. You should now have two completed scenarios of incidents from the past that have aroused your anger. Each scenario is based on an incident from your past that has aroused your anger to some degree.

Your two completed scenarios of incidents from your past should each include one or two descriptive paragraphs that enable you to "see" yourself getting angry. Your descriptions should recall both the internal sensations as well as the outward manifestations of your anger.

Your scenarios should also include at least two or three anger-increasing or anger-up thoughts, such as those defined above. You may combine two or more types of anger-up thoughts in one statement.

Practice Relaxation. Tomorrow, you will see how to combine the relaxation exercises with your anger-producing scenarios. It is important to practice the Relaxation Breath and Progressive Relaxation. The more adept you become at self-induced relaxation, the better you will be at anger management.

Summary of Day 15

♦ Select two incidents from your past in which your anger was aroused; at least one should be reflective of a high degree of anger.

♦ Write a scenario for each incident that enables you to "see" yourself in the situation when your anger peaked. Use good visual and sensory description. Recall the internal sensations of anger as well as the outward manifestations.

♦ Include two or three statements of anger-up thinking in each scenario.

♦ Practice your relaxation exercises.

Anger-Down

Today you will teach yourself first to become angry and then to interrupt and reverse the arousal. You will do this by alternating the anger-induction scenarios with relaxation breathing and "anger-down" thoughts.

When you complete today's training, you will have far less basis to fear your own anger. You will know that you have the power to make yourself angry *and*, more importantly, that you have the ability to interrupt escalating anger and calm yourself down.

"Anger-Down" Thoughts

Yesterday, you incorporated "anger-up" thoughts—flawed thinking that increases the intensity of anger—into your scenarios. Today, you will learn to counter the anger-up thinking with calming, rational statements to yourself that take specific aim at the toxic anger-intensifying thoughts.

Here are examples of anger-down thoughts:

◆ *Countering Thoughts That Make Bad Situations Much Worse.* Counteract extreme, dramatic thinking that turns a problem into a catastrophe. Keep problems downsized into irritations or disappointments with which you can cope. Examples include:

"This *isn't* the worst thing that's ever happened. It's just an irritating problem that I can handle."

"This is a bit upsetting but it's not terrible/horrible/awful. I can get over being upset. This is like lots of things that I have handled well before now."

"Stay cool. I can deal with this. Life brings plenty of tragedies and catastrophes but this isn't one of them. It's just a problem that I can think of as a challenge."

♦ *Countering Sabotaging Shoulds.* Reframe demands as preferences or wishes. Remind yourself that you are not in charge of the world and that other people are not required to do things or feel certain ways just because you say they *should.* Examples to anger-down include:

"I wish that people wouldn't criticize me, but I can find a way to benefit from their feedback."

"I would feel better if I knew that people would be there if I needed them, but I can't make them do something just because I say they should."

"I wish he had treated me differently, but I'm not in charge of other people."

♦ *Countering Negative Labeling and Obscenities.* Answer back to your swearing and obscenities; disabuse yourself from using arbitrary negative labels that just serve to make you angrier. Examples of anger-down thoughts include:

"He's not a slimy creep; he's just a guy that's irritating me."

"This computer is simply broken and it can be fixed. It's actually quite an impressive and useful machine, not a piece of crap."

♦ *Countering Magnification and Exaggeration.* Don't allow exaggerated words to stand. People rarely fit the "always" or "never" categories. Replace the exaggerated, magnified statements with measured, accurate ones. Examples of anger-down thoughts include:

"He's late frequently, but not always. Besides, I don't have to let his tardiness ruin my whole day. I can get over feeling this time pressure."

"She seems to think of herself first a lot of the time. But I don't know how she *always* thinks. Still, she isn't someone I can count on as a good friend."

"It may be difficult for me to forgive him; but in time the memory will fade and the hurt will go away. Someday maybe I'll forgive him, but not right now."

♦ *Countering Mind Reading, Assuming Facts, and One-Sided Thinking.* Don't allow yourself to assume facts without verifying them. It is very unusual for only one person to be at fault or to blame for something bad that happens. There is usually more than one reason for something happening. Examples of anger-down thoughts include:

"The whole thing wasn't *just* his fault. He may have contributed to the problem, but he's not entirely to blame."

"I am too quick to blame myself for bad things that happen. I'm not powerful enough to have caused all of this to happen. But I will take a look at my behavior and see if I had a hand in the problem so I won't do the same thing again."

"This guy is irritating me, but he doesn't know me well enough or even care to try to make me 'lose it.' He's just a guy doing something that is bothering me, but I can cope with it and not 'lose it' at all."

Writing Anger-Up and Anger-Down Statements. Take out both of your written scenarios from yesterday. Look at Scenario One and underline the anger-up thoughts. Do the same for Scenario Two.

Now, take a fresh sheet of paper and divide it down the middle with a vertical line. On the left side, write the title, "Anger-Up Thoughts" and on the right side, write the title, "Anger-Down Thoughts."

One at a time, copy the underlined statements from your scenarios to the anger-up side of your paper. For each anger-up statement, write a countering anger-down thought based on the explanations and examples above.

Check your anger-down thoughts to be sure that they are accurate and do not contain inflammatory or exaggerating words or ideas.

Putting It Together: Anger-Up, Anger-Down

You are now ready to put your anger management skills together. Begin by doing your Relaxation Breath exercise for about three to five minutes.

When you feel quite relaxed, sit up. With one of your scenarios in mind, read the accompanying anger-up statements out loud. Say them like you mean them; feel the anger build. Your intention is to re-create the feeling of anger. Your breathing rate should increase; you may notice your stomach tightening and your muscles tensing throughout your body. Feel your anger for at least one minute.

Once you feel angry, the next step is to calm yourself down. Recline again and resume your Relaxation Breath. Visualize the tide washing up the shore and out again to sea. Focus your concentration on your limbs as they grow heavy and warm. Notice how relaxed you are beginning to feel.

After a minute or so, say the anger-down thoughts from Scenario One out loud. You are using these anger-down thoughts to specifically counter the anger-up statements you just used to induce angry feelings. Be sure that you are no longer clenching your fists or jaw and that your muscles have relaxed throughout your body.

Let yourself relax for at least a few minutes. When you feel fully relaxed again, sit up and repeat the anger-up statements from your first scenario out loud again. Raise your voice and clench your fists. Get into it: Really try to become angry again. Try pounding your fists on a table or stomping your feet on the floor to emphasize your anger.

After a minute or two of feeling angry, resume the relaxation position. Once again, resume your relaxed deep breathing and say the anger-down thoughts out loud, using a calm, soft soothing voice.

Do the cycle of relaxation/anger/relaxation twice using Scenario One. Then, repeat the exercise using Scenario Two. Always begin and end with relaxation.

Don't be afraid to make yourself angry. If you can create feelings of anger on cue, you can get rid of them on demand as well. Doing both—arousing anger and then reducing it again—demonstrates that you are in control of your anger, rather than your anger being in control of you.

When you have completed the anger-up, anger-down sequences with both scenarios, take a moment to recognize what an enormously important skill you are learning. You have the ability to calm yourself down when your anger has been aroused. You have learned the relaxation exercises so that you can apply them when you need to calm down. By teaching yourself how to induce relaxation, you have created a behavioral tranquilizer for your anger.

Summary of Day 16

♦ Write anger-down corrective thoughts to counter anger-up toxic thoughts.

♦ Make a two-column list of anger-up statements on the left and anger-down statements on the right that you take from your anger-incident scenarios.

- Put the anger management training session together by alternating anger-up and anger-down cycles of relaxation and anger arousal. Creating anger with anger-up thoughts followed by defusing and calming with relaxation and anger-down thoughts is the basis of anger management training.

- You now know that you can interrupt escalating anger and calm yourself down. You have demonstrated your ability to do this. With continued practice, you will gain confidence in your anger management skills.

TIME OUT

As a recovered people-pleaser, you will no longer need to resort to appeasement tactics in order to avoid conflict or confrontation. This doesn't mean that you will now look for reasons to become angry or to start fights with people close to you. Nor does it mean that you will engage in hostile confrontations with family, friends, or strangers.

Keep in mind that it takes at least two people to have an angry confrontation or a destructive conflict. While you cannot directly control what other people do, you *can* exercise a good deal of influence over them by controlling and managing your own behavior.

If there are people close to you with whom you have had destructive conflicts in the past or with whom you fear that you might have a confrontation, you may solicit their cooperation and participation in preventative conflict management. For example, you may wish to teach them the TIME OUT procedure you will learn today.

How to Take a TIME OUT

The TIME OUT is one of the most effective methods of conflict management. The concept is to stop or interrupt a conflict that is escalating by physically removing yourself from the scene for a period of time. The purpose of the TIME OUT is to give yourself the opportunity to regain control of your own anger *and/or* to indirectly encourage the other person to gain control of his or her anger as well.

Here are the six basic steps for taking a TIME OUT:

1. Identify the cues that your anger (or the other person's anger) is escalating.

2. Use prepared exit lines to announce your departure and the approximate time of your return; give the other person face-saving exit cues.

3. Deflect negative reactions with the Broken Record technique.

4. Leave the scene.

5. Use anger reduction methods to cool down.

6. Return to the scene and call TIME IN

The steps for taking a TIME OUT may sound somewhat easier than the reality of doing it during an actual confrontation situation. However, by practicing, preparing, and rehearsing, you will soon develop the invaluable ability to take a TIME OUT and effectively defuse a conflict. Now, let's review the steps one at a time.

Step 1. The first step calls for you to identify the earliest signs and signals that either you or the other person is starting to escalate on the anger meter. You have already developed a personalized anger scale and you know where your own set-point for taking action is. The action you will take when you approach your set-point is the TIME OUT.

Although it is not your responsibility to control the anger of another adult, you can still use the TIME OUT procedure to interrupt a situation where you recognize threatening signals of escalating anger in another person.

These signs are generally not subtle. As anger rises, so typically does voice volume. Angry people also often use hostile language and aggressive, animated, and accusatory gestures such as stabbing the air with a pointed finger.

Trust your instincts to recognize escalating anger in another person. As a human being, you come equipped to detect aggression from others with much the same hardwiring as dogs or other animals. When a dog senses aggression coming from another dog, the hair stands up on his back and all his senses are on full alert.

You, too, will know by your own defensive reactions if another person is becoming aggressive and threatening toward you. You may feel your own hair quite literally stand up on the back of your neck. Or, you may find yourself physically backing away from a person who is frightening to you.

Even if you know yourself to be easily intimidated, it is best to err on the side of caution in containing conflict. The bottom line here is simple: if you feel scared, it's a good time to call TIME OUT.

Note that *you* will take responsibility for needing the break. You will *not* tell the other person that he or she is becoming too angry, or overreacting, or "losing it." These accusatory statements are only likely to provoke further aggression. Very few people respond positively to the admonition to calm down, especially when their anger is already aroused. Telling someone that he or she is overreacting invalidates the person's own feelings and almost guarantees enragement.

However, by calling a TIME OUT for yourself and explaining that *you* need to gain better control of your own anger, you will be role-modeling an appropriate coping response for the other person. When you indicate that you need time to cool down so that you don't say things you will later regret, you will indirectly suggest that he or she do the same.

Step 2. The second step of the TIME OUT procedure is to use well-rehearsed exit lines to announce that you will be leaving for a certain period of time. It is best if you can convey how much time you will require before you return. It is imperative that you promise to return within a reasonable time to resume the discussion, otherwise it will frustrate the other person and fuel his or her anger.

Here are some exit lines to practice. Note that some have indirect, face-saving exit invitations to the other person as well:

♦ "I need some time to think this over. I'll get back to you by tomorrow/[specific time]/within a few hours, and we'll finish our conversation."

♦ "I'm starting to lose my temper, and I'm not going to allow myself to do that. I'm going to take some time to calm down so we can have a constructive conversation and resolve our problem."

♦ "I need to leave for a little while to get my act together. I don't want to say things in anger that I will regret. I'm sure you can understand. I'll call you later and we'll set up a time to talk again and to get things worked out."

♦ "I'm starting to get angry now and I don't want to 'go there.' I need to go for a walk so I can cool down. When I get back, we'll finish our talk."

♦ "This discussion is turning hostile and I'm not going to let myself get caught up in this. I need some time to get it together. I'll be back later/specific time/tomorrow/in a few hours."

♦ "I have to call a TIME OUT now. I need some time to calm down so I can think clearly. I can't listen when I'm angry, and I want to hear what you're saying. I'll get back to you when I calm down."

Step 3. The third step is critical. Sometimes, especially when the other person has not heard of a TIME OUT or agreed to the procedure previously, he or she may resist your attempt to leave. The other person may even try to use your announcement to bait or provoke your anger by saying such things as, "Don't try to run away like a baby/coward/child," or, "What do you mean you're leaving? Nobody walks out on me when I'm talking. Forget about it."

You must be prepared for this resistance and counter with your Broken Record technique. You can use these lines or any others you devise to counter resistance. Just remember, do not rise to the bait, or get defensive, or engage in a debate about the content of the other person's allegations.

♦ "I understand you're surprised. Call me whatever you will, I am *not* getting sucked into a fight. I need to leave to control my anger. I promise I'll be back in [specific time]."

♦ "I understand that you feel angry. We both do, that's precisely why I need to leave for a little while so I can get control and be able to listen and not say things I'll regret. I'll be back and we'll work this out."

♦ "I understand you think I'm walking away from you. I'm doing this out of respect for you and for myself. I'm walking away from my own anger, not from you, so that I can get myself under control. When I come back, we can work this out like reasonable people."

▶ *It is vital that you believe and present taking TIME OUT as an honorable thing to do. This is your opportunity to interrupt and control a conflict. It is not the same as "giving in," "selling out," "running away," or "rolling over" in defeat.*

Think of TIME OUT as a sports metaphor. Coaches call TIME OUT when they need to advise their team, give the team an attitude adjustment, break the offensive rhythm of the other team, or otherwise help the team to win the game. Just as in a sports conflict, when you call TIME OUT, you are exercising your right to adjust your tactics and strategy, as well as take a breather.

Don't apologize; you have every right to take a break before things get out of control and its too late. Don't overexplain either. When you have announced your intention to leave and responded one or two times to negative resistance maneuvers, just stop talking and exit.

Step 4. The fourth step is straightforward: Leave. Refrain from dramatic, angry, and provocative exit gestures such as slamming a door or gunning a car accelerator as you drive away. If you are on the telephone, merely announce that you are going to hang up. Then, say goodbye and place the receiver gently on the hook. Don't slam it down.

If the other person's anger is so escalated that he or she attempts to physically block your exit, do not engage in any physical attempts yourself to clear your path. You will certainly know that a TIME OUT is past due if the other person has lost control to this extent.

Nonetheless, if your path is blocked, your only recourse is to "leave" the conversation by refusing to talk. Tell the person something like,

There is no point in trying to keep me here to continue this discussion. I can no longer listen or talk to you until I have the time I need to cool down. You will benefit as much as I will if I have time to calm down. I promise I will come back and resume the conversation.

Step 5. This step is, by now, well rehearsed. You know what to do to interrupt your escalating anger. This is what you have been practicing in your anger management sessions. Do not use the TIME OUT to brood, devise retaliatory schemes, curse, or throw or kick objects. Those are simply wastes of time that will only serve to further agitate and increase your anger.

Use your Relaxation Breath exercise and Progressive Relaxation to calm down and regroup. Use anger-down thoughts to lower your arousal level.

Even if your real purpose in calling a TIME OUT is to interrupt the other person's escalating anger, you still are well advised to use the time to cool down your own engine. If you felt threatened, you were no doubt defensively aroused to protect yourself. *Anger is highly contagious.* If the other person has "lost it," you can assume that you are angrier than you might even realize.

Step 6. This final step is mandatory. You must return to a TIME IN. You must return to your conversation with the stated intention of resolving the conflict. If you feel too threatened by the other person's anger to resume a face-to-face dialogue, you may telephone and attempt to resolve the issue with the safety that physical separation temporarily provides.

When you call the TIME IN, you should indicate that *you* are ready to resume. However, you should ask the other person if he or she is ready to resume a constructive dialogue aimed at resolving the problem. You will be learning more about effective problem-solving methods in a few days.

When you return, it is wise to thank the person for taking a TIME OUT, too, but not for "allowing" you to take one. You may simply assume that, by default, he or she took a TIME OUT when you did.

You also should indicate that your intention is to work out a resolution to the issue. At the same time, you should advise the other person that if the conflict goes off track again in anger, you might require another TIME OUT to regain control of *yourself.* Do not present this as a threat or ultimatum; merely as a point of information with the implicit leverage that everyone will be better off if tempers are kept contained.

It is a good idea to share what you have learned about taking a TIME OUT with the people that you are close to and with whom you may, on occasion, have conflict. If both parties agree in principle ahead of time to the TIME OUT, things will go more smoothly if and when you (or the other person) exercise(s) your rights to a TIME OUT in an actual conflict situation. Once you have standing agreements with others to take TIME OUT, as well as the shared experience of having used the procedure successfully, your fear of conflict will be greatly reduced as your sense of control increases.

The Dos and Don'ts of Conflict Resolution

When you call a TIME IN, you will need to stay focused on resolving the conflict. Here are some important tips on communication that will greatly increase the effectiveness of your problem-solving efforts:

1. **DON'T** use exaggerated language such as "you never . . . ," "you always . . . ," or "every time you/I. . . ."

2. **DON'T** assign responsibility for your feelings to the other person by using sentences such as "You make me feel so stupid" or "You hurt my feelings."

3. **DO** assume responsibility for your feelings as reactions to his/her behavior. Be specific in describing both the other person's behavior and your feelings in response to it. For example, "When you raise your voice, I feel disrespected" or "When you tease me, I feel hurt and angry."

4. **DO** use the **A,B,C, and D** communication approach: "When you do **A,** I feel **B;** if you would do **C** instead, I would feel **D.**" For example, "When you walk out of the room, I feel frustrated and angry; if you would tell me that you need a TIME OUT, I would feel relieved and grateful for the time to collect myself as well."

5. **DO** use empathy. Try to see the problem through the other person's perspective; try to feel as he/she feels.

6. **DO** listen carefully. Try not to interrupt. Ask for further explanation if you don't understand something that is said.

7. **DON'T** make a judgment about the validity of the other person's feelings. For example, don't say, "You're overreacting" or "You are silly to get so upset about this."

8. **DO** check that you understand the other person's statement of the problem by paraphrasing back what you think you hear. For example, use phrases like, "So, what you are saying is . . ." or "If I understand what you're saying, you feel. . . ."

9. **DO** agree on a plan and stick with it. Use "stop action" methods to monitor the conflict process. For example, if the conversation is drifting say, "I think we're getting off the track. Let's go back to how you see the problem" or "We're trying to work through the steps to reach a creative resolution. Let's go back and see what steps we've covered and what we do next."

10. **DO** ask for suggestions from the other person for correcting something that you are doing if it is causing a problem for him/her. For example, you might say something like, "So, when I say xyz, your feelings are hurt. What would you like me to say instead?"

Summary of Day 17

♦ Learn the six steps of the TIME OUT procedure for managing conflict.

♦ Practice the TIME OUT exit and Broken Record lines by yourself and, if possible, with a supportive friend. Rehearse the lines at least three to five times until you can announce that you will take a TIME OUT firmly, directly, unapologetically, and nondefensively. Also, be careful not to display hostility, and do not raise your vocal inflection as though you were asking for permission or making a request to leave.

♦ Notice that with repetition and practice of the TIME OUT procedure and the anger management training, your anxiety and stress over being in a potentially angry, confrontational situation decreases.

♦ Follow the Do's and Don'ts for effective communication and problem solving when it is time to call TIME IN. Keeping your communication on a constructive note will reduce the chances that either of you will get angry again and increase the probability of a successful resolution to the conflict.

Stress Inoculation

Today you will learn how to use anger-down self-statements during a simulated conflict situation. The statements will help prepare you for handling the stress of an actual confrontation. The anger-down self-statements are also intended to help you monitor and control the escalation of your own anger during a conflict. They will keep in check any tendency of yours toward provocative or aggressive responses that, in turn, might ignite and compel angry, hostile behaviors in another person.

The idea of stress inoculation, like its biological parallel, is to be exposed to a little bit of the situation you fear in order to desensitize yourself and to develop stress resistance to it.

The "Gardol Shield" and the Coach on Your Shoulder. With these powerful techniques, you will no longer have to face anxiety-producing conflict situations unprotected and unprepared. By using two potent images, you will greatly increase your confidence and ability to assertively handle even confrontational incidents.

The first comforting image is the protective "Gardol Shield." This concept is based on a toothpaste commercial that was shown on early television a generation or so ago, back when advertising was anything but subtle. In the Gardol commercial a woman with a lovely, gleaming smile—complete with light sparkles bouncing off her pearly white teeth—stands behind a transparent plastic barrier—the Gardol Shield.

As the woman flaunts her gleaming smile, someone off-camera throws tomatoes and other mushy foods directly at her face. Instead of besmirching her lovely smile, the food merely splatters all over the plastic wall while the woman unflinchingly maintains her glowing smile.

Visualize yourself protected by an invisible and impenetrable psychological Gardol Shield whenever you find yourself in a potential confrontation. (If you're a *Star Trek* fan, just think "Shields Up!") Imagine further that while other people can hurl emotional tomatoes at you in the form of provocations, insults, criticisms, and other hostile remarks, nothing can get past that protective shield to hurt you emotionally. As you stand behind the invisible shield, envision your angry adversary's hostile comments splattering back on him or her like mushy tomatoes.

The second comforting image is a tiny version of you, attired as an athletic coach, standing on your right shoulder and reaching up to whisper into your right ear. The coach will accompany you through each phase of a potential confrontation, monitoring your play-by-play behavior and offering supportive and directive anger-down statements.

The sport in question, however, is neither competitive nor aggressive. Therefore, this coach doesn't counsel you to fight in order to win. On the contrary, the name of this game is to stay out of a destructive, angry fight. Instead of a zero-sum game where someone wins and someone loses, the goal in constructive conflict is to reach an effective resolution to a problem so that everyone benefits.

With the coach on your shoulder counseling you with anger-down self-statements every step along the way, and with the emotional protection of an impenetrable psychological Gardol Shield, your fear and vulnerability to the stress of conflict will diminish.

Coaching You to Anger-Down. Envision the miniature version of you as your own coach whispering anger-down advice into your ear during a conflict or confrontation.

Here are some examples of the kinds of things your coach might tell you at various phases of conflict escalation.

1. *Preparation for Anticipated Conflict.* The purpose of these self-statements is to adjust your attitude and lower your tension before an anticipated confrontation occurs. These statements keep you centered and stable so that you are not vulnerable to a knockout on the first blow from the other side. Examples include:

   ♦ "This might upset me a bit, but I can handle it."

- "If I find myself getting angry or upset, I know I can take a TIME OUT."
- "I can work out a plan to deal with this problem."
- "There won't be any reason for a fight or argument; it takes two people to fight and I believe that I can control my own responses."
- "Stay flexible and calm. Take a deep breath or two. Getting rigid only closes down alternatives and options."
- "Whatever he/she says, I have my Gardol Shield to protect me so I won't get hurt or angry."

2. *When the Other Person Confronts You in Anger.* These statements should remind you of how well prepared you are to handle anger and conflict. This is the phase at which your anger-down self-statements should be most directly aimed at maintaining control and not letting your anger get overly escalated. Here are some examples:

- "Stay cool and relax. There's no point in getting mad, too."
- "Don't let him/her get to me."
- "Stay in control. My mind is on top of this situation and everything will be okay."
- "As long as I keep calm, I'm in control. There's no benefit to getting worked up."
- "It's really too bad that he/she has to act like this. I'm not going to let him/her have the power over me to get me nuts and upset."
- "Keep this in proportion. Don't blow up the importance of this. It will all work out."
- "I don't need to prove that I'm right and he/she is wrong. I can just acknowledge that we have an issue that needs resolution."

3. *If Your Anger Gets Aroused.* These self-statements will interrupt your developing anger and help you regain control. Self-statements should directly focus on keeping your anger within optimal boundaries—you may need to be angry enough to stand up for yourself, but not so angry that things become hostile and the conflict turns destructive. Examples of anger-down self-statements if your anger gets aroused are:

- "I can feel myself getting tense. I need to take a few deep breaths."
- "I may need to take a TIME OUT now. I know how to do it and I have every right to get myself back under control."

- "It's important that I not try to avoid this. I need to stay with it and trust that I can lead this discussion to a cooperative solution."

- "I will not cave in and become a people-pleaser again. There are other ways to deal with his/her anger. I don't have to feel intimated anymore. I can stand up for myself and for my rights."

- "I need to keep listening. If I get too angry, I won't be able to hear what he or she is saying."

- "Listen to my coach. Remember the Gardol Shield."

4. *When You Have Resolved the Conflict.* These self-statements should follow successful conflict resolution. Even though there may have been some touchy moments, or you took a TIME OUT to get it back together, you deserve credit and self-approval for making it through without capitulating into people-pleasing appeasement. Examples of this line of self-statement are:

- "I feel pretty good about this one. We actually got it worked out without too much anger on either side."

- "I give myself credit for not running away from conflict. I was scared, but my 'coach' got me through it and I was even able to lead the problem to a workable resolution."

- "I'm getting better and more confident at handling anger and conflict situations. I'm not as fearful as I used to be."

- "I have nothing to be afraid of except the fear itself. I have worked hard on anger and conflict management, and I won't go back to my old people-pleasing ways."

5. *If the Conflict Is Only Partially Resolved, or If No Resolution Is Reached This Time.* Praise yourself with rewarding self-statements for the *process* of how you handled the conflict, not just on the *outcome*. Keep the issue in proportion and use self-statements to stop thinking or obsessing about it. Examples include:

- "I'll get better at this with time and practice. We didn't resolve things, but we didn't wind up as enemies either. We agreed to disagree and that's okay."

- "I feel proud of how I handled myself during this situation. I'm sorry that he/she wasn't more cooperative or flexible. I believe that this would have gotten resolved if he/she had been less rigid."

- "Stop thinking and focusing on this. It will only continue to upset you. You've already spent time on it. Give it a rest for now."

♦ "Not everything can be fixed; it's not my job to be the "fixer" anyway. I can accept that I couldn't get this issue resolved, and I don't need to take it as a personal failure."

You should review and practice the self-statements above and imagine how you might use them during the various phases of a confrontation or potential conflict situation. If you wish, you may write out some self-statements of your own. The more personalized and tailored to your own way of speaking and thinking your self-statements are, the more effective your "coach" will be.

Hearing Your Coach's Inner Voice

Once you learn the skill of stress inoculation through the use of a practice script, you can use it to desensitize and prepare yourself for any conflict, confrontation, or other stressful situation that you anticipate facing.

Use the script below to practice. You may enlist the help of a supportive friend or relative to play the role of "friend," in the script; or you may assume all the roles yourself.

Read the parts out loud. Note that the coach's role is intended to simulate your inner voice. The first few times you practice the script, say the coach's lines in a very low whisper, as though you were just hearing them inside your mind. After you have practiced the script a few times, stop saying the coach's lines aloud but continue to "hear" them subvocally as internal self-statements in your mind. Pay attention to how the Anger-Down statements of your inner coach help you to control your own anger.

The topic of the practice script is money. You are asking your friend, to whom you loaned money, to repay the debt. To be effective, the friend's role should be said in an angry tone. The point is to learn how to face a potentially hostile confrontation and to be able to manage it.

Before you begin reading the script, imagine the Gardol Shield around you. Keep that visualization going as you read through the script. No matter how angry the friend becomes, her statements merely bounce off the invisible shield that surrounds you.

The more you practice the script, the more potent the stress inoculation effect will be. If you wish, you may write your own script using the three roles for another potentially stressful conflict or confrontation situation.

You: I need to talk with you about the money you borrowed several months ago. We had an agreement that you would repay me within six weeks, and I haven't received any money yet.

Friend: Six weeks? I thought our agreement was six months! You know how bad my situation is. I've just started my new job, and I have a lot of debts to pay. [*getting angry*] I actually can't believe you're putting pressure on me like this. I thought you were my friend.

Coach: Okay. Stay calm. She's starting to get worked up, but I can handle it and stay calm. I need to listen carefully and stay nondefensive. Take some deep breaths.

You: I understand that you feel pressured but I need to start to get repaid. Maybe we can work out a payment schedule that will be less pressure for you.

Friend: [*angrily with voice raised*] What would be less pressure is for you to get off my back! What kind of a friend are you? You know, I've done you a lot of favors over the years. Why do you need the money now? You can afford to wait. I've got other creditors to deal with!

Coach: Don't blow it. Stay cool. No point in getting mad. She is getting very defensive, and she's just trying to make me feel guilty. I need to stick with my Broken Record technique and control my anger. If I start to lose it, this conversation is going to go downhill fast.

You: I can really understand that you feel upset. I know how it feels to have financial pressures. I have them myself which is why I need to start getting the loan repaid. I have tried to be understanding and supportive which is why I loaned you the money in the first place. Let's see if we can work out a payment schedule that you can handle and that will meet my needs, too.

Friend: [*very angry, yelling*] You don't understand anything. I'm going crazy from the pressure I'm under and you know it. And now you come at me about this money thing!

Coach: I definitely need a TIME OUT or else I'm going to lose my own temper and that's the last thing I want to do. Be calm. Convince her that we need a cooling off break.

You: We can't afford to get into an argument. And I refuse to fight with you. Let me just take a break for a few minutes so we can both regroup. I'm going to go to the bathroom. I'll be back in five minutes or so and we'll figure out a solution.

Friend: Okay. You're probably right.

Coach: Great. She'll come around after the TIME OUT.

You [After five minutes of TIME OUT] All right. Let's agree to stay calm and then I'm sure we can arrive at a solution to this issue. We certainly don't have to get into an argument. We can do better than that.

Friend: [*tearful*] I feel just terrible about this. You're making me feel so guilty. I thought you would understand my situation. I need new clothes and shoes for my new job. I have to pay my other bills. You certainly don't seem to need the money right now as much as I do.

Coach: Don't get defensive. Don't apologize or rationalize. She owes me the money. It's not my role to fund her new lifestyle. Take some deep breaths. Don't let her intimidate me. Use the Broken Record.

You: I understand that this conversation is unpleasant. It's unpleasant for me, too. I think it's important for our friendship that we get this money issue resolved. This is about a business arrangement we made—it's not personal. Let's just agree on when you will start repaying the loan, and on how much you will pay in installments. As soon as we reach an agreement, we'll both feel better.

Friend: [*reluctantly, but less angrily*] Well, I can't afford to pay back everything at once. You have to be patient with me. I'll try my hardest, but I really am stretched to the limit financially with all my new expenses.

Coach: Stay loose. She is obviously unhappy and irritable. Don't make things worse by being sarcastic about her 'new expenses.' I'm almost there—just put forth a solution that shows her respect.

You: Okay. Let's sit down and work out a payment schedule we can both live with. I'm confident that we can get past this. I know it doesn't feel good to owe money, and it doesn't feel good for me to have to ask for repayment of a loan from a friend either. We can work it out. Let's try to move to a solution because neither of us wants to argue.

The important part of the practice is to "hear" your anger-down thoughts and to train yourself to keep that inner monologue going in an actual conflict or potentially stressful confrontation.

Summary of Day 18

♦ Visualize an invisible "Gardol Shield" that protects you and deflects another's hostility.

♦ Visualize and "hear" the "Coach on your shoulder" maintain a continuous subvocal monologue of anger-down statements to keep you and your anger in control during a potential confrontation.

♦ Learn anger-down self-statements for various phases of a potential confrontation so that you can monitor your anger and control the conflict.

♦ Practice the stress inoculation script by saying the Coach's role either in a whisper or subvocally, and the other role(s) out loud. Notice how repeated practice "inoculates" you and reduces the level of stress you feel.

Solve a Problem with a Friend, Not for a Friend

Friends and relatives frequently present you with their problems because you have been a people-pleaser for such a long time. The main reason they do so is their expectation that you will fix all the problems, manage all the crises, and solve all the dilemmas *for* them. You have created this expectation through your past actions.

As a recovered people-pleaser, you need to teach the people that come to you with their problems to expect a different, healthier response from you.

Prioritize the People You Most Want to Help

You certainly may still choose to help the people you love and care about most with their problems. However, you cannot continue to solve or fix *everyone's* problems, *all* of the time. Some people will just have to help themselves.

The final determination of how much you decide to help with others' problems will, in most cases, depend on the circumstances presented on a case-by-case basis. Of course, there is still a short list of people in your life for whom you would do almost anything to help with nearly any problem.

Write your list, which should be *very short*, in your journal under the title, "The People I Most Want to Help." If you need two hands or more to count, you have too many people on your list again. Remember, your list should represent the select few—the most central and special people in your life. These are the people for whom you want to preserve your time and energy in case they truly *need* your help with crises or with other significant life problems.

Keep in mind that when you overextend yourself trying to fix the problems of others that are *not* on your select list, you are potentially diminishing your ability—and availability—to help those closest to you should they suddenly need your help.

The people on your select list also value and love you. When they see you exhausted and depleted from helping so many others with their problems, those on the select list—the special people that you really *do* want to help—may be less inclined to turn to you because of the onerous burden they see you are already carrying.

When a Friend Asks for Help with a Problem

The next time a friend or family member brings you a problem you will need a different script to replace your habitual reflex response. Your old response, of course, was to automatically adopt the burden as your own. You new response will be one of two alternatives:

1. *Say No.* Empathize with the person's feelings but leave the problem where it belongs: with the other person. Wish the person good luck and express your confidence that she/he will get things worked out. Be prepared to say "no" if your friend directly asks you to help; or

2. *Buy Time* to think about how much you want to become involved in helping the person *with* the problem. You already know the basics of buying time from your prior training, which are:

   a. Acknowledge and empathize with the person's distress.

   b. Make no commitment other than to say that you need time to think about the problem.

   c. Promise to recontact the person within a relatively short period of time. Be as specific as possible in offering a date or approximate time estimate for getting back to the person.

Saying "No" to a Friend with a Problem

Here are two examples of how to shift the responsibility for solving a problem back to the person who "owns" it. Read these out loud. Write one or two more ways to shift the responsibility for solving another's problem away from you:

- "It's really understandable that this is upsetting you. I just know you'll find a way to work it out."

- "I'm so sorry this is happening to you. I can only imagine how unhappy [the situation] is making you feel. I really hope things get better for you as soon as possible."

If you wish, you can write a few more scripts on your own that are specific to your own life. When you practice these scripts, it is important that you *not* apologize or overexplain why you are not jumping in to solve the problem for the other person. You have every right to preserve yourself for your own problems and to help those on your short select list.

Keep in mind that just by listening, you are already doing something helpful for someone with a problem.

"Buying Time" to Respond to a Friend with a Problem

Here are three examples of "buying time" responses when a friend or someone else comes to you with a problem:

- "I understand that you're upset and that you want me to help you with this problem. I need some time to think about how I can best help you. I'll get back to you by [day of week/time of day]"

- "I know this problem seems very overwhelming to you. Let me think about how I might best be of help. I need to check my current commitments. I'll get back to you [day of week]."

- "I can feel how upsetting this must be for you. I know that you need some answers or solutions to this problem. Let me think about it for a day or two and then we'll talk again."

Again, you may write more scripts for buying time. It will be helpful if you have specific people and/or problems in mind.

Practice the "buying time" scripts so that they are familiar enough for you to use them the next time someone asks for help and you want to think of how much you want to get involved.

The 7-Step Problem-Solving Model

One of the most helpful things you can do to help a friend solve a problem is to offer a structured approach that is logical and effective. As you will see below, you can use the model to determine how much you want to become personally involved in the actual problem-solving process.

Here are the 7 steps of effective problem solving:

1. Define the problem as a decision to be made.
2. Brainstorm *all* possible alternative solutions.
3. Collect relevant information within a reasonable time frame.
4. Weigh the pros and cons of each alternative.
5. Select the best (or least *undesirable*) alternative.
6. Implement your decision.
7. Evaluate how the solution is working; define new problems as decisions to be made (return to Step 1).

Choose How Much to Help

You can now choose from one of three levels or degrees of involvement with another person's problem. The third or highest level of involvement should generally be restricted to those on your *short select* list. Your goal, with even the third level, is to help solve your friends' or relatives' problems *with* them, not *for* them.

Here are the three levels of involvement and how to implement each:

Level 1: *Your Friend Is on Her/His Own.* This is the lowest level of involvement in which you essentially draw a clear boundary that says, "This is *your* problem to solve. I can be a sympathetic friend, but I can't solve the problem for you or even with you." Here is the basic scenario of what to do after the person asks for your help:

♦ Recontact your friend/relative/coworker.

♦ Restate their problem to acknowledge that you listened carefully.

♦ Empathize with the person's feelings (e.g., I know how upset you are).

♦ Indicate clearly and firmly that you cannot do more than offer some basic problem-solving advice, and call in a few weeks to see how things are going. For example,

"You might find it helpful to talk to a therapist or counselor."

"It's a good idea to brainstorm as many possible ideas for solving the problem as you can. Try not to evaluate what is a good idea and what isn't until you've brainstormed every alternative you can think of. Let me know how things work out."

"Sometimes I find it helpful to write down the pros and cons of a particular solution so I can look at it objectively. Give me a call to let me know how everything worked out."

Level 2: *Brainstorm with a Friend.* Here, you offer to help by defining the problem and by brainstorming together with your friend. Give the person the "gift" of the 7-step model and offer your encouragement. The basic scenario for Level 2 involvement is:

♦ Recontact the person.

♦ Tell the person about the 7-step model and how it works.

♦ Offer to discuss the problem and/or to brainstorm possible alternative solutions. But limit your involvement *explicitly* to discussion and brainstorming only.

♦ Remove yourself from the problem-solving setting. Shift responsibility to the other person for collecting information, evaluating alternatives, choosing a solution, and implementing the solution.

Level 3: *Solve a Problem with a Friend.* Offer to help by working through the full problem-solving process jointly with the other person (this would be especially instructive and helpful with your children.) *Note:* This is a very high level of involvement and should be reserved for a very short list of special people. Even with them, however, you are *not* taking over the responsibility for solving the problem or fixing the crisis. That is Disease to Please behavior and you don't do it anymore. Here is the Level 3 scenario:

♦ Recontact the person.

♦ Offer to work collaboratively with the other person through the whole 7-step process.

♦ Indicate that you will be a participant in the process but that the ultimate responsibility—and credit—for solving the problem will be the other person's and not yours.

♦ Be sure the other person assumes responsibility for the final choice of a solution.

♦ Limit your participation in the implementation of the solution to a *supportive* rather than central role.

Summary of Day 19

♦ Read and learn the 7-step problem-solving method.

♦ Make a *short* list in your journal of the very select, special people in your life for whom you want to be available to help when they have problems;

♦ Practice buying time for you to think of how much you want to get involved.

♦ Practice the three levels of involvement after you recontact the person.

♦ Be aware of your words, tone, and inflections. Be careful not to sound apologetic or guilty for not fixing everything *for* other people. Remember, your goal is to recover from your Disease to Please while still being a good, supportive friend or family member.

Correcting Faulty Assumptions

Today you will learn to test your predictions about how other people will respond when you behave like the new person you have become: a recovered people-pleaser.

In the past, you have tended to overestimate the likelihood that people would get angry with you, reject you, disapprove of or abandon you if you failed to please them or comply with their wishes. By now, in all likelihood, you have been relieved to learn that nobody has responded aggressively or tried to angrily intimidate you into submission when you have said "no" or turned down a request; nor have they disapproved, abandoned, or rejected you.

Have faith in your family and friends. People who really love and care about you will support your efforts. They *will* adjust to the new reality as long as you don't slip and regress to your old people-pleasing habits. They will get over whatever temporary reactions they may have to the changed you, *and* they will still love you.

Trust that curing your Disease to Please is the right thing to do for everybody in the long run. Other people will only have more respect for you when you show them that you respect yourself.

To conquer your fears, you will need the courage to test your predictions.

▶ *Over time, with mounting evidence that your fears are unfounded, your anxiety will decrease and eventually disappear altogether.*

Check the Accuracy of Your Assumptions

Test Your Predictions. In your personal journal, divide a new page into three columns. Make the left and right column wide; the center column can be quite narrow—enough to fit the words "yes" or "no."

Title the left column "My Predictions;" the middle column "Yes/No;" and the right column "Actual Outcomes."

Select one behavior from the following list that you will commit to do within the next week:

1. Say "no" to a request, demand, invitation, favor, etc.

2. Delegate a job, chore, or task.

3. Ask for help.

4. Ask someone to stop doing something that is bothering you, and offer a suggested alternative behavior.

5. Listen to someone's problem without offering advice or jumping in to solve or fix it; just show empathy and shift responsibility back to him/her.

6. Express a negative emotion to someone (e.g., anger, disappointment, criticism, disapproval) and make a constructive suggestion for change.

7. Make a counterproposal on *your* terms to a request or demand on your time and resources.

The list represents seven behaviors that you have practiced and, in some cases, have already incorporated into your life. If you have not yet completed your delegation or saying "no" assignments from previous days' training, now is your chance to do so.

The point is simply for you to commit to doing just one boundary-setting/non-people-pleasing behavior so that you can test your predictions of the consequences of your actions.

When you have selected one behavior from the list, put the behavior in a specific situational context with a specific target person. For example, let's say you selected "ask for help" as your behavior. You place it in the context of, "I will ask my husband to help me get ready for my performance review at work. I need his support to role-play with me so I can ask my boss for a raise." Finally, you add the prediction, "I think my husband will be annoyed and won't have the time to spend over my anxiety. He will be impatient and he will get angry if I ask him to role-play and he will probably refuse to do it."

The next step, of course, is critical. *You must do the behavior and test your prediction by observing the consequences.*

In the middle column, record a "yes" if your predictions were correct and accurate; record a "no" if your predictions were wrong. In the right column, write down what actually happened and exactly what was said and done.

It may be the case that you are not sure how to interpret the other person's emotional reaction. For example, you fear (and therefore predict) that your husband will be annoyed and angry. However, when you actually ask for his help, he agrees to role-play and spends an hour preparing you to ask for a raise.

Clearly, your prediction that he will refuse to role-play was in error. But, suppose you still do not know his emotional reaction. Since you fear that he will be annoyed and angry, you may read those feelings into your perception of his behavior.

If you are not clear about the emotional response, ask. In this case, you could use the occasion to thank him and to reinforce his willingness to help. At the same time, you could ask him to describe his feelings at the time. Was he, in fact, annoyed and angry? You may learn that, quite to the contrary, he was gratified that you listened to his suggestions and that you gave him the opportunity to be helpful to you in a concrete demonstrable way.

Continue to Test Your Predictions. You should use your journal to record predictions and outcomes every time you establish a personal boundary or do other behaviors that demonstrate that you are a recovered people-pleaser.

There are two purposes for continuing to record your predictions and the actual outcomes. First, the prediction-testing exercise will help sustain your commitment to your newly acquired repertoire of recovery behaviors. Therefore, by testing your predictions, you will actually do the new behaviors repeatedly over time.

The second reason to continue monitoring your predictions and the actual outcomes is to develop a body of real evidence to prove that your people-pleasing beliefs were wrong and self-defeating. It took you years to develop deeply ingrained people-pleasing beliefs about your relationships with other people. It is going to take repeated life experience to show you that you do not have to remain oppressed by the Disease to Please in order to retain the affection and respect of the people important in your life. Your prediction-testing journal entries are ways to collect actual data that prove your negative predictions to be false.

Flashcards to Stay in Control

You are now very near completion of your 21-Day Action Plan. Even when you are through, you will need to remind yourself on a regular basis to control your people-pleasing tendencies.

Teachers use flashcards to drill basic math, word recognition, and other rote memory skills into the supple minds and spongelike memories of children. Think of yourself as being in the early developmental stages of recovery from the Disease to Please.

Like a young child learning multiplication tables, you have been learning the new rules of being your own person—the words and phrases that help you remember how to be a recovered people-pleaser—and of no longer compulsively catering to the needs of others. You will have to drill the new rules into your memory so that they become second nature.

To make your flashcards, you will need a felt marking pen and a stack of 3 × 5 index cards. The flashcards you will make are one-sided—you will not need to flip the card over to reveal an answer.

Below is a list of 50 words and phrases to copy onto your cards. Some of the words will be more meaningful or significant to you than others. However, it is a good idea to make a complete set of flashcards that contain all 50 items.

You may add to your stack of flashcards at any time. The more personalized you can make your flashcards the better. Any words or phrases that particularly remind you of how you transformed from a compulsive people-pleaser into a recovered people-pleaser who has reclaimed control over your life are appropriate for flashcards.

Words and Phrases for Flashcards

1. Say "NO"
2. TIME OUT
3. Delegate
4. It's okay not to be nice
5. I need my *own* approval
6. Time
7. Set limits
8. Anger down
9. Control
10. Listen to my coach
11. Problems are challenges
12. Self-respect
13. My Gardol Shield
14. 7-Step Method
15. Count to 10
16. Make good choices
17. Flexibility
18. On *my* terms in *my* life
19. No "SHOULDS"
20. Broken Record
21. Relax
22. Sandwich Technique
23. Pleasurable activities
24. Breathe
25. Self-approval
26. Litmus test
27. Select list
28. Self-preservation
29. Recovering in small steps

30. RPP	36. My anger set-point for action	43. Courage to change
31. Act as if I'm an RPP	37. Interrupt anger	44. Like myself
32. Relaxation Breath	38. "Time-In" for problem solving	45. Respect myself
33. Constructive conflict	39. Stop and anger down	46. Options
34. Appropriate anger	40. I am *not* what I do	47. No guilt
35. My anger scale	41. Take care of me too	48. Rehearse
	42. I'm not indispensable	49. Stress inoculation
		50. It's my choice to care

Flashcard Reviews. During the next month to six weeks, you will benefit most from reviewing your flashcards at least once a day. You can carry the cards with you and flip through a few at a time during random breaks during your day. You can keep the flashcards on your night table and review them once all the way through before you retire each evening.

What is important is that you merely keep yourself mindful of the key concepts that changed your life for the better. As you progress in your newly established self-concept as a recovered people-pleaser, you may find that a particular day's events may make two or three flashcards particularly relevant. On another day, different catch words and phrases may stand out.

If you wish, you may make more than one set of flashcards so that they are readily available to you whenever you want or need to consult them. Retaining a heightened state of awareness about making good choices and about interrupting your old people-pleasing habits is the best protection against relapse.

After a month to six weeks from now, you may feel that the flashcard words and phrases are fairly well drilled into your awareness. Still, you will benefit by continuing regular review sessions at least two or three times weekly.

Booster Sessions: Continue to Work Your Action Plan

It is important that you continue to work the program by doing the activities prescribed in Days 1 through 20 of the 21-Day Action Plan. Schedule two or three booster sessions per week and repeat exercises and activities from the program that have been most helpful or that help shore up areas of vulnerability and weakness.

Do your pleasurable activities and relaxation exercises as regularly as possible. Ideally these should be incorporated into your daily regimen.

By now you will have a good sense of which activities have been most beneficial for your particular habits and vulnerabilities. While you no doubt share a great deal of behavior in common with other people-pleasers, you also have your own special version or form of the Disease to Please.

Your most deeply ingrained people-pleasing habits should be the ones you work on repeatedly. Don't expect that you will automatically become skilled at delegating or at saying "no," for example, on the basis of just one or two practice exercises. Continual practice will help you integrate your new habits into your daily lifestyle.

Review the summaries at the end of each day in the 21-Day Action Plan. The summaries are handy reminders of the exercises and direction contained in that portion of the program. You will benefit most by eventually repeating all the exercises during booster sessions spread out over several months.

The booster sessions will help reinforce the skills you have acquired and the important changes you have made. The more you reinforce your new behaviors, the more ingrained your new, healthy ways of treating yourself and of interacting with others will become.

Summary of Day 20

♦ Test your predictions by making a commitment to do a specific boundary-setting, need expression, or other self-preserving action— e.g., delegating a chore or task, saying "no" to a request, expressing a negative emotion—during the next seven days.

♦ Write down what you plan to do and predict how you believe the other person(s) will react to your action.

♦ Observe the data of your experience. Record whether your prediction was confirmed or not confirmed. Then record in more detail what actually happened.

♦ Make a set of 50 flashcards with the words and phrases provided above that are key to your recovery from the Disease to Please. Add whatever words or phrases have further value to you in helping you stay aware of your new choices as a recovered people-pleaser.

♦ Review your flashcards at least once daily for the next month to six weeks; review them at least two or three times weekly thereafter. Staying aware of how you transformed yourself is the best protection against slipping back into old habits.

♦ Review the summaries of Days 1 through 20. Schedule booster sessions two or three times per week in which you repeat exercises and activities from the 21-Day Action Plan.

Celebrate Your Cure

To borrow a phrase, today is the first day of the rest of your new life . . . as a recovered people-pleaser. *Congratulations!*

You have worked hard to get through this program and you deserve to celebrate. Select a date on the calendar, as close as possible to one month from today. Make that date a special time to celebrate and reward yourself for the transformation you have made.

▶ *To celebrate your cure, plan a day to please you.*

Indulge yourself in a wonderful day. Do things that will make you feel relaxed and happy; plan activities that you like to do best. Spend money on yourself; you deserve it!

Whatever you choose to do, spend your celebration day reflecting on how much you have changed and on how much you value recovering from the Disease to Please. Remember, the approval you give to yourself is the most important affirmation you can earn.

Measure the Changes You Have Made

Take the "Do I Have the Disease to Please?" quiz in Chapter 1 again. Compare your score now with your baseline score when you first began to read the book. Pay attention to the ways that your behavior, thoughts, and feelings (the components of the Disease to Please triangle) have altered.

Of course, it is likely that there is room for still more improvement. That is exciting news because you now know how empowering it feels to treat problems as challenges and to employ effective strategies for self-improvement and personal growth. As industrialist Henry Kaiser once said, "I always view problems as opportunities in work clothes."

Develop a Support Group

The next most important and potent source of support for your recovery will be other people. Talk to your friends and coworkers and find out about their own experiences with their Disease to Please.

The saying is, "It takes one to know one." If you know people who are still caught in the web of people-pleasing, you may wish to offer your support of their efforts to change. In turn, they can become a support system for you.

The people who really care about you will want to help you stay healthier and happier. Tell them how they can be supportive. Ask them for help directly. These very actions are evidence that you have recovered from the Disease to Please.

People in 12-step programs telephone members of their support group whenever they feel vulnerable to a relapse. Make a pact with a friend or family member—ideally, with someone who is also a recovered people-pleaser—so that you will have someone to contact and talk to should you find yourself slipping into old patterns.

If possible, you will find it very beneficial to have regular meetings with your support group. Make the meetings enjoyable and convenient. Scheduling support group meetings over lunch on a monthly basis, for example, works for many people. Or, you might organize an informal meeting in the evening at members' homes on a rotating basis, once a month.

Being a member of a group of people who understand and who have a basis for empathy with your experience is a highly effective way to sustain personal change.

diseasetoplease.com

The concept of a support group takes on an entirely new dimension in the age of the Internet. The Web site, **diseasetoplease.com,** is your access to a universe of recovered and recovering people-pleasers with whom you can share support.

Through the Web, you can also provide support to people currently caught in the grip of the Disease to Please. By sharing your experiences and offering others the benefit of your knowledge, you will greatly enhance and expand the impact of your own recovery.

The **diseasetoplease.com** Web site also will support and help sustain your recovery by offering advice, Q and A, additional self-help activities and exercises, specific suggestions for handling people-pleasing challenges, and other useful information. I hope you will be an active visitor and contributor to the site.

Open in Case of a Backslide: Write a Letter to Yourself

Sit down now and write a letter to yourself that you will open and read in the event that you feel yourself backsliding into old habits.

Do not panic if you slip. Prior to this program, you had been a committed, compulsive people-pleaser for a number of years, probably even most or all of your life. Do not engage in perfectionist, self-defeating thinking. You don't need to be *perfect* in order to be recovered.

If you have changed just some of your basic thoughts, feelings, and behaviors that form the Disease to Please triangle, you are on the path to permanent recovery. You may slip along the way and find yourself saying "yes" when you really want to say "no," or agreeing to do too much for a worthy organization, family member, or a friend.

Being generous and giving is, after all, in your nature and that's a *good* thing.

But you must retain your newly drawn boundaries. A slip here and there in the first few months of your recovery won't turn into an overwhelming landslide of people-pleasing regression unless you allow it to happen.

Staying aware and on top of how you are thinking, feeling, and behaving means that you will notice if and when a slip does occur. At those moments, don't make the mistake of becoming self-disparaging, negative, and brutally critical of yourself.

Instead open the letter that you are currently writing. This letter should have a gentle but firm tone. You should recall to yourself in this letter how it felt to be so out of control and burdened when your Disease to Please consumed your life.

Use some examples to illustrate how unreasonable your demands on yourself had become. Refer back to your original answers to the Chapter 1 quiz. Describe the negative effects of being a compulsive people-pleaser. Remind yourself that being nice didn't always or necessarily protect you from unkind treatment from others. It simply made the negative treatment more difficult to understand and justify. Believing that nice people are always treated fairly sets you up for self-blame, guilt, and depression.

Now write yourself a message that will wake you up if you start to backslide. You do not want to resume the negative, self-defeating pattern of people-pleasing. You do not want to take on the mantle of guilt and persistent inadequacy that the Disease to Please creates and that you have just worked so hard to shed.

You have learned the value of earning your own approval. And you have worked hard to liberate yourself from your addiction to the approval of other people and the compulsion to make everyone like you. In the letter, write that you are counting on yourself to sustain these hard-fought victories. Remind yourself that overcoming the Disease to Please is done in small steps—one step at a time, one day at a time. Big changes and even full transformations are merely the accumulation of small steps.

If you slip, you simply need to notice, recommit to recovery, and make good choices the next time a people-pleasing challenge comes your way. A mistake only becomes as error when it is overlooked and repeated. You can learn from mistakes. Tell yourself that in the letter.

Direct yourself right back to the flashcards and booster sessions. If you had a slip, it only means that you need to become more careful so that you don't find yourself on the slippery slope back to a way of living that made you feel unhappy, insecure, inadequate, and exhausted.

Remind yourself in the letter to check the Internet site, **diseasetoplease .com,** and to use the information, exercises, tips, and supportive advice that you will find there. If you feel comfortable, you can share your "in case of a slip" letter with your support group and/or with others on the Web site.

By sharing your story and making a gift of your own experiences in overcoming the Disease to Please, you can continue to meaningfully help others while still taking care of yourself.

Summary of Day 21

♦ Celebrate your recovery from the Disease to Please!

♦ Set aside a day—or a good part of one—to enjoy, reward, and indulge yourself.

♦ Develop a support group of other recovered people-pleasers—or those just beginning their recovery—with whom you can exchange stories, experiences, and mutual help and advice.

♦ Visit **diseasetoplease.com** regularly to sustain your recovery.

♦ Write a letter to open in case of a slip. Don't be a perfectionist. You may very well slip now and then into some people-pleasing behavior. Notice your slip; learn from your mistake; and commit yourself again to changing any part of the Disease to Please Triangle—thoughts, feelings, behavior—and you will be right back on the right track.

Some Final Thoughts

While you have come to the end of this book, I trust that this is the beginning of a new way of living in which you feel happier with yourself and your relationships with others. You have transformed into a *recovered people-pleaser*, more in control over your life and far more aware of your personal power to change.

Now you know the process of identifying something about yourself that you want to fix or improve and how to follow a systematic strategy for unlearning bad habits and replacing them with better ones. If you have changed your long-standing Disease to Please, you can gain or reclaim control over almost any other aspect of your behavior, appearance, health habits, relationships, thoughts, or feelings with which you currently feel dissatisfied.

When you started this book, I directed you to one of the three sections and then to the 21-Day Action Plan. If you have not already done so, now is a good time to go back and read what you skipped. Every people-pleaser will benefit from reading *all three sections*—People-Pleasing Mindsets, Habits, and Feelings, and you should not shortchange yourself.

Experiencing—not just reading about—a process of personal change is empowering. I congratulate you for demonstrating the commitment, discipline, and courage necessary to overcome your Disease to Please. And I encourage you to *cherish* and *protect* your newly recovered status especially from anything or anybody who would rather see you resume your old people-pleasing habits.

Practice and stay aware of your new intentions to take care of yourself and to be selective in responding to the needs of other people. Replace the compulsive people-pleasing habit with good choices based on caring for yourself as well as others.

Endnotes

Chapter 2

1. For more on cognitive therapy and cognitive-behavior therapy, see A. T. Beck, *Cognitive Therapy and the Emotional Disorders* (New York: International Universities Press, 1976); D. Burns, *Feeling Good: The New Mood Therapy* (New York: Avon Press, 1992); and D. Burns, *The Feeling Good Handbook* (New York: Plume Press, 1990).
2. See K. Horney, *The Neurotic Personality of Our Time* (New York: Norton, 1993).
3. See A. Ellis, *Reason and Emotion in Psychotherapy* (New York: Birch Lane Press, 1994) and A. Ellis and S. Blau (eds.), *The Albert Ellis Reader: A Guide to Well-Being Using Rational-Emotive Behavior Therapy* (New Jersey: Citadel Press, 1998).
4. A. Ellis, *Keynote speech* (Los Angeles County Psychological Association, Annual Convention, Anaheim, California, 1999).

Chapter 3

5. H. Selye, *The Stress of Life* (New York: McGraw-Hill, 1978) and H. Selye, Personal interview, *Psychology Today* 11 (10) (March 1978): 60–70.
6. H. Braiker, *Lethal Lovers and Poisonous People* (New York: Pocketbooks, Hardcover, 1991).

Chapter 11

7. D. Burns, *Therapist's Toolkit* (Los Altos Hills: Burns (self-published), 1997 upgrade).

Chapter 12

8. M. T. Friedman and R. Rosenman, *Type A Behavior and Your Heart* (New York: Knopf, 1974).

Chapter 14

9. For a more detailed examination of the three-tiered conflict model, see H. Braiker and H. Kelley, "Conflict in the Development of Close Relationships," in *Social Exchange in Developing Relationships* ed. R. L. Burgess and T. E. Huston (New York: Academic Press, 1979).